THE
MOUNTAIN
BIKER'S

TRAINING BIBLE

A complete training guide for the competitive mountain biker

BY JOE FRIEL

Foreword by Ned Overend

VELO
press

VELOPRESS • BOULDER, COLORADO • USA

International Standard Book Number: 1-884737-71-4

     Library of Congress Cataloging-in Publication Data

Friel, Joe.
  The mountain biker's training bible : a complete training guide for the competitive
mountain bikers / by Joe Friel ; foreword by Ned Overend.
    p. cm.
  Includes bibliographical references and index.
  ISBN 1-884737-71-4
   1. All terrain cycling--Training. I. Title.

GV1056 .F75 2000
613.7'11--dc 21

                                       00-028317

Printed in the U.S.A.

Distributed in the United States and Canada by Publishers Group West.

VeloPress
1830 N 55th Street
Boulder, Colorado 80301-2700

303/440-0601 • fax 303/444-6788 • e-mail: velopress@7dogs.com

To purchase additional copies of this book or other VeloPress products,
call 800/234-8356 or visit us on the Web at www.velogear.com

Design by Erin Johnson
Cover photograph © Karl Weatherly/Corbis Images
Photo Credits: Back cover and page xviii by John Gibson;
page 18 by Karen Schulenberg; page 126 by Tom Moran; page 162 by John Gibson.
Illustrations by Todd Telander.

Before embarking on any strenuous exercise program, including the training described in this book, everyone, particularly anyone with a known abnormal heart or blood pressure condition, should be examined by a physician.

This one, at last, is for my parents,
George and Betty Friel.
Thanks for everything.

CONTENTS

ACKNOWLEDGMENTS

This book and the training concepts described in it are possible because of the help of others. There are many to thank, but I especially want to acknowledge Dr. Tudor Bompa for sharing his many insights into the theory of training and periodization, Gale Bernhardt for reading and often clarifying the many details of the training method we have discussed for years, Dr. Loren Cordain for opening my eyes to a different way of seeing nutrition, and Ned Overend for supporting my training ideas and writing the Foreword. The quotes at the start of each chapter are from Bill Strickland's excellent book, *The Quotable Cyclist* (Breakaway Books, 1997).

This book was also made a reality due to the loving support of my wife, Joyce, who put up with 4 a.m. wake-up alarms daily for six months. My son, Dirk, continues to be a "proving ground" and sounding board for my training ideas. Thanks.

Most of all I want to thank the many athletes I have coached for the past 20-some years. Their questions, insights, and dedication to excellence have inspired most of what is written here.

FOREWORD

The greatest and most rewarding challenge for cyclists is finding and expanding the limits of our physical abilities.

In my 17-year racing career I have been fortunate to find the combination of training factors that has led to my success in mountain bike racing. The right training has helped me take gold and bronze medals at world championships, win four World Cup races and six national championship titles, and, most recently, win two XTERRA Mountain Bike Triathlon Championships.

From the very beginning of my career I've had a voracious appetite for coaching information. I have sought out and absorbed every book and magazine article I could find on the subject. I've listened to everyone who had advice to give. By filtering through this information and experimenting with a variety of methods, I have devised a personal training program that I continue to fine-tune by learning more about training techniques.

Joe Friel's first book, *The Cyclist's Training Bible*, even though aimed primarily at road racers, has been my most valuable source for training information and was instrumental in refining my self-coaching strategy in the last few years. I waited with much anticipation for Joe's mountain bike version—and he does not disappoint. This book goes well beyond what he has written before.

While reading *The Mountain Biker's Training Bible* my heart rate rose and I started to sweat. I imagined myself in race situations using the fitness gained from the training strategies described here. This is a book I will reference again and again.

When writing for the serious rider, it is not enough to just explain the science of *how* to train. Joe knows that, and he takes training theory out of the classroom and onto the trail, using real-world examples to show *why* his method is effective. He lays out his scientifically based training guidelines in a step-by-step format that simplifies the job of developing a personalized self-coaching program.

Parts of the book that I found particularly helpful focus on hitting several peaks throughout the season; recovering quickly using nutrition, stretching and massage; improving individual weaknesses; recognizing the early symptoms of overtraining; and objectively evaluating race performances.

Over the past fifteen years I have seen scores of talented riders become frustrated at their lack of progress and quit racing. Many of these athletes were more physically gifted than I was at the time. They possessed the talent, the drive and the willingness to endure intense training, but they didn't have the knowledge to create a program tailored to their specific needs. If they had had access to this book and the discipline to follow its strategies, many of them would be racing successfully today.

Whether your goal is to qualify for the Olympic team or to be more competitive on your lunch hour ride, *The Mountain Biker's Training Bible* will guide you to dramatic performance improvements. Even if you are fortunate enough to have a coach who writes your schedule and monitors your progress, it is still important to read this book. It will give you a deeper understanding of why your coach uses certain workouts. You will also learn how to provide feedback to your coach about each training session and your state of recovery.

I still love to ride, develop fitness, and test myself against other mountain bikers—I always will. That's one of the most valuable benefits of Joe's complete coaching approach: A long life of being fit and healthy and enjoying the rides.

—Ned Overend

PREFACE

There is a feeling of great responsibility that comes with writing a book on how to train—especially one that calls itself "the Bible." I know that many readers will take what I've said at face value, never questioning how it may fit with their unique lifestyle. Others, more skeptical, will pick and choose, keeping some and letting the rest go.

Some will purchase this book assuming I have some deep training "secrets" that will miraculously elevate their racing performances. Within a few chapters they will come to realize that this is not the case and that, in fact, the training program prescribed is rather fundamental. Instead of unbelievably difficult workouts, massive training volumes and unusual methods, the emphasis of my program is on establishing a well-defined direction, and following it with consistency and moderation.

Recently a friend sent me a posting from an Internet discussion group in which a rider described how to use the methods I described in *The Cyclist's Training Bible* for mountain bike training. His boiled-down explanation was humorous and concise. Here's what he said:

"Work out, work out, work out, recover.

Work out harder, work out harder, recover.

Work out even harder, recover.

Work out really, really hard, recover.

Recover, recover, race."

How I prepare athletes to race is almost that simple, but that is sometimes difficult for athletes to accept when they are bent on finding "The Secret." Once, after I gave an all-day clinic on training for a cycling club, a rider came up to me and asked in a hushed voice how I *really* trained athletes. Despite having written three books on the subject and spoken to hundreds of athletes at clinics, I still encounter this disbelief that it is really so simple.

Although we would all like to find the "magic bullet" workout that puts us on the podium every week, it doesn't exist. It still comes down to a few basic concepts. My purpose in this book is to describe those concepts. But before we start up this long trail together, it might be helpful if you know more about me and how my training ideas came about.

The training philosophy and methods I use began to develop with my own competitive aspirations in the 1970s. I went back to school to get a master's degree in exercise science to learn how to better coach myself. In 1980 I bought a running store and, soon after, the bike shop next door. I hired some of the best athletes in the area to work as salespeople. For the next eight years this store was an incubator for my training ideas. Nearly every day those who worked there would discuss, and even argue about, the optimal ways to train. Even our customers would become embroiled in these lengthy debates about the minutiae of training. My coaching philosophy, which is described in Chapter 1, developed in these years. It was further refined when I decided to leave retail and spend more time coaching the local athletes who served as my "lab rats."

What's popular in training is always changing. When I was a collegiate runner in the 1960s, nearly all of my coach's training program was based on intervals. Long, slow distance (nicknamed LSD) was in vogue during the 1970s and many seemed to thrive on it. The notion was that doing all of one's training at a low to moderate intensity for hour after hour would develop superior aerobic fitness. In recent years there has been a rebirth of interest in LSD. In the 1980s high-intensity training with an emphasis on intervals came into fashion once again.

As sport science, a relatively young field of study, began to mature in the 1990s, training became more scientific and less intuitive. Many top athletes began working under the tutelage of exercise physiologists and physicians instead of with former elite athletes who had retired into coaching. The scientific approach continues to mold our current methods.

Developing parallel to these training changes throughout this 30-year period was the concept of "periodization." I was, and continue to be, fascinated by the notion that we can manipulate the elements of training—frequency, intensity, duration and mode—throughout the season to produce peak fitness at predetermined times. I have read everything on this topic I could get my hands on, including the seminal work of the Romanian Dr. Tudor Bompa, *Theory and Methodology of Training*. A few years ago I was fortunate to spend some time with Dr. Bompa picking his brain about the origins of periodization. Much of this book is based on his work.

Out of this background grew the concepts you will find discussed in this book.

The Mountain Biker's Training Bible is the third book in a series I have been working on since 1995. The first in the series was *The Cyclist's Training Bible,* and the second was *The Triathlete's Training Bible.* Some of what is included here is based on those previous books, with information updated when appropriate, but there is also a great deal that is entirely new.

Part I explores the subjective side of being a successful self-coached athlete. Not only is it important to develop a personal training philosophy, it is also necessary to be realistic about what it takes to succeed—ability and motivation.

In Part II the scientific side of training is examined. Basic concepts regarding physiology, stress, fatigue, and the principles of training are discussed in Chapter 3. Chapter 4 describes perhaps the most misunderstood side of training—intensity.

Part III begins describing the process of self-coaching with an analysis of who you are as an athlete and what is necessary for racing success.

How to periodize your training is described in a step-by-step manner in Part IV. In some ways this is the heart of the book—the part you will return to year after year to develop training plans for each new season. It ends with detailed case studies of two athletes I coached through their 1999 racing seasons. The purpose is to provide examples of how periodization works in the real world.

In Part V we examine the highs and lows of training. Chapter 10 looks at how to prepare for a successful race, from peaking to warm-up to strategy to post-race evaluation; and Chapter 11 delves into the darker side—illness, burnout and overtraining.

Part VI covers five topics that will help to further refine your training program. These include the problems and solutions for winter training, strength and stretching, the unique needs of subgroups within mountain biking, using a training diary, and fueling the body.

This book was written specifically for the serious and dedicated mountain biker. It assumes that the reader has experience in the sport and that basic bike-handling skills are established. Those who are brand-new to the sport are advised to simply spend time riding, preferably under the tutelage of a local coach or with more experienced riders.

The book also assumes that your health is sound. If there is any reason at all to believe that this is not the case, you are strongly advised to consult with your physician before beginning the demanding training program described here-in.

The purpose of *The Mountain Biker's Training Bible* is to make you a better self-coach and, ultimately, a more successful mountain bike racer. To that end I have tried to make this book both understandable and practical. I hope I have succeeded and that your enjoyment of mountain biking continues to grow for many years to come.

Joe Friel
Fort Collins, Colorado
March 2000

THE SELF-COACHED ATHLETE

Most elite mountain bikers train under the watchful eye of a coach because they recognize the value of having another point of view. They also understand that a coach is usually more experienced and objective so he or she can make wiser day-to-day decisions. And since the athlete's racing career depends on staying healthy, injury-free and fit while avoiding overtraining and burnout, the best coach possible is hired. Self-coaching, however, is far more common among nonelite racers due to budget constraints, the mistaken belief that coaches only work with elites, and the challenge of coaching oneself.

Self-coaching can be effective if its many pitfalls are avoided. The obvious ones have to do with anticipating common training mistakes that lead to frequent breakdowns. Chapter 1 addresses this issue by proposing a philosophy of training that will guide your daily decisions and keep you on track. Chapter 2 offers guidance in understanding yourself—especially your potential in the sport.

SMART TRAINING

*People write and call me and ask me to describe a general training week.
But they don't need my general training week, they need their general
training week. They need to figure their ideal training situation.*

—NED OVEREND

Just as Ned Overend does, I frequently get e-mail and fax communications from riders asking me how they should train. They want to perform as well as some of the riders I have been fortunate to work with. While I'm flattered that they have so much confidence in my coaching ability, I have to tell them that it is difficult, if not impossible, to provide such guidance for someone I don't know.

When I begin to train athletes, I start getting to know them fairly well—but it still takes weeks to determine exactly how they should train. There are many individual factors to consider in developing an effective training program, which is why it is difficult to do for a stranger. A few of these factors are:

- Years of experience in the sport
- Age and maturational level
- How training has progressed in the long term
- Most recent training program
- Personal strengths and weaknesses
- Local terrain and weather conditions
- Schedule of important races are scheduled
- Details of the most important races: duration, terrain, competition, previous results
- Recent and current health status
- Lifestyle stress (work and family issues, for example)

**Individual factors must
be considered in training.**

The list could go on and on. There are simply too many unknowns for me or anyone else to advise a stranger on how best to prepare for competition. After all, right now no one knows you as well as you do. Only you can make such decisions. All that is needed are the tools. That's why I wrote *The Mountain Biker's Training Bible*—so that you might do a better job of self-coaching.

Before we get into the details of day-to-day training, however, it is important for you to establish an understanding of what goes into making smart training decisions.

SYSTEMATIC TRAINING

Some structure is necessary for peak performance.

This book is about systematic and methodical training. Some riders think of that as boring and would rather work out spontaneously. They prefer to train by the seats of their pants—no planning, no forethought and minimal structure. I won't deny that it is possible to become a good rider without a highly structured system and method. I have known many who have been successful with such an approach. But I've also noticed that when these same athletes decide to compete at the highest levels, they nearly always increase the structure of their training. Structured systems and methods are critical for achieving peak performance. It won't happen haphazardly.

But it should also be pointed out that the system and methods described in this book are not the only ones that will produce peak racing performance. There are many systems that work; there are as many as there are coaches and elite athletes. There is no one "right" way—no system that will guarantee success for everyone.

The "secret" to successful training is a comprehensive program.

There are also no secrets. You won't find any magic workouts, miracle diet supplements or all-purpose periodization schemes. Everything in this book is already known and used by at least some riders. No coach, athlete or scientist has a winning secret—at least not one that is legal. Many have developed effective systems, however. Effective training systems are marked by comprehensively integrated components. They are not merely collections of workouts. All of the parts of effective programs fit together neatly, like the pieces of a complex jigsaw puzzle. Furthermore, there is an underlying philosophy that ties the parts together. All aspects of a sound program are based on this philosophy.

TRAINING PHILOSOPHY

Does fatigue produce fitness?

Is there a relationship between fatigue and speed? Are there studies showing that if a rider gets really tired in training and does that often enough, he or she will get faster? Does starting workouts with chronically tired legs somehow improve power and other aspects of race fitness?

I pose these questions because so many athletes tell me that there's no improvement unless they feel at least a little sluggish all the time. But when I ask these same athletes why they train the answer always is, "To get faster for racing." Chronic fatigue seems to be a strange way to get faster.

Recently I did a Web search of the sports science journals to see if any research has found a positive relationship between fatigue and athletic performance. Of the 2036 studies I came across on these subjects, not a single one showed that an athlete performed better if he or she got tired often enough.

All of this leads me to believe that athletes who keep themselves chronically tired and leg weary must be making a mistake. Either that or they have a training secret. But I doubt it. More than likely the reason for their excessive training is a combination of an overly developed work ethic and obsessive-compulsive behavior.

In fact, there are a few athletes I have been unable to train for this reason. When I allow them to rest in order to go into a hard workout fresh, they interpret the lack of fatigue as a loss of fitness and become paranoid. After a few episodes of their putting in "extra" intervals, miles, hours and workouts, we part company. My purpose in coaching is not to help otherwise well-intentioned athletes keep their addiction going. I'd like to see them race faster, not just be more tired. **Training or addiction?**

On the other hand, I have trained many athletes in a variety of sports on a program of less training than they were accustomed to. It's amazing to see what they can accomplish once they fully commit to their actual training purpose—to get faster. When riders go into hard workouts feeling fresh and snappy the speeds and power produced are exceptional. As a result, the muscles, nervous system, cardiovascular system and energy systems are all optimally stressed. Once they have a few more days of recovery to allow for adaptation, we do it again. And guess what—they are even faster.

My training methodology is not complicated. It's based on this philosophy:

Do the least amount of the most effective training at the appropriate times. **Training philosophy stated.**

What this means is that there are times when it's right to do higher volume training, but not necessarily the highest possible. Thi is usually in the Base or general preparation period of training. There are also times when high volume is not wise, but faster, more race-specific training is right. These are the Build and Peak or specific preparation" periods. (Periods are explained in Chapter 7.)

While it seems so simple, there are many who can't seem to get it right. They put in lots of miles when they should be trying to get faster. And when they should be building a base of general fitness, they're going fast—usually in group hammer sessions.

So what do you use to gauge your progress—how tired you are or fast you are? If it's the former you're doomed to a career of less-than-stellar racing. Once you figure out that fatigue gets in the way of getting faster and you make the necessary changes, you'll be flying.

CONSISTENT TRAINING

Theoretically, you can probably accept the philosophy expressed here. But chances are, when it comes time to train, you often adopt a "more is better" philosophy. For example, what choice do you typically make when you:

- Feel tired, but have a hard workout planned?
- Are afraid of losing fitness while taking time off even though you feel wasted?
- Believe your competition is putting in more training time than you?
- Feel like your training partners are riding too fast?
- Sense there is only one interval left in you?
- Think you could do more, but aren't sure?
- Have a "bad" race?
- Seem to have plateaued or even lost fitness?

Answers to everyday training questions indicate philosophy.

If your personal philosophy is "more is better," you will answer these questions differently than if it is "do the least amount of the most effective training at the appropriate times." Do you see the difference?

This is not to say that you shouldn't do hard workouts or that it isn't necessary to push the limits on occasion and experience fatigue as a result. It's obvious that if coming close to your riding potential is your goal, then you must often face and conquer training challenges. The problem arises when you don't know when to back off, when to rest, and when to do less than planned. The inevitable consequences of "more is better" are burnout, overtraining, illness and injury. Extended or frequent downtime due to such problems inevitably results in a loss of fitness and the need to rebuild by returning to previous, lower levels of training. Riders who experience these problems with some regularity seldom achieve their potential in the sport.

Consistent training produces great fitness.

Training consistently, not extremely, is the route to the highest possible fitness and your ultimate racing performances. The key to consistency is moderation and rest. That may not be what you want to hear about in a book on training, but read on to better understand how consistency will make you faster.

MODERATION AND CONSISTENCY

Your body has physiological limits. Muscles will only contract forcefully a certain number of times before they refuse to pull hard again. When glycogen, the body's storage form of carbohydrate energy, begins to run low, no amount of willpower can fuel the body. Slowing down is the only option. If such limits are approached frequently and over a long enough period of time, the body's ability to adapt is exceeded, recovery is greatly delayed, and training consistency is interrupted.

By usually staying within your limits, and infrequently stretching them, you can avoid breakdowns and achieve consistent training results. You should finish most workouts feeling like you could have done a bit more. For example, when there is only one hill repeat left in you, and digging really deep is the only way to complete it, stop. Don't do it. The risk of breaking training consistency is greater than the possible gain from one more effort.

Know when to stop.

The time to abandon a training session is when your speed or power has noticeably decreased, or pedaling and handling techniques are becoming sloppy. Some riders are so focused and determined that they lose control of the workout in such situations and mistakenly believe that continuing will make them faster. It won't.

This is a good example of why training under the watchful and objective eye of a coach allows some athletes to race so well. It's not because the coach pushes them, but rather because he or she knows when to stop the workout and when the athlete should do less.

The self-coached mountain biker must learn to think objectively and unemotionally. It should be as if you are two people—one is the rider and the other is the coach. The coach must be in charge. When the rider says, "Do more," the coach should question whether that's wise. Doubt is a good enough reason to discontinue the session. When in doubt—leave it out.

Do every workout conservatively, but with a cocky attitude. When the coach stops the hill repeats workout at just the right time, and the rider says, "I could have done more," stopping is not a loss—it's a victory.

Train conservatively— ride cocky.

Hard workouts progress through a discomfort-hurt-agony sequence. Be assured that when "agony" is reached, nothing happens that is more physiologically advantageous than the benefits achieved at the "hurt" level, but the risk of a training breakdown rises dramatically. There is no scientific evidence to support the need for frequent supreme efforts in training, but there is a great deal of support for the notion that moderate stress is beneficial in the long term.

In fact, during most of the year training is best devoted to building or maintaining the more basic elements of fitness with moderate effort and duration.

REST AND CONSISTENCY

What's the first aspect of daily life most athletes cut back on when they are pressed for time and feel the need to fit in a workout? The answer is sleep. They get up earlier or go to bed later in order to wedge more into each day.

Sleep must not be compromised.

The problem with this way of "creating" time is that it compromises recovery and adaptation. It's during rest, especially sleep, that the body mends and grows stronger. While we sleep, human growth hormone is released in spurts. If our time spent snoozing is shortened, it takes us longer to recover and our consistency in training suffers. Glycogen stores aren't fully replenished between workouts, leading to decayed endurance performance over several days. Damaged cells take longer to heal, raising the risk of injury and illness. If the training workload remains high despite decreased sleep time, overtraining becomes a real threat. Burnout is waiting just around the corner.

A well-rested rider looks forward to workouts, enjoys being on the bike, is powerful, has good endurance, and grows progressively stronger as a result of training. Never underestimate your need for sleep.

The average person needs seven or more hours of sleep every day. A hard-riding mountain biker may need more. As the intensity and volume of training rise so does the need for slumber. Because they realize how critical it is to their success, many professional riders get in 10 or more hours of sleep a day—including a daily nap.

The quality of sleep may be improved by:

How to improve the quality of sleep.

- Going to bed at a regular time every night, including the night before races
- Darkening the room in the last hour before bedtime and narrowing your focus by reading or engaging in light conversation
- Sleeping in a dark, well-ventilated room that is 60 to 64 degrees Fahrenheit (16 to 18 Celsius)
- Taking a warm bath before bed
- Progressively contracting and relaxing muscles to induce total body relaxation
- Avoiding stimulants such as coffee and tea in the last several hours before going to bed
- Restricting alcohol (which interferes with sleep patterns) prior to retiring

YOU MUST OVERREACH

I hope I've not led you to believe that doing the least amount of the most effective training is easy. The training philosophy described above does not mean that you should never challenge yourself. In fact, in order to become the best rider possible, it's not only important, but necessary to "overreach." That means occasionally taking a risk and attempting more than you think is possible. This shouldn't be done every day.

Once every 14 to 21 days, push the limits of the envelope. This will leave you extremely fatigued and in need of extra recovery days. That's okay. Just plan for it. In a later chapter I'll describe overreaching cycles, recovery and transition periods. All of this must be understood if you're to overreach successfully—and safely.

Periodic overreaching is necessary for success.

COMMITMENT

Striving for peak performance is a 24-hour-a-day, 352-day-a-year task. Racing at the highest possible levels demands a full-time commitment that is not just training related. The higher the goals, the more life must revolve around eating, sleeping and working out. Eating nutritious food fuels the body for training and helps speed recovery by replenishing depleted energy and nutrient stores and by providing the building blocks for a stronger body. Sleeping and working out have a synergistic effect on fitness.

Lifestyle is a part of "training."

Every day you have lifestyle choices to make about diet, sleep, and other physical and mental activities. The decisions you make, often without even thinking, will impact how well you ride.

A fully committed rider is a student of the sport. Read everything you can get your hands on. Talk with coaches, trainers, athletes, mechanics, race officials, salespeople, and anyone else who may have a unique perspective. Ask questions, but be a bit skeptical. If you're to grow as an athlete, change is necessary. Other knowledgeable people are often the sources for this change.

Learn all you can about the sport.

Training to improve includes keeping a training log. Record workout details, perceptions of effort, stress signals, race results and analyses, signs of increasing or decreasing fitness, equipment changes, and anything else that describes your daily experience. It may all prove helpful down the road. Most athletes also find that keeping a log provides them with a sharper training focus and more rapid growth toward their goals.

Keep a log.

Each of us has a comfortable level of commitment. There are times when we need to check our "want to" against our "have to." Jobs, families and other responsibilities cannot be forsaken just to ride a bike. Passion must be restrained or we'll quickly alienate others who aren't equally zealous—we will become "bike bums."

Suggested Daily Routines

	Two Workouts Daily		One Workout Daily	
	Work day	No-work day	Work day	No-work day
6:00 am	Awake	Awake	Awake	Awake
:30	Workout 1	Eat	Workout	Eat
7:00	I	Stretch	I	Stretch
:30	I	Personal	I	Personal
8:00	Eat	I	Eat	I
:30	Shower	Workout 1	Shower	Workout
9:00	Work	I	Work	I
:30	I	I	I	I
10:00	I	I	I	I
:30	I	Eat	I	I
11:00	I	Shower	I	I
:30	Eat	Nap	I	Eat
12:00 pm	Nap	Stretch	Eat	Shower
:30	Work	Personal	Nap	Nap
1:00	I	Eat	Work	Personal
:30	I	Personal	I	I
2:00	I	I	I	I
:30	I	Workout 2	I	I
3:00	Eat	I	I	I
:30	I	I	Eat	Eat
4:00	I	I	I	Personal
:30	I	Eat	I	I
5:00	End work	Shower	End work	I
:30	Workout 2	Nap	Personal	I
6:00	I	Stretch	I	I
:30	Eat	Personal	Eat	Eat
7:00	Shower	I	Personal	Personal
:30	Personal	Eat	I	I
8:00	I	Personal	I	I
:30	Eat	I	I	I
9:00	To bed	To bed	To bed	To bed

REFERENCES

Bunt, J. C., et al. "Sex and Training Differences in Human Growth Hormone Levels During Prolonged Exercise." *Journal of Applied Physiology* 61 (1986): 1796.

Farrell, P. A., et al. "Enkephalins, Catecholamines, and Psychological Mood Alterations: Effects of Prolonged Exercise." *Medicine and Science in Sports and Exercise* 19 (1987): 347.

Heath, G. W., et al. "Exercise and the Incidence of Upper Respiratory Tract Infections." *Medicine and Science in Sports and Exercise* 23 (1991): 152.

Houmard, J. A., et al. "Testosterone, Cortisol, and Creatine Kinase Levels in Male Distance Runners During Reduced Training." *International Journal of Sports Medicine* 11 (1990): 41.

MacIntyre, J. G. "Growth Hormone and Athletes." *Sports Medicine* 4 (1987): 129.

Weltman, A., et al. "Endurance Training Amplifies the Pulsatile Release of Growth Hormone: Effects of Training Intensity." *Journal of Applied Physiology* 72 (1992): 2188.

ABILITY
AND MOTIVATION

*It becomes a part of your body, and all the movements just
become one hundred percent natural. When you get to that
point on a mountain bike, then you're a good rider.*

—JOHN TOMAC

How good can you become at mountain bike racing? Do you have the genes to
excel? After all, racing off-road is physically demanding—you can't fake it. There
isn't a team to protect you, and there are no wheels to follow closely to reduce your effort.
It's just the bike, your breathing and your thumping heart.

What motivates you to endure all of the suffering? Why do you train and race? Is it
for self-satisfaction, to impress others, to gather trophies, to seek and overcome challenges, or simply to have fun? Maybe it's some combination of these, or something
entirely different.

In the final analysis, success simply comes down to these two ingredients—ability
and motivation. The champions in the sport are blessed with ample ability and they are
highly motivated. These people are easy to pick out at an early age because of their
enthusiasm for sport and their easy successes.

There are also riders with great ability but little motivation. They display brief
glimpses of potential when they are mentally "on," yet they seldom stand atop the podium. Such riders get down on themselves and frequently need pep talks from others to
get back on track. They often fail to finish races and their workout consistency is poor.

Then there are those who have limited ability but a burning desire to excel. This
group may account for the majority of those who put a bike on the start line. In their
desire to become champions, these riders are prone to overtraining, burnout and injury.
They don't know when to stop. The philosophy expressed in Chapter 1 is critical for

**Success depends on ability
and motivation.**

keeping these riders on track.

The low-motivation, low-ability group seldom makes it in mountain biking. In fact, most aren't even attracted to the sport. There are very few of these people on the trails.

You're probably in either the first (high ability, high motivation) or third (low ability, high motivation) group, since the other two don't read books on how to train—they don't care. How well you do in mountain biking depends on your personal mix of these two ingredients, tempered by a third—opportunity. Let's take a closer look.

ABILITY

Genetics have a lot to do with achievement in sport. There are some obvious examples of this: Tall basketball players, huge sumo wrestlers, small jockeys and long-armed swimmers are but a few. Such athletes were born with at least one of the physical traits necessary to succeed in their chosen sport.

Physical characteristics and racing.

What are the physical traits common to most of those who are at the pinnacle of mountain bike racing? The most obvious is a small and lean stature. The top racers typically have a low body mass. One simple way to express body mass is by comparing body weight to height. The podium finishers in the elite field are usually less than 2 pounds per inch of height (0.35kg/cm). This is often the case because the ability to powerfully propel the combined weight of bike and body uphill is a significant determiner of race outcome.

It should be pointed out, however, that the smallest rider isn't always the victor. There are other physical traits that aren't quite as obvious as stature. In the example of climbing hills, muscular power is another key trait. We can't see power in a rider in the same way we can see body mass. There are other physiological traits that define ability in mountain bike racing, including aerobic capacity (VO_2 max), lactate threshold and economy (see Chapter 3 for details). These are somewhat determined by genetics, but they may also be improved by training.

So how much natural ability do you have? How close are you to reaching your potential? No one can say for sure. The best indicator may be how you've done in the sport in the past relative to your training. Good results combined with mediocre training usually indicate untapped potential. Excellent training with poor results is also revealing of potential.

Compare results and training to get a glimpse of potential.

If you are new to the sport with less than three years of racing, your results may not tell you much about your ability and potential. In the first three years there are a lot of changes happening at the cellular level—changes that will eventually reveal a rider's ability. This means that even if someone new to the sport is successful, he or she may not continue to dominate. Other beginners may eventually catch up to and surpass the most successful novices. This is often due to the different rates at which the human body responds to training.

Some people are "fast responders" and others are "slow responders." Fast responders gain fitness quickly because, for some unknown reason, their cells are capable of changing rapidly. Others take much longer, perhaps years, to realize the same gains. The problem for slow responders is that they often give up before reaping the benefits of training. Figure 2.1 illustrates the response curve.

Fast and slow responders.

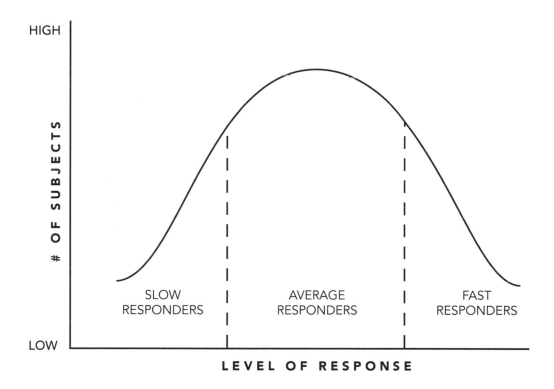

FIGURE 2.1
Theoretical bell-shaped curve indicating level of response to a given training stimulus.

MOTIVATION

The highly motivated mountain biker has a passion for the sport. Passion is generally evident in how much time is devoted to riding, caring for the bike, reading books and magazines about mountain biking, associating with other riders and simply thinking about the sport.

Those who are passionate about the sport also frequently have a well-developed work ethic. They believe that hard training is what produces good results. Up to a point that is a valuable trait to have, as success does indeed demand consistency in training, as pointed out in Chapter 1. The problem is that the combination of passion for mountain biking and a strong work ethic sometimes leads to obsessive-compulsive training. These riders just can't stop riding. If they do, their sense of guilt can become overwhelming. For such athletes, training interruptions—such as injuries, business trips or vacations—are emotionally devastating. This is because their training pattern may be disrupted, but their obsessive motivation is still intact.

Passion and work ethic are a potentially harmful combination.

This obsessive-compulsive trait is most common in riders who are new to the sport. They believe that they discovered the sport too late in life and need to catch up with others by training a lot. No wonder overtraining is rampant among those in their first three years of racing.

Regardless of when in life you started or how burning your desire is to be good, it's critical that you view excellence in athletics as a journey, not a destination. You will never arrive at the point where you are fully satisfied with performance. That's the nature of highly motivated people. So obsessive-compulsive training in order to achieve racing nirvana—where you can finally back off—is not going to happen. Once you realize this

Excellence is a journey— not a destination.

and take a long-term approach to training, your breakdowns from overtraining, burnout and illness will diminish, allowing you to achieve training greater consistency and better race performances. You will also experience less mental anguish and frustration when the inevitable setbacks occur.

Mountain biking is a life-long sport to be enjoyed for what it brings to your life— superb fitness, excellent health, enjoyable times and good friends. It is not an opponent to be subdued and conquered.

OPPORTUNITY

The chances are great that the best potential athlete in the world is an overweight and sedentary smoker. Right now, sitting in front of a television somewhere is this person born to be the world champion in mountain biking and to dominate the sport as no one ever has. At birth he was blessed with a huge aerobic capacity and all of the other physiological ingredients necessary for success. The problem is that he never had the opportunity to discover his ability, even though the motivation may have been there.

Ability and motivation without opportunity mean nothing.

Maybe he was born into poverty and forced to work at an early age to help feed the family. Maybe he lives in a war-ravaged corner of the world where staying alive is the number one priority. Or perhaps mountain biking just never caught his attention and he instead found some success in soccer. We'll never know what he could have been because the opportunity never presented itself.

The lack of opportunity need not be so extreme to hold back your growth as a mountain biker, however. If any of the following are missing, your opportunity to realize full potential may be compromised:

- Off-road trails
- Terrain variety—flats, hills and technical trail sections
- Adequate nutrition
- Good equipment
- Coaching
- Training partners
- Weight-room equipment
- Time to train
- Available races
- A low-stress environment
- Supportive family and friends

This list could go on and on—there are many environmental elements that contribute to your overall opportunity to achieve your potential in mountain biking. The greater your desire to excel, the more important it becomes to mold your lifestyle and environment to match your aspirations. That's what the remainder of this book is all about.

One's total environment determines opportunity.

REFERENCES

Atkinson, J. W. and W.R. Reitman. "Performance as a Function of Motive Strength and Expectancy of Goal Attainment." *Journal of Abnormal and Social Psychology* 53 (1956): 361–366.

Coyle, E. F., et al. "Physiological and Biomechanical Factors Associated with Elite Endurance Cycling Performance." *Medicine and Science in Sports and Exercise* 23, no. 1 (1991): 93–107.

Mahoney, M. J. and M. Avener. "Psychology of the Elite Athlete: An Exploratory Study." *Cognitive Therapy and Research* 1 (1977): 135–141.

part II

FROM LAB TO TRAIL

Athletes now have more knowledge available to them than at any time in history. In the last 20 years, sport science has taught us more about how the human body works during exercise than we learned in the preceding millennium. In the late twentieth century, elite athletes and their coaches challenged the ways we think about intervals, strength development, recovery, and myriad other training topics. During that same period, sports equipment manufacturers designed products that changed the way we think about training.

Much of this information is now readily accessible through Internet news groups on the World Wide Web, and in books, periodicals, popular magazines, videos and seminars. As a result, training continues to improve, but it also becomes more complex and confusing. For the self-coached rider, it may seem that there is just too much information available.

The purpose of Part II is to go back to the basics of what is known about human performance—demystifying and simplifying what often appears to be a very puzzling subject. Chapter 3 examines several exercise physiology topics that form the basis for the training program presented in the remainder of the book. Chapter 4 looks at one of the most misunderstood aspects of exercise—intensity.

For the reader with little interest in sport science or training theory, this part of The Mountain Biker's Training Bible *may present a challenge. But a solid base of understanding will help in the development of an effective training program, producing better race results.*

THE SCIENCE OF TRAINING

*Having all the sport science knowledge in the world, having all the best coaches,
having all the equipment, will that win a gold medal for you?
No. But not having all that can lose it for you.*

—CHRIS CARMICHAEL

Effective mountain bike training requires both wisdom and knowledge. Wisdom involves knowing the sport and yourself well enough to produce sound, commonsense decisions every day. The athlete lacking in wisdom frequently makes poor choices based on fleeting emotions. As a result, easy days become too hard, personal weaknesses are left unexplored, and planned workouts turn into purposeless play.

The first two chapters of this book are about wisdom, but this chapter and the next address knowledge. A solid grip on the science of training will help you understand why training plans, weekly patterns, and workouts are done in particular ways. This may prove to be difficult reading, but bear with it. Grasping the "why" of training will be helpful in later chapters.

PHYSIOLOGY AND FITNESS

How can we measure physical fitness? Science has discovered three of its most basic components—aerobic capacity, lactate threshold and economy. The top riders have excellent values for all three of these physiological traits.

AEROBIC CAPACITY

Aerobic capacity is a measure of the amount of oxygen the body can consume during all-out endurance exercise. It is also referred to as "VO_2 max"—the maximal volume of oxygen. VO_2 max can be measured in the lab during a "graded" test in which the athlete, wearing a device that measures oxygen uptake, increases the intensity of exercise every few minutes until exhaustion. VO_2 max is expressed in terms of milliliters of oxygen used per kilogram of body weight per minute (ml/kg/min). World-class male riders usually produce numbers in the 70 to 80 ml/kg/min range. By comparison, normally active male college students are typically test in the range of 40 to 50 ml/kg/min. On average, women's aerobic capacities are about 10 percent lower than men's.

Aerobic capacity is largely determined by genetics and is limited by such physiological factors as heart size, heart rate, heart stroke volume, blood hemoglobin content, aerobic enzyme concentrations, mitochondrial density and muscle fiber type. It is, however, trainable to a certain extent. Typically, it takes six to eight weeks of high-intensity training to produce VO_2 max peak values.

As we get older, aerobic capacity usually drops—by as much as 1 percent per year after age 25 in sedentary people. For those who train seriously, especially by regularly including high intensity workouts, the loss is far smaller and may not occur at all until the late 30s.

LACTATE THRESHOLD

Aerobic capacity is not a good predictor of endurance performance. If all of the riders in a race category were tested for aerobic capacity, the race finishing results would not necessarily correlate to their VO_2 max test values. The athletes with the highest VO_2 max values would not necessarily finish high in the rankings. But the highest value of VO_2 max that one can maintain for an extended period of time is a good predictor of racing capacity. This sustainable high value is a reflection of the lactate threshold.

Lactate threshold, sometimes also called "anaerobic threshold" (or "onset blood lactate accumulation" or "lactate turn point" or "ventilatory threshold"), is the level of exercise intensity above which lactate begins to rapidly accumulate in the blood. At this point metabolism rapidly shifts from dependence on the combustion of fat and oxygen in the production of energy to dependence on glycogen—the storage form of carbohydrate. The higher this threshold is, as a percentage of VO_2max, the faster the athlete can ride for an extended period of time, as in a race. Once the lactate reaches a high enough level, there is no option but to slow down in order to clear it from the blood.

Sedentary individuals experience lactate threshold at 40 to 50 percent of VO_2max. In trained athletes, the lactate threshold typically occurs at 80 to 90 percent of VO_2max. So it is obvious that if two riders have the same aerobic capacity, but rider A's lactate threshold is 90 percent and B's is 80 percent, then A should be able to maintain a higher

VO2 max is the same thing as aerobic capacity.

Lactate threshold is a good predictor of performance.

average velocity and has quite a physiological advantage in a head-to-head race.

Compared with aerobic capacity, lactate threshold is highly trainable. Much of the training detailed in this book is intended to elevate the lactate threshold.

ECONOMY

Compared with recreational riders, elite mountain bikers use less oxygen to hold a given, steady, submaximal velocity. The elite riders are using less energy to produce the same power output. This is similar to automobile fuel efficiency ratings that tell prospective buyers which cars are the gas guzzlers. Using less fuel to produce the same amount of power is an obvious advantage in competition.

Economy is a measure of fuel efficiency.

Studies reveal that an endurance athlete's economy improves if he or she:

- Has a high percentage of slow twitch muscle fibers (largely determined by genetics)
- Has a low body mass (weight to height relationship)
- Has low psychological stress
- Uses light and aerodynamic equipment that fits properly
- Limits body frontal area exposed to the wind at higher velocities
- Eliminates useless and energy-wasting movements

Fatigue negatively impacts economy as muscles that are not normally called on are recruited to carry the load. That's why it's critical to go into important races well rested. Near the end of a race, when economy deteriorates due to fatigue, you may sense that your pedaling and technical handling skills are "getting sloppy." The longer the race is, the more critical economy becomes in determining the outcome.

Just as with lactate threshold, economy is highly trainable. Not only does it improve by increasing all aspects of endurance, but it also rises as you refine bike skills. This is why I emphasize drill work for pedaling in the winter training months and a commitment to improving handling skills year round.

PERSPECTIVE

The preceding discussion probably makes it sound as if fitness can be easily quantified and, perhaps, used to predict or even produce top athletes. Fortunately, that's not the case. The best scientists in the world can take a group of the most fit mountain bikers into a state-of-the-art lab, test, poke, prod, measure, and analyze them, then predict how they will do in a race—and fail miserably. Labs are just not the real world of racing, where many variables beyond the ken of science escape quantification.

TRAINING STRESS

There are five terms used repeatedly in this book that relate to the stresses applied in training; you need to understand these terms. By carefully changing workout *frequency*, *duration* and *intensity* throughout the season, the body's comfortable state is disturbed, forcing it to adapt with the positive changes we call "fitness." This manipulation has to do with *volume* and *workload*. Let's briefly examine each of these terms.

FREQUENCY

This refers to how often training sessions are done. Novice riders may work out five or six times a week and experience a rapid change in fitness, perhaps in the range of 10 to 20 percent improvement. Experienced mountain bikers train with greater frequency, often doing 2 workouts a day at certain times of the year. Seven to 12 sessions in a week are more common at this level. But such high frequency may only produce a 1-percent gain in fitness, since these athletes are already so close to their potential.

How often do you ride?

Should a novice try to train at the same high level as the more experienced rider, he or she may actually see a decrease in fitness due to overtraining. If the experienced rider trains for a substantial length of time at the novice's low level, there will also be a loss of fitness because of undertraining—the stress frequency is too low.

The frequency at which you work out is dependent on what your body is currently adapted to. For example, even if you're an experienced rider but have not trained for several weeks, it's best to start with a lower frequency and gradually increase it.

DURATION

Training sessions may vary considerably in length. Some last several hours in order to improve aerobic endurance. Others are short, to allow for higher efforts or to promote recovery. Just as frequency is, workout duration is determined by experience level, with seasoned riders generally doing the longest sessions.

How long do you ride?

Duration may be measured in time or in distance covered. *The Mountain Biker's Training Bible* bases training sessions on time.

The appropriate time for long rides is largely determined by the anticipated duration of your races. Workout durations equal to, or up to twice as long as, your longest race are common. But there are obvious exceptions, especially at the high end. If you are training for the Leadville 100-mile Trail Race, your longest rides will seldom, if ever, be as long as the anticipated race time.

INTENSITY

Frequency and duration are easy to quantify, so athletes often refer to them in describing their training program. They may, for example, say that they rode seven times last week for a total of 14 hours. This actually only describes a portion of their training—the portion called "volume." Volume is the combination of frequency and duration, and it does, indeed, provide an idea of what an athlete's training is like. But volume is an incomplete description of the stress of training.

Volume = Frequency x Duration.

A better summary of one's training is "workload," defined as the combination of volume and intensity. By also knowing how hard the rider trained—how much effort or power went into each workout—the stress magnitude is more completely defined. The problem for the average rider is that it's difficult to quantify intensity in the same way that frequency and duration are quantified. One way to do this is to assign an average exertion level to each training session when it is completed, using a 1 to 10 scale with 1 being extremely easy and 10 an all-out race effort. By multiplying the number of minutes of the session by the exertion level, workload is adequately quantified.

Workload = Volume x Intensity

For example, let's say you rode for 60 minutes including a warm-up, several high-intensity hill repeats, and a cool-down. And assume that you assigned an average effort level of 7 to this entire session. Your workload would then be 420 (7 x 60).

To determine weekly workload, which includes frequency, add up the daily workload values. By comparing the workloads for a number of weeks, you can see how the stress experienced by the body changes.

Training intensity is the stressor that athletes most often get wrong. They ride a little too intensely when they should be taking it easy and, as a consequence, are slightly tired when a high intensity workout is needed. All training shifts toward mediocrity as the easy rides become too hard and the hard rides too easy. For most mountain bikers, getting the intensity right is the key to moving up to the next level of performance. Chapter 4 offers greater detail on this complex issue.

How hard do you ride?

Volume versus Intensity

Which is more important—volume or intensity? Given the finite amounts of physical resources available to the rider, should he or she get in as many miles as possible or ride fewer miles with high intensity?

The answers to such questions depend on the rider's level of experience in the sport. Those new to cycling will improve rapidly merely by riding frequently and with relatively high durations. As the rider becomes more experienced—and fit—increases

Novices should focus on volume, veterans on intensity.

in volume have less and less impact on performance and variations in training intensity become more critical.

FATIGUE

Resistance to fatigue is a marker of fitness.

Were it not for fatigue we would all be champions. How quickly and to what extent we experience fatigue is a great determiner of our fitness level—it is a primary reason for training. The fittest athletes are those who can best resist its slowing effects.

There are several causes of fatigue, but the ones the mountain biker is most concerned with are:

- Lactate accumulation
- Glycogen depletion
- Muscle failure

A sound training program improves fitness by stressing the body's systems associated with these causes of fatigue. Let's briefly examine each.

Lactate Accumulation

Energy for pedaling the bike comes largely from two sources—fat and carbohydrate. The body's storage form of carbohydrate is called "glycogen." As glycogen is broken down to produce energy, lactic acid appears in the working muscle cells. The lactic

Lactate interferes with muscle contraction.

acid gradually seeps out of the cells and into the surrounding body fluids, where it is picked up by the blood stream. As it leaves the cells, hydrogen ions are released and the resulting salt is called "lactate." If the concentration of lactate becomes great enough, its acidic nature reduces the muscle cells' ability to contract, causing the rider to slow down.

Lactate is always present in the blood as the body, uses carbohydrate along with fat for fuel at all levels of exertion—including while you are reading this page. But during exercise, as the use of glycogen increases, there is a concurrent rise in blood lactate levels. At low levels the body has no trouble removing and buffering the acid. But as the intensity of exercise shifts from aerobic (light breathing) to anaerobic (labored breathing), the lactate eventually reaches so great a level that the body is no longer able to remove it at the same rate it is produced. The resulting lactate accumulation causes short-term fatigue. The only way the rider can deal with it now is to slow down so lactate production is decreased and the body can catch up.

This type of fatigue occurs during brief, but extremely high intensity efforts, such as sprinting or climbing a hill. Thus, the way to improve your body's ability to clear

How to train lactate clearance and buffering.

and buffer lactate is by doing short-duration, interval workouts that replicate these race conditions. The Anaerobic Endurance workouts that appear in Appendix B address this cause of fatigue.

Depletion of glycogen

Fat is the primary source of fuel for every ride you do, but as the intensity of the ride varies, the contribution of carbohydrate to the energy demand rises and falls considerably. Figure 3.1 illustrates this shift.

Carbohydrate is stored in the muscles and liver as glycogen and in the blood as glucose. A well-nourished athlete has about 1500 to 2000 kilocalories of glycogen and glucose packed away, depending on body size and fitness level.

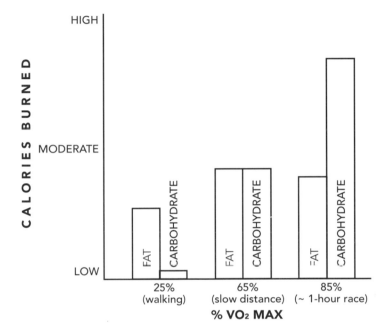

FIGURE 3.1
Relative contribution of fat and carbohydrate (glycogen and glucose) to exercise fuel at three levels of aerobic capacity (VO₂ max). (Adapted from Romijn, J.A., et al. 1993, Regulation of Endogenous Fat and Carbohydrate Metabolism in Relation to Exercise Intensity and Duration. American Journal of Psysiology 265: E380.)

That's not much energy. Most of this, about 75 percent, is in the muscles.

The problem is that when glycogen and glucose stores run low, exercise slows considerably, since the body must now rely primarily on fat for fuel, as shown in Figure 3.1. This is called "bonking."

Low glycogen stores cause the bonk.

A two-and-a-half-hour, cross-country race may have an energy cost of 3000 kilocalories, with perhaps half of that coming from carbohydrate sources. If the rider starts with a low level of glycogen on board and these carbohydrate calories are not replaced during the race, he or she may be forced to abandon the race. The same sorry results may also occur if the rider handles the bike uneconomically or if general aerobic fitness is poor.

Research reveals that a well-trained athlete is capable of storing greater amounts of carbohydrate while using it more sparingly than an untrained person. The diet you habitually eat also determines how much fuel is socked away and how rapidly it is used up. This is discussed in greater detail in Chapter 16.

The athlete's body can be trained to spare glycogen.

Muscle Failure

Exactly what causes the rider's working muscles to fail to contract forcefully near the end of a long and grueling race is unknown. It is probably related to chemical failure at the point of connection between the nerve and the muscle, or by a protective mechanism in the central nervous system intended to prevent muscle damage.

High intensity training may help to fortify the body against muscle failure by training the nervous system to recruit more muscles for endurance activity. Working out at high intensity, as when doing intervals, involves more fast twitch muscles than riding long and slow, which favors slow twitch muscles. Fast twitch muscles are not called on until the effort becomes so great that the slow twitch muscles can no longer handle the effort. As fast twitchers are recruited to support the slow twitchers during what is basically an endurance activity—such as intervals—they begin to take on some of the slow twitch characteristics. This is of great benefit to the endurance athlete.

Fast twitch muscles can be trained to take on slow twitch characteristics.

PRINCIPLES OF TRAINING

Science is incapable of devising a training program that works for all athletes all the time. While such a formula would make it easy to get in shape, it would take all of the fun out of training for competition. Discovering exactly what works and doesn't is the art of training—a critical aspect that will be addressed in later chapters.

But science has provided some general guidelines or principles that, if understood and followed, will keep your training on track.

Progressive Overload

Improving race fitness depends on a balance between "catabolism" and "anabolism." Catabolism refers to the breaking down of cells with stress coming from workouts such as intervals, hills, weights and overdistance rides. Following these training sessions that overload the body's capacity to cope, there is a temporary loss of fitness that may last 24 to 48 hours, depending on the magnitude of the stress applied and other individual factors.

This cell breakdown and accompanying drop in fitness is balanced by the cells slowly regaining and surpassing their previous levels of function. The process by which cells adapt to new stress levels and build to a stronger level is called anabolism. The resulting increase in fitness resulting from anabolism is referred to as "overcompensation." Figure 3.2 illustrates the adaptive process.

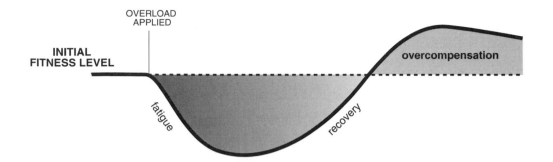

FIGURE 3.2
Overcompensation resulting from a training overload.

If the overload that causes catabolism is too great, or the time allowed for anabolism is too short, causing either condition to last for an extended period of time, overtraining is possible. But when the overload is increased gradually over days, weeks and months, and sufficient time is allowed for the anabolic process of adaptation, fitness steadily increases. This is why I emphasized a conservative approach to training and consistency in Chapter 1.

The overload necessary to produce changes in fitness must progress steadily.

Always keep in mind that the body's cells are sensitive. They do respond to a stressful overload by growing stronger, but only when the proper amount of stress is applied. Too much stress included in too-frequent training causes the cells to struggle for days, perhaps weeks, to recover. No matter how strong your desire to reach peak fitness, the catabolic-anabolic process cannot be rushed. Be patient and train with a long-term perspective.

A long-term perspective is necessary for growth as an athlete.

Specificity

The principle of specificity simply says that in order to achieve peak fitness for mountain bike racing, you must ride a bike. You can't do it by running, jumping rope, skiing or taking aerobics classes. That's not to say that such activities won't help some—they will. But the physiological gains are mostly limited to the heart, lungs and blood. The muscles, nerves and energy systems necessary for cycling receive little or no benefit.

Furthermore, to maximize fitness for mountain bike racing, the greatest portion of the training stress must have a joint and muscle movement pattern exactly like that of riding a mountain bike. Although running and cross-country skiing also depend on the legs for movement, the pattern of usage of the leg's muscles and joints is not the same as in cycling.

The principle of specificity, however, does not intend that you should never cross train. Very early in the season, when the focus of training is on developing the heart, lungs, and blood, activities other than cycling are quite effective. That's why the train-

Cross training has limited value for the serious mountain biker.

ing programs suggested in subsequent chapters encourage sports other than cycling at certain times of the year.

Reversibility

From time to time, all riders experience breaks in training due to illness, injury, job responsibilities, family vacations, and other planned or unplanned interruptions. If the time away from training is long enough, fitness begins to erode. Noticeable losses of fitness are evident within two weeks of missed workouts. By three weeks, race performance begins to suffer badly. Without continued stress from working out, there soon comes a time when the body loses its previous gains. This is the principle of reversibility.

Without physiological stress there is a gradual loss of fitness.

Each of the body's systems and functions has a unique rate of decline when training stress is absent. For example, aerobic fitness is lost faster than anaerobic fitness. According to one study, strength declines faster than power. In addition, the more fit an athlete is, the faster the rate of fitness loss. Table 3.1 lists some of the changes that commonly occur during a period of detraining.

TABLE 3.1

Changes resulting from three weeks of not training

(Adapted from Wilber, R.L. and R.J. Moffatt. 1994. Physiological and biochemical consequences of detraining in aerobically trained individuals. Journal of Strength Conditioning Research 8: 110.)

Measure of Fitness	Change
Aerobic capacity (VO_2 max)	-8 %
Heart stroke volume (blood pumped per beat)	-10 %
Submaximum heart rate (beats/minute)	+4 %
Blood plasma volume	-12 %
Muscle capillary density	-7 %
Oxidative enzymes	-29 %
Blood insulin at rest	+17-120 %
Blood lactate during exercise	+88 %
Lactate threshold	-7 %
Use of fat for fuel during exercise	-52 %
Time to fatigue (minutes)	-10 %

Individuality

While the principles described so far offer general training guidelines, we're all individuals when it comes to deciding exactly what to do in training. What works for one will not work for all others.

This is perhaps the most important principle and the one that serious riders frequently ignore. For example, a steady diet of group "hammer" sessions makes it difficult, if not impossible, to reach peak fitness. You must work to improve race weaknesses while maintaining strengths. This, of necessity, requires that you often train alone.

It's often necessary to train alone.

REFERENCES

Bompa, T. "Physiological Intensity Values Employed to Plan Endurance Training." *New Studies in Athletics* 3, no.4 (1998): 37–52.

Bompa, T. *Theory and Methodology of Training.* Dubuque, IA: Kendall/Hunt, 1983.

Bouchard, C., et al. "Aerobic Performance in Brothers, Dizygotic and Monozygotic Twins." *Medicine and Science in Sports and Exercise* 18 (1986): 639–646.

Brynteson, P. and W. E. Sinning. "The Effects of Training Frequencies on The Retention of Cardiovascular Fitness." *Medicine and Science in Sports and Exercise* 5 (1973): 29–33.

Costill, D. L., et al. "Effects of Reduced Training on Muscular Power in Swimmers." *Physician and Sports Medicine* 13, no. 2 (1985): 94–101.

Costill, D. L., et al. "Adaptations to Swimming Training: Influence of Training Volume." *Medicine and Science in Sports and Exercise* 23 (1991): 371–377.

Coyle, E. F., et al. "Time Course of Loss of Adaptations After Stopping Prolonged Intense Endurance Training." *Journal of Applied Physiology* 57 (1984): 1857.

Coyle, E. F., et al. "Physiological and Biomechanical Factors Associated with Elite Endurance Cycling Performance." *Medicine and Science in Sports and Exercise* 23, no. 1 (1991): 93–107.

Coyle, E. F., et al. "Cycling Efficiency Is Related to the Percentage of Type I Muscle Fibers." *Medicine and Science in Sports and Exercise* 24 (1992): 782.

Daniels, J. "Training Distance Runners—A Primer." *Sports Science Exchange,* 1, no. 11 (1989*):* 1–4.

Fitts, R. H., et al. "Effect of Swim-Exercise Training on Human Muscle Fiber Function." *Journal of Applied Physiology* 66 (1989): 465–475.

Gonzalez, H. and M.L. Hull. "Bivariate Optimization of Pedaling Rate And Crank-Arm Length in Cycling." *Journal of Biomechanics.* 21, no. 10 (1988): 839–849.

Heil, D. P., et al. "Cardiorespiratory Responses to Seat-Tube Angle Variation During Steady-State Cycling." *Medicine and Science in Sports and Exercise* 27 no. 5 (1995): 730–735.

Hickson, R. C., et al. "Reduced Training Intensities and Loss of Aerobic Power, Endurance, snd Cardiac Growth." *Journal of Applied Physiology* 58 (1985): 492–499.

Hopkins, W. G. "Advances in Training for Endurance Athletes." *New Zealand Journal of Sports Medicine* 24, no. 3 (1996): 29–31.

Houmard, J. A., et al. "Reduced Training Maintains Performance in Distance Runners." *International Journal of Sports Medicine* 11 (1990): 46–51.

Houmard, J. A., et al. "The Effects of Taper on Performance in Distance Runners." *Medicine and Science in Sports and Exercise* 26, no. 5 (1994): 624–631.

Jacobs, I., et al. "Blood Lactate: Implications for Training and Sports Performance." *Sports Medicine* 3 (1986): 10–25.

Kearney, J. T. "Training the Olympic Athlete." *The Scientific American,* June 1996: 52–63.

Klissouras, V. "Adaptability of Genetic Variation." *Journal of Applied Physiology* 31 (1971): 338–344.

Loftin, M. and B. Warren. "Comparison of a Simulated 16.1km Time Trial, VO2 Max and Related Factors in Cyclists with Different Ventilatory Thresholds." *International Journal of Sports Medicine* 15, no. 8 (1994): 498–503.

MacLaren, C. P., et al. "A Review of Metabolic and Physiologic Factors in Fatigue." *Exercise and Sports Science Review* 17 (1989): 29.

McArdle, W., F. Katch and V. Katch. *Exercise Physiology.* Baltimore: Eilliams & Wilkins, 1996.

Matveyev, L. *Fundamentals of Sports Training.* Moscow: Progress Publishers, 1977.

Neufer, P. D., et al. "Effects of Reduced Training on Muscular Strength and Endurance in Competitive Swimmers." *Medicine and Science in Sports and Exercise* 19 (1987): 486–490.

Nicholls, J. F., et al. "Relationship Between Blood Lactate Response to Exercise and Endurance Performance in Competitive Female Master Cyclists." *International Journal of Sports Medicine* 18 (1997): 458–463.

Poole, et al. "Determinants of Oxygen Uptake." *Sports Medicine* 24 (1996): 308–320.

Romijn, J. A., et al. "Regulation of Endogenous Fat and Carbohydrate Metabolism in Relation to Exercise Intensity and Duration." *American Journal of Physiology* 265: E380.

Tanaka, K., et al. "A Longitudinal Assessment of Anaerobic Threshold And Distance-Running Performance." *Medicine and Science in Sports and Exercise* 16, no. 3 (1984): 278–282.

Weltman, A. *The Blood Lactate Response to Exercise.* Champaign, IL: Human Kinetics, 1995.

Wenger, H. A., et al. "The Interactions of Intensity, Frequency and Duration of Exercise Training in Altering Cardiorespiratory Fitness." *Sports Medicine* 3, no. 5 (1986): 346–356.

Weston, A. R., et al. "Skeletal Muscle Buffering Capacity and Endurance Performance after High-Intensity Training by Well-Trained Cyclists." *European Journal of Applied Physiology* 75 (1997): 7–13.

Wilber, R. L. and R.J. Moffatt. "Physiological and Biochemical Consequences of Detraining in Aerobically Trained Individuals." *Journal of Strength Conditioning Research* 8 (1994): 110.

Wilmore, J. and D. L. Costill. *Training for Sport and Activity: The physiological Basis of the Conditioning Process.* Champaign, IL: Human Kinetics, 1988.

Wilmore, J. and D. L. Costill. *Physiology of Sport and Exercise.* Champaign, IL: Human Kinetics, 1994.

Wyatt, F. B., et al. "Metabolic Threshold Defined by Disproportionate Increases in Physiological Parameters: A Meta-Analytic Review." *Medicine and Science in Sports and Exercise* 29, no. 5 (1997): S1342.

INTENSITY

If you desire to be groovy and flowing instead of battling and conquering, miles-per-hour is the last equation you want to pay attention to.

—BOB ROLL

Which is more important—volume or intensity? Given the finite amount of energy available to the serious mountain biker, should he or she get in as many miles as possible or ride fewer miles with greater intensity? The answers to these questions depend on the time in the season relative to important races and, more importantly, on the rider's years of experience in the sport. Those new to mountain biking will improve rapidly merely by riding frequently and with relatively high duration. As the rider's experience—and fitness—increases, volume has less and less impact on performance and the intensity of training takes on a greater significance.

HARD TRAINING

Scientific research supports the notion that high intensity training done at the appropriate times is better than relying on long and frequent sessions for producing peak performances in the seasoned athlete. What nearly all studies on this topic have found is that one's average workout velocity, especially in key workouts, is a better predictor of race outcome than one's average training miles.

Volume is a poor predictor of race performance.

One reason that high intensity sessions are so critical has to do with the specificity principle discussed in the last chapter. Recall that this tenet states that a significant portion of the demands placed on the body in training need to reflect what is expected of it in racing. Mountain bike racing is almost always highly intense—it's not a long, slow event. Therefore, at the appropriate times of the year, at least a couple of your weekly training sessions should include race efforts. You simply won't become a great mountain biker by merely focusing on weekly training volume.

Also, as described in Chapter 3, in order to attain peak fitness, three physiological variables must be optimized—VO_2 max, lactate threshold and economy. According to scientific research, the optimal intensity for boosting VO_2 max is 90 to 100 percent of VO_2 max (about 93 to 100 percent of maximum heart rate). Lactate threshold may be improved with workouts that include portions that are 87 to 90 percent of VO_2 max (about 90 to 93 percent of maximum heart rate). And economy is improved with short, high-speed repetitions. Notice that the intensities for optimally developing all three of these are quite high—similar to what is experienced in a race. A steady diet of only low and moderate intensities will not produce peak fitness for the typical mountain bike race, which lasts one to three hours.

Additionally, hard workouts, but not moderate or easy ones, cause the pituitary gland to release large amounts of human growth hormone. This is the stuff that builds muscles, repairs bones, maintains ligaments and heals tendons. Human growth hormone also speeds up the metabolism, making the body into a better fat-burner and thereby improving body composition and power. According to research, the optimal intensity for producing human growth hormone is above 90 percent of maximum heart rate.

Bear in mind that a steady diet of hard training without adequate rest and recovery is a formula for the overtraining, burnout and illness that interrupt the consistency of training, causing a setback. Hard days must be balanced against easy ones. Chapter 11 discusses this in greater detail.

INTENSITY LANDMARKS

There are three intensity levels that are critical markers for gauging training efforts—aerobic threshold, lactate threshold and velocity at VO_2 max.

AEROBIC THRESHOLD

The aerobic threshold is the minimum intensity necessary for aerobic fitness improvement.

How slow and easy can you go and still get a fitness benefit by improving the efficiency of the aerobic energy-producing systems and boosting cardiorespiratory (heart and lung) endurance? For a well-trained athlete, the answer is that an intensity of about 55 percent of VO_2 max, which is about 70 percent of maximum heart rate, is necessary to produce enough stress to cause adaptation. This will vary somewhat with individuals. Bear in mind that the changes experienced at this intensity—the aerobic threshold—are minimal. Below this level of exertion the seasoned rider is engaging in "active recovery."

LACTATE THRESHOLD

The last chapter briefly touched on the lactate threshold, also sometimes referred to as the anaerobic threshold. You'll recall that this is the level of exercise intensity above which lactate begins to accumulate rapidly in the blood, and that lactate is a potent producer of fatigue. The higher your lactate threshold is as a percentage of VO_2 max, the greater the average speed you'll maintain in a long endurance event such as a cross country race.

The key determiner of lactate threshold fitness is how rapidly your body can remove lactate from the blood once it begins appearing there in prodigious quantities. Blood lactate is cleared as neighboring muscles that aren't working so intensely, as well as the heart, convert it back into a useable energy source. Training near or above the lactate threshold enhances blood lactate clearance capability.

Lactate clearance is the key to a high lactate threshold.

VELOCITY AT VO2 MAX

Chapter 3 described VO_2 max as a measure of the amount of oxygen the body can consume during all-out endurance exercise. Recall that this is one of the three key markers for endurance performance, the other two being lactate threshold and economy.

A very effective way of using VO_2 max in training is based on the velocity or power you can maintain at that maximal level of aerobic effort. For example, if your training produces an increase in the speed or power you can hold during a relatively long all-out effort, such as a steep 400-meter hill climb, faster race times and better results are possible. In fact, we could rather accurately predict the outcome of a cross-country race by knowing the speed or power the riders could sustain when at their VO_2 max, since research has revealed that this also reflects one's lactate threshold velocity and economy rating. In other words, the greater the velocity at VO_2 max, the higher the velocity when lactate threshold is achieved and the more economical one is. All three performance-critical variables are intrinsically tied to one measure.

Velocity at VO2 max is a good predictor of performance.

A recent French study used elite runners to reveal that four weekly sessions including five three-minute intervals done at velocity at VO_2 max, with three-minute recoveries, dramatically improved economy and velocities at both VO_2 max and lactate threshold. This workout and variations on it designed for mountain bikers are described in the Anaerobic Endurance section of Appendix B.

The obvious question then is—how do you go about determining velocity at VO_2 max? There is still a lot to be learned about this for cyclists, especially mountain bikers, since most studies have employed runners as subjects, but it appears that a simple six-minute time trial serves as a good measure. Since speed varies considerably with wind conditions on a bicycle, however, the best way of determining this measure is by gauging power (power-measuring devices are described in the next section). In a "field" test, the highest average power that can be maintained for six minutes adequately represents your velocity at VO_2 max. Chapter 5 describes how to do this and other field tests.

Average power for six minutes represents velocity at VO2max.

MONITORING INTENSITY

It's not enough to merely know the critical intensity landmarks described above. Each of them, and all other levels of intensity, must be monitored during training to ensure that the benefits sought are achieved. There are a number of practical ways for the mountain bike rider to accomplish this. These include regulating intensity by monitoring either perceived exertion, heart rate or power. Each has certain advantages and disadvantages. Let's take a closer look.

Perceived Exertion

Experienced athletes are good at knowing how hard they are working out relative to their highest possible exertion. During a training session, for example, one might say that he or she is riding at an "easy," "moderate" or "hard" effort. The same athlete would be able to compare today's hard effort to the one two days prior and know which was harder. Empirically, this rider would know how much harder, but would find it difficult to adequately express the intensity in words. Language just isn't a good medium for describing fine variations in exertion perceived during exercise.

Perceived exertion is based on breathing and other physical sensations of effort.

The way to get around this language limitation is to describe the effort one feels using numbers. Such a system is called "ratings of perceived exertion" (RPE). Using a scale with a 0 to 10 rating is easy for most veteran athletes. By assigning a number to the effort experienced at any given time on a ride, exertion may be described. Here is a suggested scale:

Suggested RPE scale.

0	No exertion at all	5	
1	Very light	6	Very hard
2	Light	8	
3	Moderate	9	Extremely hard
4	Somewhat hard	10	Maximal exertion

The "anchor" for this scale is 10—the highest exertion you have ever experienced. All other exertions are compared to it. Once you get good at using this scale, it's even possible to assign an RPE between the fixed points above, such as "7.5."

The greatest problem with using RPE is the tendency of some athletes to underestimate their exertion level to appear tough or brave. Value judgments should not effect such decisions. Assigning an RPE must be a cold and scientific endeavor.

Heart Rate

In the early 1980s, the wireless heart rate monitor was introduced and soon began changing the way athletes trained. Prior to its introduction, athletes in many endurance sports had used heart rate as an indicator of intensity. But taking the pulse manually at the throat or wrist required stopping activity and counting heartbeats. Pulse naturally decreased when activity was interrupted, and counting for a few seconds and then extrapolating to a minute introduced more errors. With the heart rate monitor, no manual counting was necessary and activity could continue without interruption.

As coaches and athletes got better at using heart rate to measure intensity, training changed. The heart rate monitor allowed an accurate and objective assessment of intensities ranging from very low to high.

Heart rate is a fairly effective measure of effort. As the intensity of a ride increases or decreases, heart rate rises and falls. In fact, there is a nearly linear relationship between the two. Figure 4.1 provides an example of this relationship during a steady increase in intensity.

Heart rate reflects workout intensity.

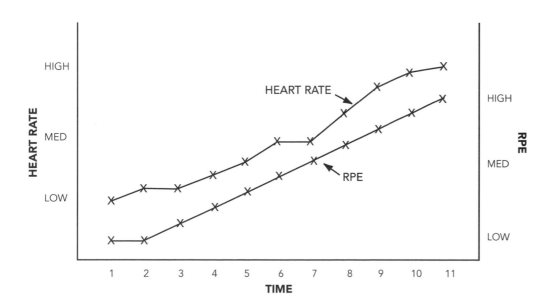

FIGURE 4.1
Example of relationship between heart rate and RPE during a steady increase in RPE.

There are drawbacks to heart rate monitoring.

Heart rate–based training is not perfect, however. Heart rate is affected by many external and internal environmental factors. Conditions including extremes of air temperature, humidity, nervousness and diet can modify the relationship between heart rate and RPE, resulting in some confusion for the rider. Also, there is a time lag that occurs between a change in intensity and the heart rate's response. For example, when going from riding at a "moderate" RPE to climbing a hill at a "very hard" RPE, heart rate takes several seconds, or even minutes, to catch up. This lag is depicted in several places in Figure 4.1. And on the descent side of the hill heart rate remains elevated for some time even though the RPE is low.

For intervals shorter than about two minutes, heart rate is a poor intensity indicator. It is of no value at all for short, sprint-type repetitions lasting a few seconds. For long effort, steady types of training, however, heart rate is effective for monitoring intensity.

Use lactate threshold as a heart rate standard.

The most common way to train with heart rate is by using "zones" that are tied to some measure of the user's unique physiology. Maximum heart rate is most often used for this, but I believe that is a mistake. Attempting to achieve such an effort is seldom possible, and often is not good for the rider's training. A better indicator is the individual lactate threshold—one of the intensity landmarks described earlier. An example may help to show why lactate threshold is preferable to maximum heart rate in determining heart rate training zones.

Assume we have two riders with exactly the same maximum heart rate, but where lactate thresholds are significantly different. Rider A goes anaerobic (lactate accumulates quickly) at 90 percent of maximum heart rate, but rider B experiences lactate threshold at 80 percent. If both are assigned a workout intensity of 85 percent of maximum heart rate, rider A is comfortably aerobic, while rider B is suffering. But if both ride at or below their lactate thresholds, they experience the same exertion level and reap the same benefits. Using a percentage of maximum heart rate just isn't as precise as basing heart rate training zones on the lactate threshold heart rate.

Finding your lactate threshold heart rate demands some precision, but don't let that stop you from using it. The procedure for discovering it is fairly simple, and is described in the next chapter.

Table 4.1 provides training zones based on lactate threshold heart rate (LTHR). Once you've discovered your LTHR in Chapter 5, return to this table to find your individual zones.

TABLE 4.1

Cycling Heart Rate Zones

Find your LT pulse (bold) in the "5a Zone" column. Read across, left and right, for training zones.

1 Zone	2 Zone	3 Zone	4 Zone	5a Zone	5b Zone	5c Zone.
Active Recovery	Extensive Endurance	Intensive Endurance	Threshold Training	Threshold Training	VO2max Intervals	Anaerobic Repetitions
<109	109-122	123-128	129-136	137-140	141-145	146+
<110	110-123	124-129	130-137	138-141	142-146	147+
<110	110-124	125-130	131-138	139-142	143-147	148+
<111	111-125	126-130	131-139	140-143	144-147	148+
<112	112-125	126-131	132-140	141-144	145-148	149+
<113	113-126	127-132	133-141	142-145	146-149	150+
<113	113-127	128-133	134-142	143-145	146-150	151+
<114	114-128	129-134	135-143	144-147	148-151	152+
<115	115-129	130-135	136-144	145-148	149-152	153+
<116	116-130	131-136	137-145	146-149	150-154	155+
<117	117-131	132-137	138-146	147-150	151-155	156+
<118	118-132	133 138	139-147	148-151	152-156	157+
<119	119-133	134-139	140-148	149-152	153-157	158+
<120	120-134	135-140	141-149	150-153	154-158	159+
<121	121-134	135-141	142-150	151-154	155-159	160+
<122	122-135	136-142	143-151	152-155	156-160	161+
<123	123-136	137-142	143-152	153-156	157-161	162+
<124	124-137	138-143	144-153	154-157	158-162	163+
<125	125-138	139-144	145-154	155-158	159-163	164+
<126	126-138	139-145	146-155	156-159	160-164	165+
<127	127-140	141-146	147-156	157-160	161-165	166+
<128	128-141	142-147	148-157	158-161	162-167	168+
<129	129-142	143-148	149-158	159-162	163-168	169+
<130	130-143	144-148	149-159	160-163	164-169	170+
<130	130-143	144-150	151-160	161-164	165-170	171+
<131	131-144	145-151	152-161	162-165	166-171	172+
<132	132-145	146-152	153-162	163-166	167-172	173+
<133	133-146	147-153	154-163	164-167	168-173	174+
<134	134-147	148-154	155-164	165-168	169-174	175+
<135	135-148	149-154	155-165	166-169	170-175	176+
<136	136-149	150-155	156-166	167-170	171-176	177+
<137	137-150	151-156	157-167	168-171	172-177	178+
<138	138-151	152-157	158-168	169-172	173-178	179+
<139	139-151	152-158	159-169	170-173	174-179	180+
<140	140-152	153-160	161-170	171-174	175-180	181+
<141	141-153	154-160	161-171	172-175	176-181	182+
<142	142-154	155-161	162-172	173-176	177-182	183+
<143	143-155	156-162	163-173	174-177	178-183	184+
<144	144-156	157-163	164-174	175-178	179-184	185+
<145	145-157	158-164	165-175	176-179	180-185	186+
<146	146-158	159-165	166-176	177-180	181-186	187+
<147	147-159	160-166	167-177	178-181	182-187	188+
<148	148-160	161-166	167-178	179-182	183-188	189+
<149	149-160	161-167	168-179	180-183	184-190	191+
<150	150-161	162-168	169-180	181-184	185-191	192+
<151	151-162	163-170	171-181	182-185	186-192	193+
<152	152-163	164-171	172-182	183-186	187-193	194+
<153	153-164	165-172	173-183	184-187	188-194	195+
<154	154-165	166-172	173-184	185-188	186-195	196+
<155	155-166	167-173	174-185	186-189	190-196	197+
<156	156-167	168-174	175-186	187-190	191-197	198+
<157	157-168	169-175	176-187	188-191	192-198	199+
<158	158-169	170-176	177-188	189-192	193-199	200+
<159	159-170	171-177	178-189	190-193	194-200	201+
<160	160-170	171-178	179-190	191-194	195-201	202+
<161	161-171	172-178	179-191	192-195	196-202	203+
<162	162-172	173-179	180-192	193-196	197-203	204+
<163	163-173	174-180	181-193	194-197	198-204	205+
<164	164-174	175-181	182-194	195-198	199-205	206+

POWER

Power is a measure of work compared to time. It is expressed in units called "watts," named for James Watt, the inventor of the steam engine. In physics, power is described in a formula as:

$$power = \frac{work}{time}$$

Gear size and cadence determine power.

At the risk of oversimplification, in cycling, "work" is essentially gear size and "time" is cadence. So if gear size is increased and cadence kept steady, power rises. Or, if cadence is increased (time per revolution of the crank is decreased) while using the same gear size, power also rises.

Several scientific studies have found that power is closely related to performance. If the average power output increases, race velocity also increases. The same cannot always be said for heart rate, as explained above; that is why power monitoring is such an excellent tool for bicycle training. It is the most effective way for the serious rider to monitor intensity.

Power is the preferred monitoring method for cycling.

The downside of power monitoring, as compared with heart rate, is equipment cost. In the early and middle 1990s, a power meter cost about 20 times as much as a heart rate monitor. With the introduction of the Tune Corporation's Power-Tap in 1999, however, the cost ratio was lowered to something approaching 4 to 1.

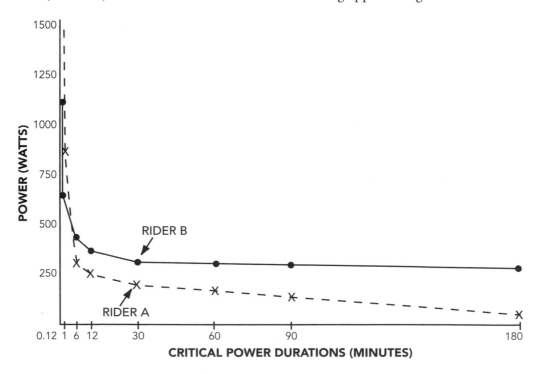

FIGURE 4.2
Critical power profiles of two riders.

Power-based training begins with determining one's "critical power profile." This is a visual representation of the ability to produce power at various durations. Finding and graphing average power output for the critical power (CP) durations of 12 seconds and 1, 6, 12, 30, 60, 90 and 180 minutes produces a curve or profile such as those shown in Figure 4.2.

Note that the profiles in Figure 4.2 are considerably different for the two riders. Rider A is capable of producing far greater power than Rider B for short durations. Although Rider B lacks short-duration power, the generally shallower slope indicates much greater endurance capability. In an all-out sprint near the finish line, Rider A has an advantage, but Rider B has the upper hand as the duration increases. Downhill racers are likely to have a Profile similar to Rider A's, while cross-country racers may be expected to have a profile like Rider B's.

Once you've determined average power for each of the above durations (Chapter 5 describes how to do this), your CP training zones can be established. For the average power at each duration, add and subtract 5 percent to establish zones. For example, if your average power for six minutes is 360 watts, then CP6 is 342 to 378 watts (360 x 0.05 = 18, 360 − 18 = 342, 360 + 18 = 378).

How to set critical power zones.

TABLE 4.2

Critical Power Zone Benefits and Race Applications

Duration	CP Zone	Fitness Benefit	Race Application
12 sec.	CP0.2	Explosive power	Finishing sprint Short hill Start
1 min.	CP1	Lactate clearance	Fast starts Short climbs
6 min.	CP6	Velocity at VO$_2$ max	Moderate duration climbs Short, high intensity segments
12 min.	CP12	Aerobic capacity (VO$_2$ max)	Long climbs
30 min.	CP30	Supralactate threshold	Long, steady efforts
60 min.	CP60	Lactate threshold	Short duration race endurance
90 min.	CP90	Sublactate threshold	Moderate duration race endurance
180 min.	CP180	Basic aerobic function	Long duration race endurance

Focusing your training on a given range of CP zones has the potential to produce fitness benefits that can be applied in certain race situations, as shown in Table 4.2.

MULTISYSTEM TRAINING

RPE, heart rate and power each offer unique benefits for the serious rider when it comes to monitoring intensity of a workout or race. RPE provides a subjective yet comprehensive view of what you are encountering when on the bike. Heart rate offers a window into the cardiovascular system and thus a glimpse of the load the body is under. A power meter reports what the body is accomplishing. Power is a measure of performance rather than an indicator of the physiological stress experienced. Each is valuable in the training process.

RPE, heart rate and power provide unique feedback.

Using all three is like seeing a picture in three dimensions instead of only one or two—training makes more sense. Whether or not a number is assigned, RPE should be an integral method of monitoring intensity in all workouts. This will pay dividends in races where closely observing heart rate and power is not possible. RPE is the "stake in the ground"—the supreme reference for all intensity monitoring. You must become good at using it.

Heart rate is best used for steady-state training particularly that done below the lactate threshold. It is especially effective during long, aerobic rides and for recovery workouts.

Focus on power for intervals, hill training, sprint-power training, and all anaerobic workouts. I've seen significant improvement in race performance when riders have begun training with power. This is unquestionably the future of bicycle training.

Mastering and appropriately applying each of these intensity monitoring systems has the potential to dramatically improve your training and, therefore, your racing.

MEASURING WORKLOAD

Now that you have three systems for monitoring intensity, it's possible to quantify workload. Recall from the previous chapter that workload is the combination of frequency, duration and intensity of training. Knowing workload allows you to keep track of and compare weekly training stress loads placed on the body. Such information is valuable for avoiding overtraining. It also helps in planning daily workouts if you know how much stress training is likely to produce. In turn, this allows you to determine how much and when recovery is needed. It also makes periodization of training more effective (see Chapter 7 for details on periodization).

Quantifying workload sharpens training focus.

The following are three workload-measuring methods, one based on each RPE, heart rate and power.

RPE

At the end of a training session, assign an average workout RPE using the 0 to 10 scale. Then multiply this RPE value by the number of minutes in the session. For example, if a 60-minute session including intervals had an average RPE of 7, the workload for this day is 420 (60 x 7 = 420).

Heart Rate

Using a heart rate monitor with a time-by-zone function, it's possible to know how many minutes were spent in at least three zones (with a three-zone monitor, all five zones may be observed by switching zones during the ride). By multiplying each of the zone's numeric identifiers (3 zone, for example) by the number of minutes spent in each zone and then adding them up, workload may be determined.

For example, if you completed a 60-minute ride that included 20 minutes in the 1 zone, 25 minutes in the 2 zone, and 15 minutes in the 3 zone, the cumulative workload is 115. Here's how that number was determined:

$$20 \text{ x } 1 = 20$$
$$25 \text{ x } 2 - 50$$
$$15 \text{ x } 3 = \underline{45}$$
$$\text{Total} \quad 115$$

Power

The Tune Power-Tap offers a quick way of monitoring workload—session kilojoules, recalled as "E" (for energy) and displayed in units called kilojoules (kJ) on the Power-Tap. This is a measure of energy expended. One kilocalorie (kcal or Calorie) is equal to 4.184 kJ. Energy used in training is a nearly perfect way of expressing workload.

Cumulative Workload

Whichever method you use, record your daily workload in a training log. By totaling the daily workloads, a cumulative workload for the week is determined. This number serves as an indicator of how difficult the week was. By comparing it with past weeks, you can quickly see what is happening to the stress load. In general, the cumulative workload should increase as the year progresses from the start of training season in early winter until the spring races. This should not be a straight-line progression, however. It instead follows a wave-like pattern that allows the body to gradually adapt

Cumulative workload shows where you've been and projects what you can manage in training.

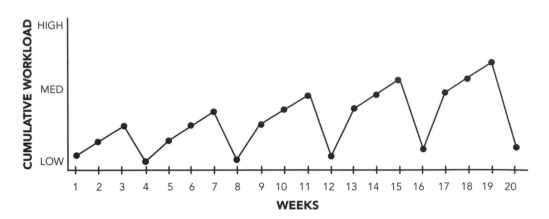

FIGURE 4.3
Example of weekly cumulative workload progression

and grow stronger. Figure 4.3 shows how the cumulative weekly workload advances through one portion of the training year.

Unfortunately, there is no rule of thumb for determining what a given athlete's workload should be. It varies considerably with the individual, so experience is the best teacher. By comparing your weekly cumulative workloads with your training and racing performances, it's possible to plan optimal training patterns while avoiding overtraining. But always bear in mind that optimal workload is a moving target that is dependent on accumulated fitness, time of the training year, health, psychological stress and other variables. Cumulative workload history provides a better starting point for determining how you should train today and in the future than does merely guessing.

REFERENCES

Billat, V. L., et al. "A Comparison of Time to Exhaustion at VO_2 Max in Elite Cyclists," Kayak Paddlers, Swimmers And Runners. *Ergonomics* 39, no. 2 (1996): 267-277.

Billat, V. L. and J.P. Koralsztein. "Significance of the Velocity at VO_2 Max and Time to Exhaustion at this Velocity." *Sports Medicine* 22, no. 2 (1996): 90–108.

Billat, V. L., et al. "Interval Training at VO_2 Max: Effects on Aerobic Performance and Overtraining Markers." *Medicine and Science in Sports and Exercise* 31, no. 1 (1999): 156–163.

Borg, G. *An Introduction to Borg's RPE Scale.* Ithaca, NY: Mouvement Publications, 1985.

Boulay, M. R., et al. "Monitoring High-Intensity Endurance Exercise With Heart Rate and Thresholds." *Medicine and Science in Sports and Exercise* 29, no. 1 (1997): 125–132.

Coyle, E. F., et al. "Physiological and Biomechanical Factors Associated with Elite Endurance Cycling Performance." *Medicine and Science in Sports and Exercise* 23, no. 1 (1991): 93–107.

Dunbar, C. C., et al. "The Validity of Regulating Exercise Intensity by Ratings of Perceived Exertion." *Medicine and Science in Sports and Exercise* 24 (1992): 94–99.

Friel, J. *The Cyclist's Training Bible*. Boulder, CO: VeloPress, 1996.

Friel, J. *Training with Power*. Cambridge, MA: Tune Corp, 1999.

Gibbons, E. S. "The Significance of Anaerobic Threshold in Exercise Prescription." *Journal of Sports Medicine* 27 (1987): 357–361.

Goforth, H. W., et al. "Simultaneous Enhancement of Aerobic and Anaerobic Capacity." *Medicine and Science in Sports and Exercise* 26, no. 5 (1994): 171.

Hagberg, J. M. "Physiological Implications of the Lactate Threshold." *International Journal of Sports Medicine* 5 (1984): 106–109.

Herman, E. A., et al. "Exercise Endurance Time as a Function of Percent Maximal Power Production." *Medicine and Science in Sports and Exercise* 19, no. 5: 480–485.

Hopkins, S. R., et al. "The Laboratory Assessment of Endurance Performance in Cyclists." *Canadian Journal of Applied Physiology* 19, no. 3: 266–274.

Ivy, J. L., et al. "Muscle Respiratory Capacity and Fiber Type as Determinants of the Lactate Threshold." *Journal of Applied Physiology* 48 (1980): 523–527.

Jacobs, I. "Blood Lactate: Implications for Training and Sports Performance." *Sports Medicine* 3 (1986): 10–25.

Lehmann, M., et al. "Training-Overtraining: Influence of a Defined Increase in Training Volume Versus Training Intensity on Performance, Catecholamines and Some Metabolic Parameters in Experienced Middle- and Long-Distance Runners." *European Journal of Applied Physiology* 64, no. 2 (1992): 169–177.

Lindsay, F. H., et al. "Improved Athletic Performance in Highly Trained Cyclists after Interval Training." *Medicine and Science in Sports and Exercise* 28, no. 11 (1996): 1427–1434.

McArdle, W. D., F.I. Katch, and V.L. Katch. *Exercise Physiology*. Baltimore: Williams & Wilkins, 1996.

Myburgh, K. H., et al. "High-Intensity Training for 1 Month Improves Performance but Not Muscle Enzyme Activities in High-Trained Cyclists." *Medicine and Science in Sports and Exercise* 27, no. 5 (1995): S370.

Niles, R. "Power as a Determinant of Endurance Performance." Unpublished study at Sonoma State University, 1991.

Pompcu, F. A., et al. "Prediction of Performance in the 5000m Run by Means of Laboratory and Field Tests in Male Distance Runners." *Medicine and Science in Sports and Exercise* 28, no. 5 (1996): S89.

Romijn, J. A., et al. "Regulation of Endogenous Fat snd Carbohydrate Metabolism in Relation to Exercise Intensity and Duration." *American Journal of Physiology* 265 (1993): E380.

Tanaka, K., et al. "A Longitudinal Assessment of Anaerobic Threshold and Distance-Running Performance." *Medicine and Science in Sports and Exercise* 16 (3) (1984): 278–282.

Weltman, A., et al. "Endurance Training Amplifies the Pulsatile Release of Growth Hormone: Effects of Training Intensity." *Journal of Applied Physiology* 72, no. 6 (1992): 2188–2196.

Weltman, A. *The Blood Lactate Response to Exercise.* Champaign, IL: Human Kinetics, 1995.

Wenger, H. A. and G.J. Bell. "The Interactions of Intensity, Frequency and Duration of Exercise Training in Altering Cardiorespiratory Fitness." *Sports Medicine* 3, no. 5 (1986): 346–356.

Weston, A. R., et al. "Skeletal Muscle Buffering Capacity and Endurance Performance after High-Intensity Interval Training by Well-Trained Cyclists." *European Journal of Applied Physiology* 75 (1997): 7–13.

Wilmore, J. and D. Costill. *Physiology of Sport and Exercise.* Champaign, IL: Human Kinetics, 1994.

PURPOSEFUL TRAINING

Time is a precious commodity. It seems that we never have enough time to train as we would like. Of the 168 hours each of us has to spend every week, about 56 are accounted for by sleep, 40 or more go into work, and another 50 or so are taken up with meals, home maintenance, transportation, shopping and personal care. That leaves 22 hours each week unaccounted for. A large portion of this time is frittered away watching television or just goofing off. The bottom line is, there aren't many hours left for training. Whether you have 15 hours or 5 left over, it's imperative that they be used in a purposeful manner. You can't afford to waste them if peak mountain bike racing performance is your goal.

The purpose of the next two chapters is to help you determine exactly what your training needs are, and to find the best ways to address them in order to get the most out of the limited time available. Chapter 5 shows how to assess your fitness and measure ongoing progress during the season. In Chapter 6, we examine how to use that information to determine the best course of action for your training. By the end of Part III, you will be prepared to design a personal training program in Part IV.

SELF-ASSESSMENT

It's hard to measure yourself if nobody is challenging you.

—JOHN TOMAC

One way to measure how good you are for cross-country mountain bike racing is to simply do a race. Questions regarding fitness are usually answered quickly: How good is my start? Do I have the endurance to race strongly, even on the last lap? Am I climbing well? How are my technical handling skills? Am I staying focused throughout the race?

The answers to these and other questions come largely from comparing your performance with that of the other riders in the same race category. Obviously, then, the size of the field and ability of the other riders are have a bearing on this method of self-measurement. If it's a well-established, national caliber race, you may come away feeling somewhat depressed about your race ability. But if the race is a small, local one, your post-race impressions may be just the opposite despite having performed the same as in the bigger race.

Races may be used to measure progress, but there are drawbacks.

Another problem with using races to measure fitness is that they don't always occur at the right times. There may not be a race available when it's time to check personal progress. This is almost always the case during the winter months in colder locales. In fact, racing in the winter is often a mistake anyway, if you are following a typical seasonal development plan, as the body and mind are not yet ready for competition.

Putting your wheel on a starting line also requires an emotional investment that has been likened to burning your "matches" over the course of a season. Each of us has only so many matches, according to this way of thinking, and when they are used up, the season must end. This is burnout. Frequent racing to determine fitness, or for any other purpose, takes a toll. Some riders are ready to quit by June every year—their matches have been expended much too early.

Racing has an emotional cost.

So it is often necessary to conduct self-tests in order to establish personal fitness standards against which progress may be measured. This is especially beneficial before the serious racing begins. Once you are into the heart of the competitive season, race results are usually the standards by which fitness is assessed.

Just like racing to measure progress, self-testing is not a perfect method of evaluation, either. To produce useable results, many test variables must be controlled, such as the equipment used, environmental conditions, warm-up procedures and diet. But when done carefully and regularly, the performance information gathered is valuable in helping you know yourself well enough to make intelligent training decisions. Let's start the measurement process.

PERSONAL PROFILE

Getting to know yourself.

The first step in self-coaching is knowing exactly who you are as a racer. This can be done by evaluating past race performances, natural abilities and mental skills. Taken together, these will help to form a clearer picture of you as a mountain bike racer. They will also help in making decisions about training.

Begin by completing the accompanying Race Ability Profile (Special Element 5.1). Rate yourself on a scale of 1 to 5 for each of the nine critical race abilities. For example, in your race category, if you are the same as most other riders as far as race endurance is

SPECIAL ELEMENT 5.1

Race Ability Profile

Compared with others in my race category, I'm...

	1 among worst at	**2**	**3** same as most at	**4**	**5** among best at
...race endurance					
...fast starts					
...finish sprints					
...short climbs					
...long climbs					
...fast single-track descents					
...dealing with mud					
...riding on roots and rocks					
...clearing obstacles					

concerned, place a check in column 3 for "race endurance." In the same way, if you are typically a little better than most but not one of the best when a race starts very fast, then place a check in column 4 for "fast starts." Continue in this manner for each of the remaining race abilities. You undoubtedly already have a sense of how you compare with others, but this exercise will help you more clearly identify your strengths and weaknesses.

In the same manner, fill in the Natural Ability Profile (Special Element 5.2) and the Mental Skills Profile (Special Element 5.3).

Natural Abilities Profile

Read each statement below and decide if you agree or disagree with it as it applies to you. Check the appropriate answer. If unsure, go with your initial feeling.

A=Agree   D=Disagree

A   D

___ ___ 1. I prefer to ride in a bigger gear with a lower cadence than most of my training partners.

___ ___ 2. I race best in criteriums and short road races.

___ ___ 3. I'm good at sprints.

___ ___ 4. I'm stronger at the end of long workouts than my training partners.

___ ___ 5. I can squat and/or leg press more weight than most in my category.

___ ___ 6. I prefer long races.

___ ___ 7. I use longer crank arms than most others my height.

___ ___ 8. I get stronger as a stage race or high volume training week progresses.

___ ___ 9. I comfortably use smaller gears with higher cadence than most others I train with.

___ ___ 10. I have always been physically quicker than most other people for any sport I've participated in.

___ ___ 11. In most sports, I've been able to finish stronger than most others.

___ ___ 12. I've always been physically stronger than most others I've played sports with.

___ ___ 13. I climb best when seated.

___ ___ 14. I prefer workouts that are short but fast.

___ ___ 15. I'm confident of my endurance at the start of long races.

SCORING: For each of the following sets of questions, count the number of "agree" answers you checked.

Question numbers		Score	
1, 5, 7, 12, 13: Number of "agrees" _____		Strength	_____
2, 3, 9, 10, 14: Number of "agrees" _____		Speed	_____
4, 6, 8, 11, 15: Number of "agrees" _____		Endurance	_____

Mental Skills Profile

Read each statement below and choose an appropriate answer from these possibilities:

1=Never 2=Rarely 3=Sometimes 4=Frequently 5=Usually 6=Always

___ 1. I believe my potential as an athlete is excellent.

___ 2. I train consistently and eagerly.

___ 3. When things don't go well in a race I stay positive.

___ 4. In hard races I can imagine myself doing well.

___ 5. Before races I remain positive and upbeat.

___ 6. I think of myself more as a success than as a failure.

___ 7. Before races I'm able to erase self-doubt.

___ 8. The morning of a race I awake enthusiastically.

___ 9. I learn something from races when I don't do well.

___ 10. I can see myself handling tough race situations.

___ 11. I'm able to race at near my ability level.

___ 12. I can easily picture myself training and racing.

___ 13. Staying focused during long races is easy for me.

___ 14. I stay in tune with my exertion levels in races.

___ 15. I mentally rehearse skills and tactics before races.

___ 16. I'm good at concentrating as a race progresses.

___ 17. I make sacrifices to attain my goals.

___ 18. Before an important race I can visualize doing well.

___ 19. I look forward to workouts.

___ 20. When I visualize myself racing, it almost feels real.

___ 21. I think of myself as a tough competitor.

___ 22. In races I tune out distractions.

___ 23. I set high goals for myself.

___ 24. I like the challenge of a hard race.

___ 25. When the race becomes difficult I concentrate even better.

___ 26. In races I am mentally tough.

___ 27. I can relax my muscles before races.

___ 28. I stay positive despite late race starts, bad weather, poor officiating, etc.

___ 29. My confidence stays high the week after a bad race.

___ 30. I strive to be the best athlete I can be.

SCORING: Add up the numerical answers you gave for each of the following sets of statements.

Statement numbers	Score*			Total	Ranking	*Score
2, 8, 17, 19, 23, 30:	Total ____	Motivation ____		32-36	Excellent	5
1, 6, 11, 21, 26, 29:	Total ____	Confidence ____		27-31	Good	4
3, 5, 9, 24, 27, 28:	Total ____	Thought habits ____		21-26	Average	3
7, 13, 14, 16, 22, 25:	Total ____	Focus ____		16-20	Fair	2
4, 10, 12, 15, 18, 20:	Total ____	Visualization ____		6-15	Poor	1

What does all of this mean? The results of the Race Ability Profile should be obvious. If any of your ratings on this profile were placed in columns 1 or 2, these must be training priorities. The higher your goals for the season are, the more ratings there must be in columns 4 and 5. In fact, any racing ability marked 3 or lower is holding you back. Sometimes all it takes is improvement in one of these areas—the one that is the weakest—and immediate improvement in race results are made. For example, if you graded performance as a 3, 4 or 5 for all abilities except "race endurance," and that was a 2, your race results will improve greatly just by working on endurance. All that's needed for the other race abilities is maintenance until endurance improves.

What's holding you back?

Success in mountain biking is determined by having the optimal mix of the three physical abilities scored in the Natural Abilities Profile:

- Endurance—the ability to resist fatigue
- Force—the ability to use muscular strength
- Speed skill—the ability to make quick moves efficiently

The most basic racing abilities.

Cross-country racing emphasizes endurance, but force development is necessary for climbing hills and speed skill is what the good technical riders have lots of. The Natural Abilities Profile discovered with SE 5.2 is unique for you, and shows which aspects of the sport you naturally excel at and which need work. Your capabilities for these three most basic elements of race fitness is determined by genetics and training. Your genetic code can't be changed, but your training can. That is covered in the next chapter.

While the mental skills measured in Special Element 5.3 are important for riders of all abilities, the higher the race category you are in, the more critical the mental aspect becomes in determining race results. At the highest level of the sport, a close battle for finishing position is often decided by psychological rather than physiological skill. The rider with the optimal combination of motivation, confidence, thought habits, focus and visualization usually comes out on top.

Mental skills.

PERFORMANCE TESTING

Performance testing serves two purposes. The first is to set standards against which fitness may be compared at some point in the future to determine progress. The second purpose is to establish intensity zones for use with a heart rate monitor and power meter.

For both purposes, the tests must be fairly accurate and dependable. If several key factors affecting the results change from time to time, the results are useless. Slight variations in warm-up, weather, equipment, overall fatigue and eating all contribute to and possibly confound the results. One way to control such variables is to have the testing

Performance test variables must be controlled.

done by a local sports medicine clinic or in a university laboratory. But this may be expensive and unavailable for many riders. Self-testing with concern for precision is a reasonable alternative.

Results are also likely to vary from day to day based mostly on your level of recovery. So it's important to be rested and ready to go when testing. Chapter 7 describes periodization—a training organizational system that provides for frequent rest and recovery periods. It's near the end of these R and R weeks, about every third or fourth week when you are not racing, that performance tests are conducted. This will be discussed in greater detail in Chapter 7.

When to test.

You will perform two or three sets of tests, depending on whether you have both a heart rate monitor and a power meter. The three tests are:

- A graded exercise test to determine your cardiovascular system's response to increasing intensity and your lactate threshold power and heart rate
- A 30-minute time trial to confirm your lactate threshold heart rate
- A set of time trials of varying durations to establish your power training zones

GRADED EXERCISE TEST

The first performance measurement is a graded exercise test (GXT) and involves monitoring heart rate and work output. It is based on the principle that as aerobic fitness improves, the cardiovascular system (heart, blood vessels, blood) doesn't have to work as hard for any given level of cycling output. This output may be measured as power or speed, using a reliable indoor trainer such as a CompuTrainer or any standard indoor training device, along with a power meter. It may even be done, although somewhat less accurately, using a stationary bike such as may be found in a health club.

The GXT measures cardiovascular fitness.

The GXT provides a nice baseline of your aerobic fitness that you can use throughout the season to measure progress, and even from year to year. If you tested with a CompuTrainer or power meter, it also provides an estimate of lactate threshold heart rate and power at lactate threshold.

The details of how to conduct a graded exercise test are found in Special Element 5.4, Graded Exercise Test.

Graded Exercise Test

Preparation

1. An assistant is needed to record information.

2. Do not eat for two hours before the test. It's generally best if the previous day was light exercise or a rest day.

3. If at any time you feel lightheaded or nauseous, stop the test immediately. You are NOT attempting a maximum heart rate on the test, but it's necessary to attain a very high effort level.

4. Use a CompuTrainer or a Power-Tap on a standard indoor training device such as a wind trainer or magnetic trainer. Warm-up for 10 minutes before the test. Note in your log what the warm-up procedure was.

Test

1. Throughout the test you will maintain a predetermined power level (plus or minus 10 watts). Start at 100 watts and increase by 20 watts every minute until you can no longer continue. Stay seated throughout the test. Shift gears at any time.

2. At the end of each minute tell your assistant how great your exertion is using the RPE scale (place this where it can be seen):

0	No exertion at all	3	
1	Very light	4	Very hard
2	Light	8	
3	Moderate	9	Extremely hard
4		10	Maximal exertion
2	Somewhat hard		

3. Your assistant records power output level, RPE, and heart rate at the end of each minute and instructs you to increase power to the next level.

4. The assistant also listens closely to your breathing to detect when it first becomes labored. This point is marked as "VT" for ventilatory threshold.

5. Continue until you can no longer hold the power level for at least 15 seconds.

6. The data collected should look something like this:

Power (watts)	Heart Rate (bpm)	Exertion (RPE)	
100	110	2	
120	118	3	
140	125	3	
160	135	4	
180	142	5	
200	147	6	
220	153	7	"VT"
240	156	9	
260	159	10	

LACTATE THRESHOLD TIME TRIAL

If you'll be training with a heart rate monitor to gauge intensity, it's a good idea to confirm your lactate threshold heart rate as determined in the Graded Exercise Test since all zones are based on it. Or, if you don't have a CompuTrainer or Power-Tap do only this test: Complete a 30-minute time trial done on the road as described in Special Element 5.5. If you are doing both tests, you may need to schedule 48 hours of recovery between the two tests.

What to do when test results don't agree.

It's likely that the lactate threshold heart rates found using these two tests won't exactly agree; each is merely an estimate. But they should be close—within about seven beats per minute of each other. If they are not that close, you'll need to repeat the tests at another time. If they are close, use the lower of the two as your lactate threshold heart rate for now. The tests should be repeated near the end of rest and recovery weeks during the Prep and Base periods described in Chapter 7.

Once you've determined your lactate threshold heart rate by doing the GXT and confirmed it with the lactate threshold time trial, you are ready to establish your personal heart rate training zones using Table 4.1.

POWER TESTS

If you have a power meter such as the Tune Power-Tap, power-based training zones should be established. Do this by completing a series of time trials as described in Special Element 5.6, Power Tests.

Suggested test days.

Note that you will complete five time trials, one each of 12 seconds and 1, 6, 12 and 30 minutes. Each test is a maximum effort for the entire duration. It's best to do these on three separate days. For example, on day 1 complete the 12-second and 6-minute tests, on day 2 the 1-minute and 12-minute tests, and on day 3 the 30-minute test. As with heart rate testing, these tests should be done near the end of a rest and recovery week in order to get good data. Some riders may need a day of recovery between test days, especially the 12-minute and 30-minute days.

There is a learning curve associated with doing this testing. It's quite possible that you will start out too fast on each of the tests and have difficulty finishing. It may take two or three training cycles to learn how to pace yourself. It's best if testing begins in the Prep and Base periods so that power zones are well established before entering the critical Build period of training. (These periods are explained in Chapter 7.)

Estimating 60-, 90- and 180-minute critical powers.

The next section describes how to graph the test results. The longer durations of 60, 90 and 180 minutes may be estimated from these graphs by extending the slope of

Lactate Threshold Time Trial on Road

Preparation

1. Find a flat stretch of road that has no turns or stop streets and little traffic. This may be a straight, multi-loop, or out-and-back course that takes 30 minutes to complete.

2. Wear a heart rate monitor and stopwatch.

3. Do not eat for two hours before the test. It's generally best if the previous day was light exercise or a rest day.

4. Warm-up for 10-20 minutes as if preparing for a race. Note in your log what the warm-up procedure was.

5. If at any time you feel lightheaded or nauseous, stop the test immediately. You are NOT attempting a maximum heart rate on the test, but rather the greatest distance you can cover in 30 minutes.

Test

1. Immediately following the warm-up, ride 30 minutes at race effort. Start your stopwatch at the beginning of the time trial and stop it as you finish.

2. Start the heart rate monitor 10 minutes into the ride so that you collect 20 minutes of data.

3. On finishing, note and record your average heart rate for the 20-minute period. This is your estimated lactate threshold heart rate.

Power Tests

Preparation

1. Do not eat for two hours before a test.

2. Conduct time trials at five durations: 12 seconds (CP0.2), 1 minute (CP1), 6 minutes (CP6), 12 minutes (CP12), and 30 minutes (CP30).

3. If at any time you feel lightheaded or nauseous, stop the test immediately. You are attempting the highest effort level possible for each test.

4. Use a Power-Tap on the road. The course should be relatively flat with few turns, little traffic, and no stop streets. Wind is of no concern.

5. Warm-up for 10 minutes before the test. Note in your log what the warm-up procedure was.

Test

1. Set the Power-Tap to the "interval" mode.

2. From a standing start complete the prescribed test duration. If doing more than one test in a session take a complete recovery before starting the next one.

3. Note and record in your log the average power output for the test.

the line without actually completing such grueling efforts. You may also get ballpark figures of the power for these durations with a little math. To estimate 60-minute power, subtract 5 percent from your 30-minute average power. For an approximation of 90-minute power, subtract 2.5 percent from the 60-minute power. Subtracting 5 percent from the 90-minute figure estimates 180-minute power.

Once you have all of these power tests completed, you are ready to determine your power training zones as shown in Table 4.2.

UNDERSTANDING TEST RESULTS

Having established a profile and completed the tests is not enough—you must now determine what all of this data means for your training. Again, keep in mind that the results of these tests are only as good as the effort put into controlling the many variables discussed earlier. Sloppy testing provides no basis for measuring fitness. Also realize that there are many variables not completely under your control, such as weather. In addition, the changes in fitness can be so slight—2 percent or less—that field testing may not be sophisticated enough to detect them. Because of these confounding factors, it might appear in subsequent tests that fitness is slipping even though you sense an improvement. Your feelings and indications of fitness from workouts are valid—don't completely disregard them in an attempt to train "scientifically."

GRADED EXERCISE TEST

As mentioned earlier, this test provides a snapshot of your aerobic fitness and helps to establish a lactate threshold heart rate. Both are applicable only to you. Comparing the heart rate data of this test with another rider's is of little or no value. Comparing your present results with those of future tests is quite revealing, however. One way to establish a basis for comparison is to graph the results. Figure 5.1 is a graph of an initial test (Test 1) and a follow-up test done several weeks later (Test 2).

In subsequent tests, improving aerobic fitness is evident if the slope of the line

Determining progress from a graded exercise test.

moves to the right and down, as shown by Test 2 in Figure 5.1. This indicates that for any given power level, heart rate has dropped. Or, to look at it another way, for any given heart rate, power is greater.

Now let's determine your lactate threshold (LT). It may be estimated from the test data by observing four indicators: RPE, ventilatory threshold or VT, time above LT and power percentage. For the experienced rider, LT typically occurs when RPE is in the range of 7 or 8. So a rough estimation of LT is made by noting the heart rates that fall in this

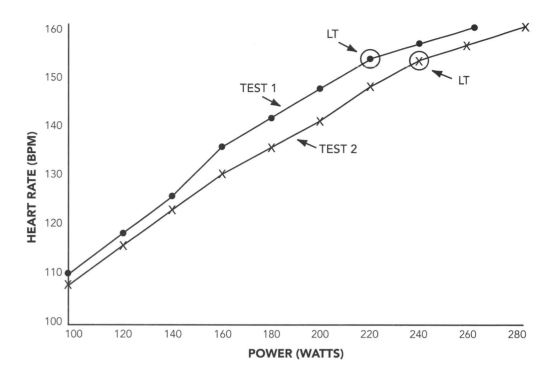

FIGURE 5.1
Graph of two graded exercise tests

RPE range. LT may also be estimated by your assistant's estimation of VT. If this falls in the range of RPE 7 or 8, it narrows the possibilities even more. Realize, however, that determining VT is quite difficult for the person who has never done it before. Another way of determining LT is that a rider will typically not be able to continue for more than five minutes once LT has been reached. So your LT is likely within the last five data points collected in the GXT. Power output may also be used to estimate LT for the experienced rider as it generally is found at about 85 percent of the maximum power achieved on the test. From these four indicators you should be able to closely estimate lactate threshold heart rate. The more times you complete this test, the more refined the estimate of LT becomes.

How to estimate LT.

Notice in Figure 5.1 that the lactate threshold heart rate has not changed from Test 1 to Test 2, although LT power has increased. This is typical of the results seen in experienced and generally well-conditioned riders during their base period. On the other hand, a novice, or someone who has had a long break from training, may expect to see the lactate threshold heart rate rise in subsequent tests.

Lactate Threshold Test on the Road

This is a simple analysis. Your heart rate average for the last 20 minutes of the 30-minute, all-out time trial done on the road as a workout is a close approximation of LT. If you compete in a time trial as a race, take 5 percent of your average heart rate and add it to the average to estimate LT. But if either of these is the only test done, it's a good idea to continue evaluating what you found your LT heart rate to be when on training rides. When riding steadily at this heart rate you should be aware of labored breathing, and a feeling of burning tightness in the legs, and your RPE should be about 7 or 8. As with all testing, the more frequently this test is done the more refined the estimate becomes.

Power Tests

The data gathered for the five power tests should be graphed to produce a Power Profile as shown in Figure 5.2. The longer critical power durations may be estimated by extending the slope of the line for CP12 to CP30. This provides rough estimations that may be a bit low or high depending on your aerobic-anaerobic fitness balance. For example, in the early winter months your aerobic fitness is probably relatively better than your anaerobic fitness. As a result, CP12 may be lower than what would be found in the summer months, thus causing the extended slope of the line to be high on the right end. Follow-up tests done over the ensuing months of the winter and spring will help to correct this overestimation.

What should your Power Profile look like? This is somewhat dependent on the courses on which you race. A short-duration race contested on a course with short, steep hills favors a rider with high CP1 and CP6 power, whereas a longer race with rolling hills and long, steady climbs favors those with high CP12 and CP30 power. If you go backwards when a race starts very fast, CP1 should be emphasized in training. If you typical-

What should your Power Profile look like?

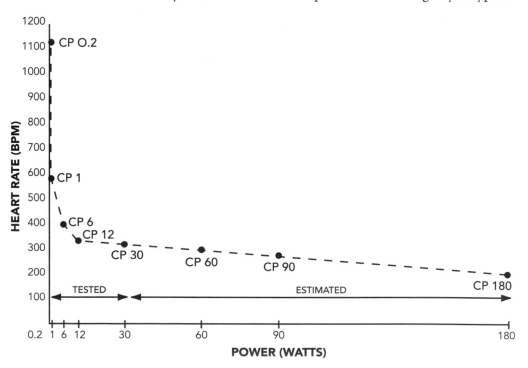

FIGURE 5.2
Power profile for hypothetical rider.

ly lose when it comes down to a one-on-one sprint for the finish line, then CP.2 needs more work. In theory, those power zones that are trained in most frequently will tend to improve the most. So comparing your Power Profile with course and race requirements of the most important races of the season provides guidance in determining exactly how to train. Chapter 6 provides greater detail on this.

SELF-ASSESSMENT

By now you've collected a lot of data on yourself. All of this is of no value unless the information is used to improve training and racing. Completing the Mountain Biker Assessment (Special Element 5.7) will provide a start toward doing that. The next chapter takes this one step further by providing a system for improvement in weak areas.

Go back to the Race Ability, Natural Ability and Mental Skills profiles and transfer the self-ratings to the Mountain Biker Assessment. There is a fourth category for self-assessment included here—Miscellaneous Factors. Most of these are quite subjective, but try to rate them using the same 1-to-5 scale as for the other profiles. The following brief comments may help you to do this.

How to rate Miscellaneous Factors.

• Nutrition. Could your nutrition improve? Do you eat a lot of junk food? On a scale of 1 to 5, how strict is your diet? If very strict with no junk food, circle 5. If nearly all you eat is junk food, circle 1.

• Technical equipment knowledge. How well do you know your bike's inner workings? Could you repair or replace anything that may need it? If you're a certified mechanic, circle 5. If you're unable to repair even a flat tire, circle 1.

• Race strategy. Before starting any race, do you have a master plan of what you will do under various circumstances? If so, mark 5. If you never give race strategy any thought and just react to what happens, circle 1.

• Body composition. Power-to-weight ratio is extremely important in mountain bike racing. Evaluate your weight side of the ratio. Are you carrying excess flab that if removed would make you a better climber? Use the following scale:

Excess Weight	Rating
10 or more pounds	1
7 to 9 pounds	2
4 to 6 pounds	3
1 to 3 pounds	4
No excess weight	5

TABLE 5.7

Mountain Biker Assessment

Race Ability Profile	Rating (5=best)	Objectives to Improve
Race endurance	? 1 2 3 4 5	_____
Fast starts	? 1 2 3 4 5	_____
Finish sprints	? 1 2 3 4 5	_____
Short climbs	? 1 2 3 4 5	_____
Long climbs	? 1 2 3 4 5	_____
Fast, single-track descents	? 1 2 3 4 5	_____
Dealing with mud	? 1 2 3 4 5	_____
Riding on roots, rocks, etc	? 1 2 3 4 5	_____
Clearing obstacles	? 1 2 3 4 5	_____

Natural Ability Profile		
Force	? 1 2 3 4 5	_____
Speed Skill	? 1 2 3 4 5	_____
Endurance	? 1 2 3 4 5	_____

Mental Skills Profile		
Motivation	? 1 2 3 4 5	_____
Confidence	? 1 2 3 4 5	_____
Thought habits	? 1 2 3 4 5	_____
Focus	? 1 2 3 4 5	_____
Visualization	? 1 2 3 4 5	_____

Miscellaneous Factors		
Nutrition	? 1 2 3 4 5	_____
Technical equipment knowledge	? 1 2 3 4 5	_____
Race strategy	? 1 2 3 4 5	_____
Body composition	? 1 2 3 4 5	_____
Support of family/friends	? 1 2 3 4 5	_____
Years of racing experience	? 1 2 3 4 5	_____

Season Goals

1. _____
2. _____
3. _____

Season Training Objectives

1. _____
2. _____
3. _____
4. _____
5. _____

• Support of family/friends. For those who are not fans of the sport, mountain bikers may seem somewhat strange. Those we are closest to have a tremendous effect on our psychological stress. How supportive of the time you spend training and racing are your family and friends? If they are 100 percent supportive, circle 5. If you have no support and are ridiculed by those who are close to you, or if they try to convince you not to devote so much time to riding, circle 1.

• Years of racing experience. How many years have you been training and racing? Circle that number. If more than five years, still circle 5. Experience plays a significant role in high-level training and racing.

• Tendency to overtrain. Do you come on strong about December—and are you ready to quit by June every year? If so, you're prone to overtraining—circle 1. Or do you frequently take rest breaks throughout the year and stay enthusiastic for training and racing right up until the last race on the calendar? If you're one of the few racers with such wisdom and patience, circle 5.

To the right of the ratings is a column called Objectives to Improve. For any item marked 3 or less, briefly indicate in the space provided what must be done to improve it. For example, if very fast starts are a problem, you need to decide why it was rated low. Is it because lactate clearance is poor? If so, write in "Improve lactate clearance." But if it is **Objectives to Improve** because you are always seeded on the start line near the back of the field, training specifically for starts won't make any difference. If you are unsure of what needs to be done, just place a question mark on the line.

At the bottom of the Mountain Biker Assessment, there are spaces for you to write in goals for the season and training objectives to help achieve them. Don't do anything with these sections yet. The next chapter takes a closer look at how to go about correcting some of the abilities that may be holding you back from better racing. In Chapter 7, the assessment will come together as you complete the last sections at the bottom of the form and begin the process of designing an annual training plan for better racing results.

REFERENCES

Costill, D. "Predicting Athletic Potential: The Value of Laboratory Testing." *Sports Medicine Digest* 11, no. 11 (1989): 7.

Daniels, J. Physiological Characteristics of Champion Male Athletes. Research Quarterly 45 (1989): 342–348.

Droghetti, P. et al. "Non-Invasive Determination of the Anaerobic Threshold in Canoeing, Cycling, Cross-Country Skiing, Roller and Ice Skating, Rowing and Walking." *European Journal of Applied Physiology* 53 (1985): 299–303.

Francis, K.T., et al. "The Relationship Between Anaerobic Threshold and Heart Rate Linearity During Cycle Ergometry." *European Journal of Applied Physiology* 59 (1989): 273–277.

Friel, J. *Training With Power.* Cambridge, MA: Tune, 1999..

Gibbons, E. S. "The Significance of Anaerobic Threshold in Exercise Prescription." *Journal of Sports Medicine* 27 (1999): 357–361.

Hagberg, J.M. "Physiological Implications of the Lactate Threshold." *International Journal of Sports Medicine* 5 (1984): 106–109.

Kuipers, H., et al. "Comparison of Heart Rate as a Non-Invasive Determination of Anaerobic Threshold with Lactate Threshold When Cycling." *European Journal of Applied Physiology* 58 (1988): 303–306.

Noakes, T.D. "Implications of Exercise Testing for Prediction of Athletic Performance: A Contemporary Perspective." *Medicine and Science in Sports and Exercise* 20, no. 4 (1988): 319–330.

Schneider, D.A., et al. "Ventilatory Threshold and Maximal Oxygen Uptake During Cycling and Running in Biathletes." *Medicine and Science in Sports and Exercise* 22, no. 2 (1990): 257–264.

Simon, J., et al. "Plasma Lactate and Ventilation Thresholds in Trained and Untrained Cyclists." *Journal of Applied Physiology* 60 (1986): 777–781.

Sleivert, G.G. and H.A. Wenger. "Physiological Predictors of Short-Course Biathlon Performance." *Medicine and Science in Sports and Exercise* 25, no. 7 (1993): 871–876.

Steed, J.C., et al. "Ratings of Perceived Exertion (RPE) as Markers of Blood Lactate Concentration During Rowing." *Medicine and Science in Sports and Exercise* 26 (1994): 797–803.

RACE FITNESS

Motivation can't take you very far if you don't have the legs.
—LANCE ARMSTRONG

Have you ever watched a house being built? If so, you know there's a well-defined order in which the many tasks of building are completed. First, the foundation is constructed of a durable material such as concrete. Great care is taken at this stage to ensure that the foundation is level, square and stable. A poorly laid foundation means the finished house will be of poor quality. Next, the wall and roof framing go up. This phase is quick, and as it's done, the house begins to take shape. With just a little imagination, you can even picture what it will look like when done. Finally, after the plumbing and electrical wiring are installed, the walls are enclosed and the finish work begins with the installation of windows, doors, cabinets and floor covers and the completion of a multitude of progressively smaller tasks. Eventually, all the work is done, and if each stage of the construction was performed carefully, the house will provide shelter for many years to come with only minor maintenance along the way.

It's remarkable how similar house building is to race fitness building. To prepare for mountain bike racing, training begins by first establishing a foundation of the most basic physical needs, and then progresses to carefully developing smaller, more refined fitness aspects that match the fitness "blueprint." Building a solid base foundation takes a long time, but if it's done correctly, such fitness is easy to maintain. Too often, novice riders want to speed up or even skip the foundation building phase of training. Even experienced athletes are tempted to do this in order to get on with the intense training that produces final race shape. But just as with a poor house foundation, slighting the base-development period means a low-quality finished product. The stronger the base, the more solid and long-lasting the final fitness is.

Building fitness is similar to building a house.

On the other hand, developing only the foundation without ever doing the finish work means that one's race potential is never realized. A season of training must include all of the phases of fitness construction at just the right times to bring about a high level of race fitness when it's needed.

The previous chapter started the blueprints for your next race season by helping to identify your mountain bike racing strengths and weaknesses. This chapter takes the process one step further by better defining what is holding you back from better racing. It also introduces the tasks to accomplish in building improved race fitness. Then Part IV (Chapters 7 through 9) finalizes the blueprints by teaching you how to organize training so the tasks are completed in an order and to a degree that produces peak race fitness.

LIMITERS

Let's examine only your identified weaknesses for a moment, as these are preventing better performances. Or are they? What if you gave yourself a score of 2 for "long climbs" in your Race Ability Profile, but the courses you race on have no long climbs. While long climbs are no less of a weakness, your race success is not limited by that weakness. Or how about if your "race endurance" score was 3, and you know that for four-hour and longer workouts, it's a struggle just to finish? That's certainly a weakness. If

Limiters are race-specific weaknesses.

your races are no more than one hour, however, and you have no trouble at this duration, multihour endurance may not be such a big deal. In other words, endurance is a weakness, but it is not limiting your performance. So it's not a concern unless, of course, you decide to train for a very long race.

It's important to know which weaknesses are holding you back for the races you do—especially your most important races. These race-specific weaknesses are your "limiters." If you devote a significant amount of training time to improving these, you will become a better racer, I guarantee it. The concept of limiter is similar to the old idea that a chain is only as strong as its weakest link. The stronger your current limiters become, the faster you go. The reverse of this is also true. Spending a lot of time working on strengths and too little time working on limiters will do little to produce better race results. Too many riders train this way by working a lot on what they are already good at. The less time your have available to train, the more important working on weaknesses becomes. Knowing and training your limiters is crucial to better racing.

TRAINING BASIC ABILITIES

Let's shift the direction of this discussion to get a better understanding of the abilities of endurance, force and speed skill. Having a good grasp of what they are all about is important to designing a training program in the next chapter.

You have probably noticed that some athletes seem to excel in long races, but are less competitive in short events. Then there are riders who thrive in the hills, leading your training group every time the terrain goes vertical, but when pedaling into the wind on flat ground, they struggle. What you're observing in each case are is individual mixes of the bike racing abilities resulting from the riders' unique combinations of genetics and training.

Each athlete has a unique set of abilities.

The abilities that you rated using the Natural Ability Profile—endurance, force, and speed skill—are basic and crucial to optimal racing performance. For the experienced mountain biker, every year must begin with the redevelopment of these abilities before progressing to the more advanced aspects of race fitness. In the first couple of years of a novice rider's career, training should consist of developing these abilities in workouts and little else. Resist the temptation to dive into high-effort workouts, such as anaerobic intervals, until your basic abilities are well established.

Rebuild the basic abilities at the start of each new season.

It may help you understand all of the abilities of racing if you think of fitness as a triangle, with the basic abilities anchoring its corners. Figure 6.1 illustrates this. In addition, knowing how racing abilities are developed in training may prove helpful before you design your training program in the next chapter. For each of the abilities described here, there are brief examples of workouts that enhance that ability. Each of these workouts and many more are explained in detail in Appendix B.

ENDURANCE

Endurance is the ability to delay the onset and reduce the effects of fatigue. Within the context of this book, when the term is used alone, endurance implies an aerobic level of exertion (heart rate zones 1 through 4 or RPE 1 through 6). Endurance training strengthens slow twitch muscle fibers—the ones that contract slowly but recover quickly. Long rides have also been shown to improve the endurance qualities of the fast twitch muscles used for high efforts. This is critical to racing. In addition, working on endurance also improves your ability to conserve the carbohydrate-based fuels, glycogen and glucose, by teaching your

FIGURE 6.1
Basic abilities triangle.

The benefits of endurance training

muscles to preferentially use fat for energy. Endurance is the most basic ability of the cross-country racer, and the most important one to train.

Endurance is specific to the event. It's unlikely that you could complete the Leadville 100-mile race on a program of short rides. On the other hand, the capacity to ride steadily for many hours is not necessary to compete in short events. It's important to match your endurance training to the demands of the events for which you train.

For beginning riders, endurance is the key to improvement. Emphasize this ability above all others in the first year or two of training. The experienced athlete rebuilds and then maintains this vital ability each season. A high level of endurance requires a relatively long time to mature.

Endurance is best developed each year by starting with general endurance training and progressing to more race-specific workouts. To build endurance, start by developing a sound cardiorespiratory system (heart, lungs and blood) with a broad range of general, or cross-training, modes such as running, cross-country skiing, rowing, swimming or aerobics classes, in addition to riding a bike. Early in the season, these workouts are done at low intensity. Later on, training becomes more specific as cross-training is reduced or eliminated and workouts gradually begin simulating races—at first in terms of duration, and later in terms of intensity.

Endurance is improved not only by long duration bike workouts, but also by consistent, chronic exposure to the activity. In other words, the weekly volume (frequency and duration) of training plays a role in the development of endurance, although not as great as workout duration alone. Exercise great care when increasing volume, since the body is not capable of rapid change when it comes to endurance adaptations. Plan on taking months and years to increase endurance, rather than days or weeks.

FORCE

Force is the ability to overcome resistance—in other words, it equals the amount of pressure you can apply to the pedal. It also plays a role in muscular economy. When the slow twitch muscles are strengthened and thus capable of carrying more of the load, faster paces are produced at aerobic efforts. This spares glycogen and glucose, which are in short supply, and keeps lactate accumulation low. All of this means that you're riding economically due to better strength.

Just as with endurance, force development progresses from general to specific throughout the training year. It begins in the early winter with weight training. While I prefer free weights for most of this work, other types of equipment may be used if free

Endurance is at the heart of mountain bike training

Endurance improves over a long time.

Strong muscles improve economy.

Force training begins with progressive resistance work, such as weight training.

weights are not available. Such equipment may include resistance machines, stretch cords, body-weight exercises or other special equipment.

By mid- to late winter, general strength development should be maximal, allowing you to begin more bike-specific force training on the trail and road. At this point, many young athletes stop lifting weights, since they are easily capable of keeping their strength with big-gear and hill training. Older athletes and many women, however, seem less capable of retaining their strength gains, and should continue general strength work throughout most of the remainder of the season, although at a maintenance level. Chapter 13 provides greater detail on general strength training in the weight room.

SPEED SKILL

Speed skill is the ability to move quickly and efficiently. It is the ability to pedal smoothly at a high cadence and to negotiate technical terrain quickly without wasted movement. It is *not* used here to mean how fast your race times or velocity are, although those are related issues. As speed skills improve, so do race times. Some aspects of this ability, such as 200-rpm pedaling, are apparently genetic. Athletes with world-class speed skill also have a high percentage of fast twitch muscles that are capable of rapid contraction, but they tend to fatigue quickly. It's possible, however, to improve speed skill. Several scientific studies have demonstrated that leg turnover is trainable given the right types of workouts and consistency of purpose. And we all know that technical trail riding improves with practice.

Speed skill is a trainable ability.

As with force, speed skill development improves pedaling economy. Frequent drill work, especially in the winter months, teaches big and small muscles exactly when to contract and when to relax. As the muscles involved in pedaling are activated with precise harmony, little precious fuel is wasted. Just as with endurance and force, speed skill training begins in the late fall or early winter, depending on the race schedule, and continues at a maintenance level throughout the rest of the season.

The timing of contraction and relaxation of muscles is crucial to Speed Skill development.

Appendix B provides several workouts for improving Speed Skill, and Chapter 12 describes how to organize training for this crucial ability.

TRAINING HIGHER ABILITIES

The basic abilities of endurance, force, and speed skill at the corners of the fitness triangle diagrammed in Figure 6.1 are only the foundation for our construction project. The sides of the triangle can be likened to the wall and roof framing. In the language of training, this framing is constructed of *muscular endurance, anaerobic endurance,* and *power.*

The higher racing abilities result from well-developed basic abilities.

These are the advanced abilities the rider emphasizes in the later periods of training, with only 10 weeks or so remaining until the most important races. Figure 6.2 shows these abilities in relation to the basic abilities. Each higher ability results from the development of the basic abilities on either side of it, and is further refined with training specific to that ability.

FIGURE 6.2
Higher abilities triangle.

MUSCULAR ENDURANCE

Muscular endurance is the ability of the muscles to maintain a relatively high load for a prolonged time. It is a combination of the basic abilities of force and endurance. Superior muscular endurance is evidenced by excellent fatigue resistance, a high lactate threshold and the ability to clear and tolerate the lactate that slowly accumulates at such intensities. Muscular endurance is *the* critical ability for the mountain bike racer. Toward the end of a race, this ability keeps the pace high. Fatigue is cumulative throughout an event, but if muscular endurance is well developed, it is kept at bay and bigger gears and higher velocity are possible.

Muscular Endurance is necessary for mountain bike racing success.

Muscular endurance work should begin in midwinter with sustained efforts of several minutes in the heart rate 3 zone or power CP180 zone. These workouts gradually increase in intensity and duration by late winter or spring (depending on when the first high-priority race is) to include mostly aerobic interval workouts in the heart rate 4 and 5a zones or power CP60 and CP90 zones. The work intervals lengthen as the recovery intervals remain quite short—about a third or a fourth of the work interval duration. By late spring, steady-state, nonstop efforts of 20 to 40 minutes in the heart rate 4 and 5a zones or power CP60 and CP90 zones are done. The effort of these workouts is much like that expended in controlled time trials and is tremendously effective in boosting both aerobic and anaerobic fitness with little risk of overtraining. Throughout the summer race period, muscular endurance is maintained.

Muscular endurance training is done at about lactate threshold.

ANAEROBIC ENDURANCE

As a blending of speed skill and endurance, *anaerobic endurance* is the ability to resist fatigue at very high efforts when cadence is high. A rider with excellent anaerobic endurance has good ability to clear and tolerate blood lactate and performs well in short-distance events and head-to-head competitions with frequent surges. For the mountain biker who specializes in ultra-endurance events, such as 100-mile off-road races, anaerobic endurance is of less importance.

There are two types of anaerobic endurance workouts. One is based on aerobic capacity–developing intervals, which are done in the heart rate 5b zone or the power CP6 zone. With about 10 to 12 weeks until the first high-priority race of the season, the experienced athlete should phase into interval training to increase VO$_2$ max. The intervals are three to six minutes long with recoveries, at first, approximately equal to the work interval. As the season progresses and fitness improves, the recovery interval length is decreased.

Anaerobic endurance training is based on intervals.

Shorter repetitions (less than one minute duration) at heart rate 5c or power CP1 zone intensity are effective for developing the capacity to manage extremely high levels of lactate, such as you might experience at the start of a race. The idea of these workouts is to produce a maximal effort that creates large amounts of lactic acid, recover briefly, and then repeat the process several times. For the shorter distance race specialist, lactate tolerance and clearance training in the spring and early summer prepares the body to remove lactate from the blood and to buffer its effects.

Short, maximal repetitions train lactate tolerance.

Anaerobic endurance workouts are quite stressful and should not be a part of the beginner's training regimen. Develop both speed skill and endurance with at least two years of training before attempting these workouts. The likely results of too much anaerobic endurance work done too soon are burnout and overtraining.

POWER

Power is the ability to quickly apply maximum strength. It results from having high levels of the basic abilities of force and speed skill. Well-developed power, or the lack of it, is obvious on short hills, in fast starts and in sudden pace changes, such as initiating a finishing sprint.

Since it includes both speed skill and force components, power is dependent on the nervous system to send the proper signals, and on the muscles to contract maximally. For this reason, improvements in power come from short, all-out efforts into the power CP.2 zone followed by very long recovery intervals to allow the nervous system and muscles to fully recover. These repetitions are quite brief—in the neighborhood of 8 to 12 seconds. Heart rate monitors are of no use in power training; use RPE, pace or power.

Short, maximum efforts train power.

Attempting to improve power while fatigued is counterproductive. Such training is, therefore, best done when you are rested, and early in a training session when the nervous system and muscles are most responsive.

LIMITERS AND RACING

Let's return to the discussion of limiters, which were previously defined as race-specific weaknesses. By now you should have a good idea of what your physical ability limiters are. The basic abilities of endurance, force and speed skill are easily identified. The advanced abilities are somewhat more difficult to recognize. But since the higher abilities are based on the combination of the basic abilities, a weakness in the latter produces a weakness in the former. For example, if your endurance is weak it will restrict both muscular endurance and anaerobic endurance. If endurance is good but force is lacking, muscular endurance and power are negatively affected. Poor speed skill means low power and inferior anaerobic endurance.

Higher ability limiters result from basic ability limiters.

As mentioned, the types of races you do determine what strengths are needed and how your weaknesses limit you. So matching your abilities to the demands of the event is critical for success. Let's examine how that works.

RACE PRESCRIPTION

Races vary not only in course length, but also in terrain. Matching your physical fitness to the demands of the most important events for which you are training produces the best results.

The longer the race is, the more it favors the basic abilities. Conversely, the shorter the race, the more important the higher abilities are. In preparing for an ultra-endurance race, endurance is paramount, but force is also necessary to deal with hills or even just undulating terrain, and good fuel economy resulting from good speed skill conserves energy. Muscular endurance plays an important role, but training for anaerobic endurance and power is of limited value.

Long races favor the basic abilities.

In the same way, a short race such as a 30-minute dirt criterium favors the higher abilities, especially anaerobic endurance and power. That doesn't mean that endurance and force aren't needed, just not to the same extent as for the ultra-endurance events. Speed skill training is critical for short races, and muscular endurance also plays a role.

Short races favor the higher abilities.

Since cross-country races typically last about two hours, they require a blending of the basic and higher abilities.

So the bottom line is that training for an important event means first deciding what is important for success and then improving your limiters that don't match the demands of the event, while maintaining strengths that already fit its demands.

TABLE 6.1

Summary of abilities

Ability	Workout Frequency*	Intervals Duration**	Zones Work	Recovery***	RPE	Heart Rate	Power	Benefit	Example
Endurance	1–4/week Continuous	20 min. to 6 hrs.	N/A	N/A	2–6	1–3	CP180	a. Delay fatigue b. Build slow twitch c. Economy	3 hrs. on flat course
Force	1–2/week Intervals	20–90 min. b. Economy	30 sec. to 2 min.	1:2	7–9	4–5b	CP12–60	a. Muscular strength	Seated hill repeats
Speed Skills	1–4/week	20–90 min.	10–30 sec.	1:2–5	9–10	N/A	CP1	a. High cadence b. Economy	30 sec. spin-ups
Muscular Endurance	1–2/week	30 min. to 2 hrs. Ints/Contin	6–20 min.	3–4:1	7–8	4–5a	CP30–60	a. Strength endurance b. Race-pace comfort c. Boost LT velocity	4 by 6 min. (2 min. RI)
Anaerobic Endurance	1–2/week	30–90 min.	3–6 min. 30–40 sec.	2:1–2 2–3:1	9	5b	CP6	a. Raise VO_2max b. VO_2 max velocity c. Lactate clearance d. Lactate tolerance	5 by 5 min. (5 min. RI) 4 by (4 by 40 sec. (20 sec. RI)) 5 min. RI betw. sets
Power	1–3/week	20–90 min.	8–12 sec.	1:10	10	N/A	CP2	a. Muscular power b. Fast starts c. Short hills d. Sprints	10 by 8 sec. (80 sec. RI)

* Varies with individual, time of season and time available to train.

** Total workout time including the portion of workout that develops the ability.

*** Work interval-to-recovery interval ratio. Example, 3:1 means rest ("off") 1 minute for every 3 minutes of work ("on") time.

Abbreviations: ' = minute, " = seconds, hrs = hours RI = recovery ("off") interval

OTHER LIMITERS

Besides the event-specific ability limiters discussed here, there are other factors that may also hold you back from achieving race goals. One of the most critical is a lack of time to train. This is perhaps the most common limiter. If this is a limiter for you, when designing a program consider that the specificity of training discussed in Chapter 3 becomes increasingly important as the hours available to work out diminish. In other words, when time becomes scarce, your training must increasingly simulate racing. So as volume declines, workout intensity increases. The next chapter helps you decide how many weekly training hours are reasonable and necessary.

Other common miscellaneous limiters are listed at the bottom of Special Element 5.7 in the previous chapter. Most are discussed in subsequent chapters.

Scarce training time is a common limiter.

REFERENCES

Bompa, T. *Theory and Methodology of Training*. Dubuque, IA: Kendall/Hunt Publishing, 1994.

Freeman, W. *Peak When It Counts*. Mountain View, CA: TAFNEWS Press, 1991.

Friel, J. *The Cyclist's Training Bible*. Boulder, CO: VeloPress, 1996.

Sleamaker, R. *Serious Training for Serious Athletes*. Champaign, IL: Leisure Press, 1989.

PLANNING

Do elite mountain bikers know something the rest of us don't about how to train? Is there a secret to success for cross-country racing? If you followed the world champion's training program, as described in a magazine, would you be as successful?

Fortunately, the answer to all of these questions is "no." There is no magic formula when it comes to training. The reason is that each athlete is an individual (remember the principle of individualization?) and must do what is best given his or her unique combination of abilities. In the previous two chapters your abilities were charted.

No, there are no secrets when it comes to training. There always have been, and always will be, five ingredients for success in sport (as in any other endeavor in life). They are the five Ps:

1. Purpose—Know exactly what your goal is.
2. Passion—Have a burning desire to achieve the goal.
3. Planning—Determine precisely how to go about achieving the goal.
4. Perspiration—Work hard (and smart) following your plan.
5. Perseverance—Willingly make sacrifices to achieve the goal.

In Part IV we develop your purpose and planning for the race season. I assume the passion is already there or you wouldn't have made it this far in the book. Subsequent parts of the book address perspiration and perseverance.

Now let's get on with producing a program that brings you to a fitness peak for the season's most important races.

PLANNING A SEASON

*The simple sport of mountain biking doesn't really exist anymore. The simple
Sunday ride will never change, but the racing already has and will continue to.*

—ALISON SYDOR

By now you should have a good understanding of the theory and science of training and have a sense of what your personal abilities are. In this chapter we bring
these together into an annual plan that will become the road map of your season.

Just as when you take a long trip by car using a map as a guide to your destination, so should you use an annual training plan to provide direction to seasonal goals.
While driving across the country, you may find it necessary to deviate from the planned
route for any number of reasons, such as road closures, bad weather or unplanned side
trips. The same may be expected when following an annual training plan. There will
undoubtedly be deviations. You'll catch a cold, unexpected travel will interrupt training, work demands will suddenly increase or Aunt Jeanne will visit for several days. I've
never coached a rider who made it all the way through the season without some
changes in the plan.

Such changes are common, so do all of the paperwork described here in pencil.
Chances are there will be many adjustments as the year progresses. Many athletes with
solid computer skills have designed programs using Excel or some other spreadsheet to
plan their season. Currently, there is no commercial software available specifically for this
need, although I expect that void to be filled in the near future.

**Expect to make changes in
the annual training plan.**

Be forewarned that there is a potential downside to planning a season as described
in this chapter. It's possible to become so married to the details of the annual training

plan produced here that you fail to make workout changes when they are obviously needed. I've seen this happen with athletes who refuse to deviate from their overly optimistic and aggressive schedule even when it is apparent that overtraining is imminent.

On the other hand, I've also known of riders developing a detailed plan and then never referring to it during the year. Planning should not be done to impress anyone or merely to feel organized. The purpose is to create an effective and dynamic guide for your training in the coming season—or what is left of it if you purchased this book well into the season.

When written down and followed, the annual training plan will constantly remind you of long-term goals and short-term directions so you don't get bogged down in working out and going to races. Most riders are myopic—they never look further ahead than the next race. Consequently, few achieve the goals they set early in the year. To be a good self-coach, you must be able to train in January with August in mind. Designing and following a plan, even if it isn't perfect, will provide you with a decided competitive advantage.

PERIODIZATION

Before you start on the annual training plan, there is one more bit of information needed—the theoretical model on which the plan is developed. There are many models that could be used, but the most effective one is based on a system called *periodization*.

Specific fitness is the purpose of periodization.

Periodization is a training concept in which the year is divided into distinct periods, with each having a particular purpose in preparing the athlete for the stresses of racing. As the training year progresses, a properly periodized program gradually causes the athlete to adapt to the specific conditions of the targeted races (according to the principle of specificity described earlier).

The basic premise of periodization is that training should progress from creating general fitness to producing fitness that exactly matches the demands of the most important races of the year. For example, in the early winter the rider may lift weights to increase fitness. This is not a specific demand of cross-country mountain biking, as weight lifting is not a part of racing. But improving one's ability to apply force (one of the three basic abilities) in the weight room is eventually converted into the ability to apply force on the bike later in the winter. By spring this force becomes part of the higher abilities of power and muscular endurance—both of which are specific demands of cross-country racing. Figure 7.1 illustrates the general-to-specific theoretical foundation of periodization.

Periodization also involves organizing training in such a way that the elements of fitness achieved in the earlier, more general periods are maintained as new, more specific fitness aspects. Small changes in the workload are introduced every three to four weeks to allow the body to adapt gradually to the increases. Figure 7.2 shows how the training year is divided into distinct periods and indicates the terms typically used to describe them. The names of the periods shown along the bottom row of this drawing ("Preparation," "Base 1," "Base 2," etc.) will be used in this book to refer to distinct blocks of time in the season.

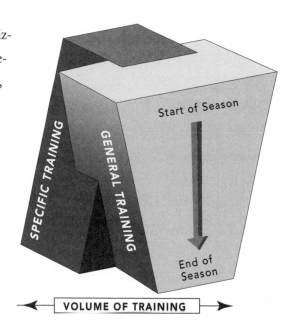

FIGURE 7.1
General to specific training emphasis throughout the training year.

The training year is divided into periods, each with a distinct purpose.

PEAKING

When periodized correctly, the rider will come to fitness peaks at the times in the season when the most important races are planned. This is the ultimate purpose of training and therefore of periodization. When a true peak comes about, you experience several changes that combine to create a nearly astonishing race performance. These changes include improved leg power, reduced lactic acid production at any given power output, increased blood volume, greater red blood cell concentration and expanded fuel stores. If you top these physiological improvements with enhanced mental skills—such as motivation, confidence and concentration—you will be in truly great race shape.

The purpose of periodizing is to peak at the right times.

This theoretical process of coming to a peak at a planned point in the future is diagrammed in Figure 7.3.

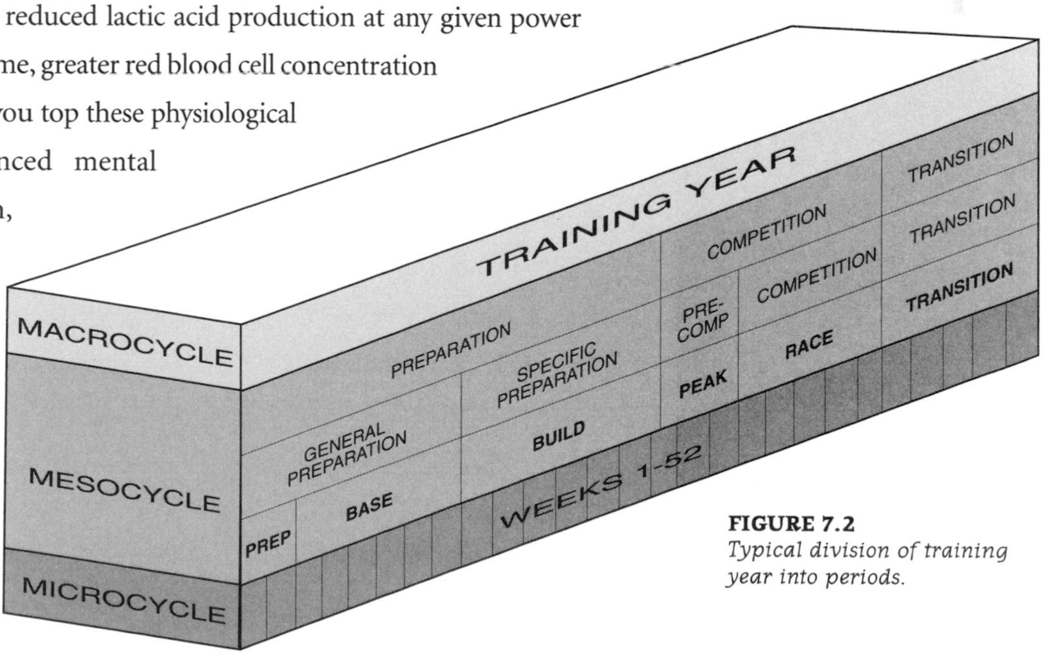

FIGURE 7.2
Typical division of training year into periods.

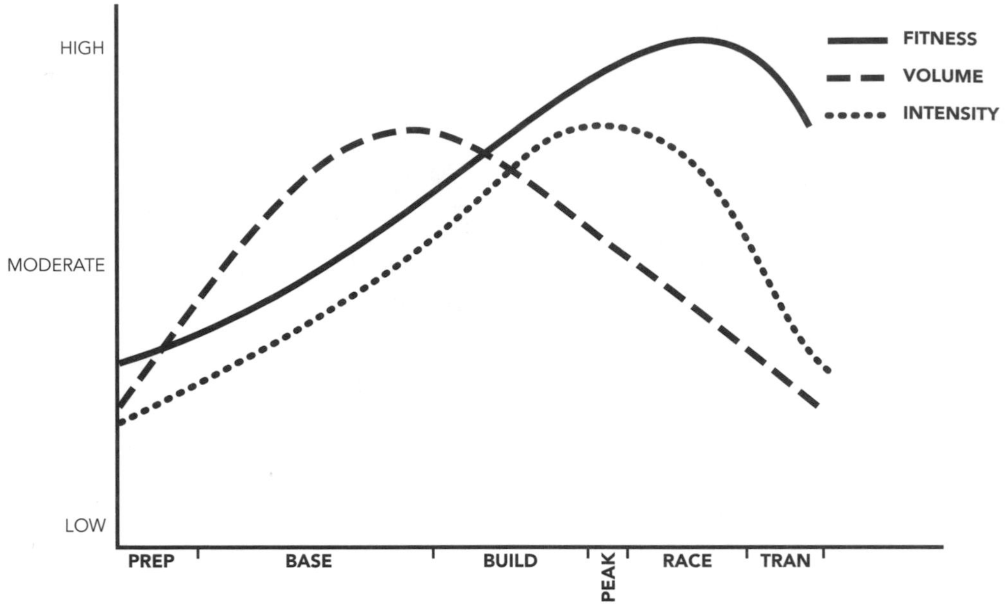

FIGURE 7.3
*A simple periodization plan
to produce a fitness peak by
varying volume and intensity*

A period of peaking is marked by both reduced training volume, to allow for rest and adaptation, and regular, race-specific workouts that accustom the body to the stresses expected in the goal race.

These peaks may be attained only briefly two or three times in a year. Each peak may last up to two or three weeks at most—a duration of a few days is more common. Attempting to maintain a peak for several weeks usually results in the loss of fitness as the reduced workload produces a detraining effect similar to that shown in Table 3.1.

PERIODS

*A description of the six
training periods.*

In the annual training plan you create in this chapter, the season will be divided into six distinct periods. These are shown in Figure 7.4.

Preparation

In the late fall or early winter, following a break from training, fitness development is the most general of the entire season. Cross-training with weights and aerobic activities such as running, skiing or swimming prepares the athlete for the next period. This is a period of "training to train" that may last three to eight weeks.

Base

In this 6- to 12-week block, on-bike training gradually replaces cross-training. Base is divided into three subperiods—Base 1, Base 2 and Base 3—of three to four weeks each.

The last few days (up to a week) of each of these is devoted to rest, recovery and testing. The training emphasis in all three is on the basic abilities of endurance, force and speed skills as described in Chapter 6. In Base 2, however, muscular endurance training is introduced, and by Base 3 it makes up a significant portion of the training program. Weight training continues, but is decreased to a maintenance level by Base 3. Races of lesser importance may begin in Base 3.

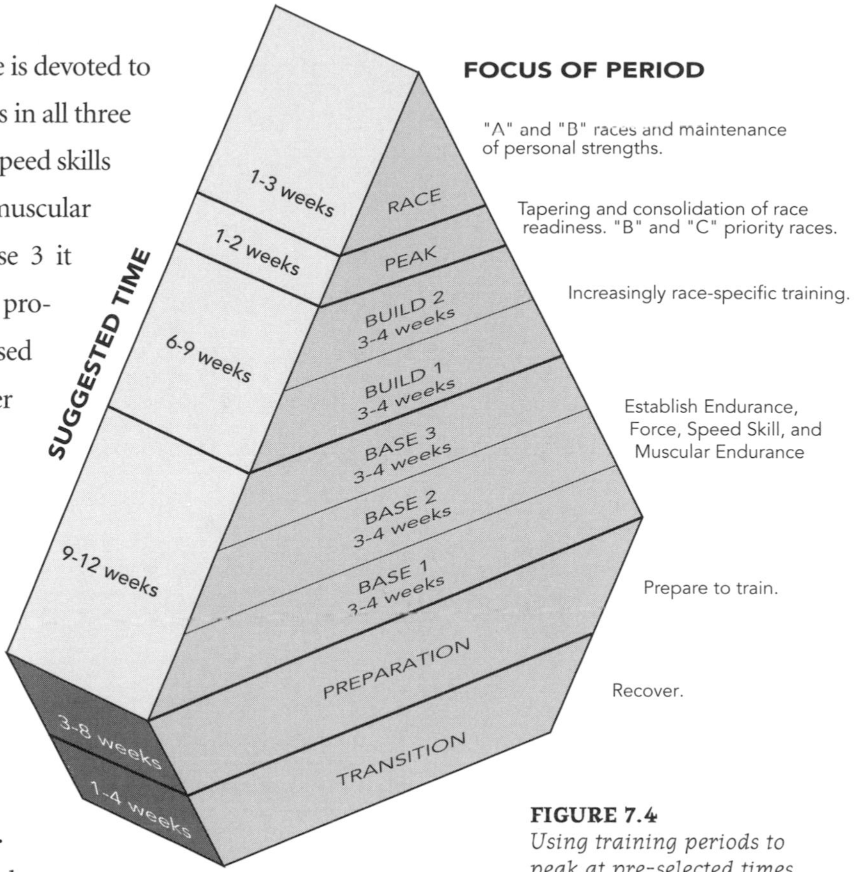

Build

In this period the specific demands of racing are paramount. That usually means more time devoted to the higher abilities of muscular endurance, anaerobic endurance and power. It is also necessary to maintain endurance, force and speed skills. Such maintenance may be accomplished with less frequent workouts in these areas, since it takes less time and effort to retain an ability than to develop it in the first place. Women and masters may continue to lift weights on a maintenance schedule of one day per week. It's been my experience that strength gains are usually well maintained in young, male riders without weight training.

Build 1, when the body is cautiously allowed to adjust to anaerobic training, is a bridge between Base 3 and Build 2. Build 1 and Build 2 may each last three to four weeks with rest and recovery in the last few days of each. Racing is common in the Build period, especially right before or at the end of a rest and recovery break. Care must be taken to allow for recovery in the days following a race.

Peak

A Peak period may last one or two weeks. During this time, volume is gradually reduced and workouts become like miniraces. In fact, low-priority racing is a great way to help produce a peak. About every 72 hours, include a workout that simulates the intensity and conditions of the targeted race but for less than race duration. This could be a series of off-road time trials on a course similar to the one you will race on. Or it

FOCUS OF PERIOD

"A" and "B" races and maintenance of personal strengths.

Tapering and consolidation of race readiness. "B" and "C" priority races.

Increasingly race-specific training.

Establish Endurance, Force, Speed Skill, and Muscular Endurance

Prepare to train.

Recover.

FIGURE 7.4
Using training periods to peak at pre-selected times.

could be a race, preferably one shorter than the targeted race. All other workouts are for recovery. The idea is to go into each of these hard workouts or races well rested in order to push your limits a bit higher while consolidating your race preparedness.

Race

This is the period for which you've been preparing for weeks. Physical fitness is high, mental skills are sharp and race readiness is high. One brief, race-specific workout about four days before the big race, with lots of rest on either side of it, will ensure a mental and physical peak. This may be a one-week period with the high-priority race at the end, a two-week period with each week culminating in an important race, or a three-week period including two or three races. But remember that the longer it is stretched out, the greater the risk of losing fitness due to decreased training.

Transition

Following a Race period, it's generally a good idea to take a break from training to allow for a physical and mental transition from the Race period before starting a buildup to a new peak. The Transition period following a midseason Race period may only be a week long. After the last race of the year, this period could last up to four weeks. The purpose of the Transition period is rest and recovery. Stay active, but at a greatly reduced level. Thi active recovery doesn't have to be on the bike and, in fact, it is probably better to employ alternate activities.

FIGURE 7.5
Hypothetical training year divided into periods showing the interplay of volume and intensity.

Figure 7.5 illustrates a season with two Race periods. It uses the periodization scheme described above while showing how volume (frequency and duration) blend with race-specific intensity to produce race fitness.

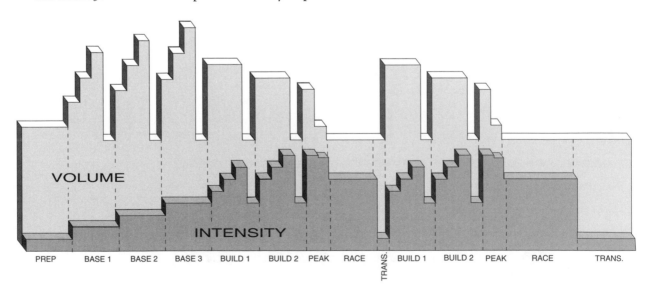

VOLUME

INTENSITY

PREP | BASE 1 | BASE 2 | BASE 3 | BUILD 1 | BUILD 2 | PEAK | RACE | TRANS. | BUILD 1 | BUILD 2 | PEAK | RACE | TRANS.

THE ANNUAL TRAINING PLAN

You should now have enough information to develop your annual training plan. To do this, you will complete seven steps. The first six are:

Step 1: Determine season goals

Step 2: Establish season training objectives

Step 3: Set annual hours

Step 4: List and prioritize races

Step 5: Divide the year into periods

Step 6: Assign weekly hours

The seventh step in this process is the planning of weekly workouts. Chapter 8 will complete your annual training plan by helping you assign weekly workouts based on your abilities as detailed in Figure 5.7. The first time you plan a season, it may take up to an hour. But every time you go through this process it gets easier, especially if the plan has been kept current throughout the year.

Working in pencil, complete the appropriate worksheet from Appendix A as you read through this chapter. There are blank annual training plan worksheets provided there for the years 2000 to 2005. The parts of the annual training plan will be addressed in the order they appear on the worksheet. At the top of each plan are annual hours, season goals, and training objectives. There are also rows for each week of the year with the week number and date of the Monday of each week indicated. The columns are where you list races, their priorities, the specific periodization period and projected training hours for each week. The small boxes on the right side are for workouts by abilities, which are addressed in Chapter 8. You should recognize most of the subheadings as the abilities discussed in the previous two chapters.

STEP 1: DETERMINE SEASON GOALS

What do you want to accomplish in racing this season? Answering this question is perhaps the most important step in the entire process, as it gives direction and meaning to everything else done here in the planning process. Don't rush into setting your goals. Give it some thought. You may even want to think about this for a day or two before returning to this page. Whatever you come up with should be clear and concise. Knowing *exactly* what your goals are unquestionably improves your likelihood of achieving them. Poorly defined goals usually contribute to a dismal season. Without an exact season "des-

Clear goals contribute to success.

tination," it's likely you'll get lost in just showing up for races, and never come to a peak.

It's good to think big at this stage, but don't confuse *goals* with *dreams*. Athletes often dream about what they want to accomplish—a win at nationals, turning pro or some other lofty vision. That's good for your future in the sport. Tall dreams keep us going and help give all of the hours spent riding a greater meaning. Everyone needs dreams, and they can become realities given enough smart and hard training. But dreams aren't goals. Dreams are so big that they take longer than one season to accomplish. If it's farfetched to believe that your wish can be achieved this season, it's not a goal but rather a dream.

Your goals can be achieved in one season.

Though you temper your hopeful optimism with realism at this point (writing an annual training plan is a decidedly objective exercise), don't forget your dreams. At some point they will become goals. Keep the flame burning in your heart. A rider without a burning passion for the future won't last long or accomplish much.

Goals lead to dreams.

Use the following four principles to help shape your goals:

Principles of goal setting.

Principle 1: The goal must be measurable.

Try to set dates and success measures for your goals. When must it be accomplished? A goal without an end point keeps getting pushed back until the season ends, usually unsuccessfully. How will you know if it's been achieved? If appropriate, use a number, such as a race time, to define the goal. Try not to use vague phrases like "get better" or "be more competitive" in your goal statement. Instead, say something like "Complete Big Bear in less than 1:45." This goal involves knowing what times you've previously done on this course. It's possible that the conditions on race day may be horrendous, so it may be necessary to redefine such a goal at the last minute.

Note that this principle doesn't mean that you should never use subjective measures of success. Sometimes it's appropriate to simply say, "Be satisfied with performance at the Fat Tire Classic." This is especially true for those who are relatively new to the sport.

Principle 2: The goal must be under your control.

Don't set goals based on what other people may or may not do. "Win my category in the Mercury Tour" sounds like a measurable goal, but what if the world's best riders in your category show up? You have no control over who races, what kind of shape they're in, or if they are "training through" or peaking for a given race. You only have control of *your* training and *your* motivation. However, there are some goals that are measurable, yet on the edge of your control. For example, if you've previously raced at nationals against all of the best riders in the country in the past and have closely followed their progress in results, then their performance may become your standard for measurement.

Principle 3: The goal must stretch you.

A goal that is too easy or too hard (a dream?) is the same as having no goal. What's "too hard" or "too easy"? It depends on you. "Finish half of my races" isn't much of a challenge for an experienced racer, but may be a stretch for a novice.

Principle 4: The goal should be stated in the positive.

A story is told of a major league baseball catcher who once told his pitcher, "Whatever you do, don't throw it low and outside to this batter." Guess where the pitcher threw it? Home run. The pitcher's mind was attracted to the wrong spot.

Your goal must maintain your concentration on what you want to happen, not what you must avoid. Setting a goal such as "Don't crash in the Trail 66 Finals" focuses attention on the wrong outcome—averting mistakes. Chances are the race will go poorly, because the focus on what was *supposed* to be done is missing. In the same way, "Don't get a knee injury" isn't as good a goal as "Lower the risk of knee injury by climbing only when recovered." The latter tells you what to do, rather than what not to do.

It's usually best if goals are based on individual or collective race outcomes. For example, "Upgrade to semipro" depends on doing well in several races. Be careful not to make objectives into goals. "Climb faster" and "Ride single-track more confidently" are really objectives that will lead to good race outcomes. The difference between goals and objectives will become more clear in the next step.

The following are examples of goals that employ the above four principles:

- Break 2:04 at Mount Snow NCS on August 22
- Finish in the top 10 at New England Finals on August 29
- Upgrade to expert category by the end of the season
- Finish all A- and B-priority races on my schedule
- Feel competitive in every A-priority race

After setting your first and most important goal, determine one or two others that are important to you. Give them the same consideration you did the first goal. Stop at three goals so things don't get too complicated in the coming months. List all your goals at the top of the appropriate annual training plan worksheet in Appendix A and at the bottom of Special Element 5.7.

STEP 2: ESTABLISH SEASON TRAINING OBJECTIVES

Let's stay with Special Element (the Mountain Biker Asessment) 5.7 for a while in order to determine your training objectives for the season. Recall that in Chapter 5 you completed several self-assessments, including the race ability profile, natural ability and mental skills profiles, and also rated the miscellaneous factors affecting your race performance. By now, these should all be entered on Special Element 5.7, along with the season goals you formulated in the last step.

In Chapter 6 we examined the concept of limiters—your current race-specific weaknesses. If a goal race calls for a certain ability and you show a weakness for that ability in the Mountain Biker Assessment worksheet (a score of 3 or less), then is a limiter. For example, a long, hilly race requires good force for climbing hills and a high level of endurance. Taken together, these mean that muscular endurance is critical to success in this event. A weakness in either force or endurance means you have a limiter for this race that must improve for success. The natural ability profile section would indicate this, but the race ability profile area (in the "race endurance" and "long climbs" rows) is another place to look for confirmation. If the two don't agree, you have to do some soul-searching to make a decision.

Season training objectives are tasks that lead to season goals by correcting limiters.

Now look at the first season goal at the bottom of the assessment form. Do any of your weaknesses (abilities scored 3 or lower) indicate limiters for this goal? Weaknesses can be found in the race ability profile, natural ability profile, mental skills profile or miscellaneous factors sections. If so, note the ability/skill/factor in the first space "season training objectives." There may be more than one limiter for Season Goal 1. In order to meet your first season goal, these limiters will need to improve. Later chapters in this book show how to do that. For now, let's just identify them.

Examples of season training objectives.

Writing down season training objectives in the Mountain Biker Assessment worksheet and the annual training plan challenges you to improve limiters by a certain time. They are specific and measurable tasks you must accomplish in order to achieve the season goal. There are several ways to measure the progress of your objectives. Chapter 5 presented graded exercise tests and time trials you could conduct to gauge gains, but low-priority races and workouts also serve as good progress indicators. As mentioned earlier, subjective measures of improvement are also often valid markers. The following are examples of season training objectives for the sample season goals used in the previous step.

Goal: Break 2:04 at Mount Snow NCS on August 22

Limiter: Muscular endurance

Season training objective: Elevate lactate threshold power to 220 watts on graded exercise test by July 6

Goal: Finish in the top 10 at New England Finals on August 29

Limiter: Fast single-track descents

Season training objective: Descend Miner's Trail in less than two minutes by August 22

Goal: Upgrade to expert category by the end of the season

Limiter: Mental skills, especially confidence

Season training objective: Read *Mental Training for Peak Performance* and complete all exercises by February 1; feel more confident and focused in spring races and group workouts

Goal: Finish all A- and B-priority races on my schedule

Limiter: Tendency to overtrain

Season training objectives: Closely follow the annual training plan, especially the R and R weeks; skip a workout when tired

Goal: Feel competitive in every A-priority race

Limiter: Time available to train.

Season training objectives: During the Base period, complete longer workouts on weekends; in the Build period, schedule group intervals on my time-management calendar; throughout the season, ride with the 5:30 a.m. group

Now write your season training objectives in a manner similar to that used here. The timing of these objectives is critical to overall success. To accomplish the goal, the season training objective must be achieved by a certain point in the season. Too late is as good as never when it comes to races.

By the time you are done with this part of the Mountain Biker Assessments, there will probably be three to five season training objectives listed. These are the short-term standards against which your progress toward your season goals is measured during the year. If these objectives are appropriate to your limiters and are accomplished on time, your season goals should be achieved. Now transfer these season training objectives to the annual training plan.

STEP 3: SET ANNUAL HOURS

Determining annual hours is one of the most critical decisions you make about training. Too many hours, and overtraining is likely; too few, and fitness—especially endurance, is low. In this step you will establish annual training volume in hours. All the physical activities carried out to improve mountain bike racing—including riding, racing, weight lifting and cross-training—are a part of the annual hours number you will write in at the top of the annual training plan.

Volume is best expressed in terms of hours rather than distance, such as miles or kilometers. There is quite a difference in the time it takes to ride on-road and off-road courses of the same distance. And since you will be riding some combination of both, training volume based on time more closely reflects what you will do in training.

To determine your annual hours start by adding up the hours you've trained in the last 12 months. Planning a small increase in volume (in the range of 10 to 15 percent) is reasonable if you are in the first three years of the sport or believe that you are capable of handling more in the coming season than in past years. If you've been training and racing successfully at the same distances for the past season or two, there is little reason to increase volume. There may even be seasons in which your annual hours decrease due to greater responsibilities at work or other lifestyle changes. The more years you've been training and racing, the less impact increases in volume have on performance.

How are annual hours determined if you haven't kept track of time in the past? A record of distance covered in the year may help, but you'll have to guess what your average time per mile was. Otherwise, about all you can do is guess and make adjustments as the season progresses. Your guess may be based on what an average week was like for you in the past year. Again, be sure to include all training time other than riding the saddle, such as weights and cross-training.

Looking back over the last three years, you can probably see trends related to training volume. For example, did you race better in the high-volume years or worse? Did you tend to overtrain or undertrain at previous volume levels? There undoubtedly were other factors in your performance at those times, but identifying these trends help you to decide on the training volume for the coming season.

If you have no idea how many hours to begin training with this season, Table 7.1 might help. It provides general guidelines typical of mountain bikers, organized by years

Annual training hours include all types of training.

Volume is based on time rather than distance.

How to determine annual hours.

TABLE 7.1

Suggested annual hours by age category and experience.

| Category | Racing Age (years of experience) | | | |
	0–1 year	2–3 years	4–5 years	6+ years
Junior (18 and under)	150–200	200–300	250–350	350–500
Senior (19–34)	200–350	350–550	500–800	600–900
Veterans (35–44)	200–350	250–450	400–600	500–700
Masters (45 and over)	200–300	250–400	350–550	400–

of experience and age. *These are not required volumes.* The suggestions here may be either way too much or too little for you. But you can start within the range listed and make changes later, if needed. They are rather broad, so you will still have to do some guesswork. It's best to start with the lowest number in the range and see how that affects you, then add or subtract hours from there.

Factors other than age and experience—such as career, family, travel, home maintenance and other responsibilities—may also have a bearing on the number of hours set aside for training. Carefully limiting the number of hours you train produces better results than struggling through an overly ambitious volume.

When in doubt, choose a lower volume.

Write in the annual hours you selected at the top of the annual training plan.

STEP 4: LIST AND PRIORITIZE RACES

On the annual training plan, list all the races you intend to do by writing them in the appropriate date rows in the column labeled "races." The date indicated in the first column on the left is the Monday for that week. Each week includes the following Saturday and Sunday, when races are usually scheduled. The races column should include all of the events you *may* do, even if you're uncertain right now. You may decide later to skip some of them, especially the lower importance ones. Write in "A," "B" or "C" in the pri (or priority) column for each race using the following criteria:

A-Priority Races

Determine the three or four races on the list that are most important to you. Two A races on the same weekend count as one race, and a stage race counts as one race. Which events get an A priority depends entirely on what is important to you or your team. The A races are usually the ones season goals are based upon, and so all training is focused on them. The purpose of training is to build up to and then peak for these races.

It's best that these races be clumped together in two- or three-week blocks or widely separated by eight or more weeks. For example, two of the races may fall into a three-week period in May with a nonrace week between them, and the other two on back-to-back weekends in August. Then again, two may be scheduled for early May, one in late July and the other in late September. The idea is that in order to come to a peak for each of these important races, a period of several weeks is needed to rebuild race fitness. During this time between A races, you may still race in B- and C-priority events, but you won't be in top form because training volume and intensity have again increased.

Realize, however, that the race schedule doesn't always work out this neatly. It's likely that two A races will be separated by only four weeks or so. This makes it difficult to either maintain a race peak or build to a new one. Such complications are what make training as much an art as a science. Chapter 9 provides case studies that address this problem. When it's time to divide the year into periods, it may be helpful to look at the examples in that chapter to see how such problems were handled.

In the pri column, write in "A" for all of your A-priority races. Remember, choose no more than four.

B-Priority Races

These races are important, but they're not as crucial as the A races for your season goals. In the last few days before each of them, you will rest, but not build to a fitness peak as with the A races. Select up to 12 of these, and, as with the A events, two B races on the same weekend or a stage race count as one event.

In the pri column, write in "B" for all these races.

C-Priority Races

All remaining races are C-priority. C races are done for experience, as hard workouts, as tests of progress, for fun, or as tune-ups for A races. You will train through these races with no peaking and minimal rest before. Riders often decide at the last moment not to do one of these low-priority events. That's okay. Over-racing often leads to burnout

Assign an A priority to three or four races.

Widely spacing A races produces best results.

B-priority races are important, but you don't peak for them.

All other races are C-priority.

early in the season. You don't have to show up just because someone puts on a race.

Assigning a race a C priority does not mean giving it less than your best shot—effort must be high in all races. It's just that you go into these races not fully race-ready, so good results are not expected. There should be a purpose and a strategy for every race you do—including the C-priority ones. If there isn't a purpose, consider skipping that race.

For the novice rider, there may be several C-priority events on the schedule. They provide a great opportunity to speed up your learning curve. The experienced racer, however, is better off keeping these races to a minimum, as the risk of crashing or simply having a bad race is greater than the potential gain.

STEP 5: DIVIDE YEAR INTO PERIODS

Once the priorities of the races are assigned, you know when peak fitness is needed—in the A-priority weeks. So it is now possible to divide the year into periods as described earlier in this chapter. This is done by working backward from the A-priority races. Table 7.2 summarizes the periods.

If you are a novice, junior, master or elite racer you should read the appropriate section in Chapter 14 before continuing, as you may need to alter the periodization routine described here.

Go to the first A race in the races column of your annual training plan, and in the

		TABLE 7.2

Periodization summary

Period	Length	Training Focus
Preparation	3–8 weeks	General adaptation with weights, cross-training and limited riding: "training to train"
Base	9–12 weeks	Establishing endurance, force and speed skills on the bike; introducing muscular endurance; maintaining gains made in Preparation period
Build	6–9 weeks	Developing race-specific fitness—usually muscular endurance, anaerobic endurance and power; maintaining gains made in Base period
Peak	1–2 weeks	Consolidation of race readiness with a reduced workload and race tune-ups
Race	1–3 weeks	Racing and recovery
Transition	1–4 weeks	Rest and rejuvenation

The first cycle of
the season.

period column write in "Race" next to it. This first Race period extends throughout your first one- to three-week grouping of A races. Count upward the page to two weeks from the Race period just entered and write "Peak" in the period column.

Using the weekly durations indicated in Figure 7.2 (or the variations suggested for special groups in Chapter 14), follow the same procedure of counting backward and moving up the page to assign the Build 2, Build 1, Base 3, Base 2, Base 1 and Prep periods. A Transition period of one week should be included following the first Race period of the season. This will help you maintain your enthusiasm for riding and fitness later in the race season. The first cycle of the year is now scheduled.

How to schedule
between Race periods.

Using the same process, go to your second A race or grouping of A races, and write in "race," and then assign the Peak and Build periods. If the first Race period was two or three weeks long, it's best to repeat the Base 3. With a two-week Peak and two or three-week Race periods, it is likely that your basic abilities will erode. Three weeks of Base 3 are often sufficient to re-establish them.

It's quite likely that the number of weeks between your two Race periods will not work out exactly right to allow four-week Build periods. So it may be necessary to assign three-week Build periods. In fact, shorter cycles are often an advantage later in the season when it's somewhat easier to maintain fitness and summer's heat is increasing the body's stress load. Just remember that the emphasis is always on boosting your limiters. The more basic these are, the more time should be dedicated to the earlier periods of Base and Build 1. If your limiters are all higher abilities, the emphasis shifts toward Build 2.

Always include a season-
ending Transition period.

Following the last Race period of the season, schedule a two- to four-week Transition period. Don't leave this out. It's important for your continued growth as an athlete.

If you are confused by the process described here, especially scheduling the second cycle of the year, look ahead to Chapter 9 where case studies with examples of annual training plans are presented. These examples may serve as models for your plan or answer specific questions.

STEP 6: ASSIGN WEEKLY HOURS

Volume and intensity
work in harmony to
produce fitness.

In previous chapters, I described the sine-wave or stair-step pattern of increasing and decreasing volume and intensity that is necessary to come to a fitness peak. Figure 7.5 illustrates this. The purpose of this pattern is to make sure the basic abilities are established and then maintained as the more race-specific higher abilities are carefully added to the training mix—all the while avoiding overtraining. In this planning step, you will assign weekly training hours based on this theoretical model.

TABLE 7.3

Weekly training hours

Period	Week	Annual hours																				
		200	250	300	350	400	450	500	550	600	650	700	750	800	850	900	950	1000	1050	1100	1150	1200
Prep.	All	3.5	4.0	5.0	6.0	7.0	7.5	8.5	9.0	10.0	11.0	12.0	12.5	13.5	14.5	15.0	16.0	17.0	17.5	18.5	19.5	20.0
Base 1	1	4.0	5.0	6.0	7.0	8.0	9.0	10.0	11.0	12.0	12.5	14.0	14.5	15.5	16.5	17.5	18.5	19.5	20.5	21.5	22.5	23.5
	2	5.0	5.0	6.0	7.0	8.5	9.5	10.5	12.0	13.0	14.5	15.5	16.5	18.0	19.1	20.0	21.5	22.5	24.0	25.0	26.0	27.5
	3	5.5	5.5	6.5	8.0	9.5	10.5	12.0	13.5	14.5	16.0	17.5	18.5	20.0	21.5	22.5	24.0	25.5	26.5	28.0	29.5	30.5
	4	3.0	3.0	3.5	4.0	5.0	5.5	6.5	7.0	8.0	8.5	9.0	10.0	10.5	11.0	12.0	12.5	13.5	14.0	14.5	15.5	16.0
Base 2	1	4.0	5.5	6.5	7.5	8.5	9.5	10.5	12.5	12.5	13.0	14.5	16.0	17.0	18.0	19.0	20.0	21.0	22.0	23.0	24.0	25.0
	2	5.0	5.0	6.5	7.5	9.0	10.0	11.5	12.5	14.0	15.0	16.5	17.5	19.0	20.0	21.5	22.5	24.0	25.0	26.6	27.5	28.8
	3	5.5	5.5	7.0	8.5	10.0	11.0	12.5	14.0	15.5	17.0	18.0	19.5	21.0	22.5	24.0	25.0	26.5	28.0	29.5	31.0	32.0
	4	3.0	3.0	3.5	4.5	5.0	5.5	6.5	7.0	8.0	8.5	9.0	10.0	10.5	11.0	12.0	12.5	13.5	14.0	15.0	15.5	16.0
Base 3	1	4.5	5.5	7.0	8.0	9.0	10.0	11.0	12.5	13.5	14.5	15.5	17.0	18.0	19.0	20.0	21.0	22.5	23.5	25.0	25.5	27.0
	2	5.0	5.0	6.5	8.0	9.5	10.5	12.0	13.5	14.5	16.0	17.0	18.5	20.0	21.5	23.0	24.0	25.0	26.5	28.0	29.5	30.5
	3	6.0	6.0	7.5	9.0	10.5	11.5	13.0	15.0	16.5	18.0	19.0	20.5	22.0	23.5	25.0	26.5	28.0	29.5	31.0	32.5	33.5
	4	3.0	3.0	3.5	4.5	5.0	5.5	6.5	7.0	8.0	8.5	9.0	10.0	10.5	11.5	12.0	12.5	13.5	14.0	15.0	15.5	16.0
Build 1	1	5.0	6.5	8.0	9.0	10.0	11.5	12.5	14.0	15.5	16.0	17.5	19.0	20.5	21.5	22.5	24.0	25.0	26.5	28.0	29.0	30.0
	2	5.0	5.0	6.5	8.0	9.0	10.0	11.5	12.5	14.0	15.5	16.0	17.5	19.0	20.5	21.5	22.5	24.0	25.0	26.5	28.0	29.0
	3	5.0	5.0	6.5	8.0	9.0	10.0	11.5	12.5	14.0	15.5	16.0	17.5	19.0	20.5	21.5	22.5	24.0	25.0	26.5	28.0	29.0
	4	3.0	3.0	3.5	4.5	5.0	5.5	6.5	7.0	8.0	8.5	9.0	10.0	10.5	11.5	12.0	12.5	13.5	14.0	15.0	15.5	16.0
Build 2	1	5.0	6.0	7.0	8.5	9.5	10.5	12.0	13.0	14.5	15.5	16.5	18.0	19.0	20.5	21.5	22.5	24.0	25.0	26.5	27.0	28.5
	2	5.0	5.0	6.0	7.0	8.5	9.5	10.5	12.0	13.0	14.5	15.5	16.5	18.0	19.0	20.5	21.5	22.5	24.0	25.0	26.5	27.0
	3	5.0	5.0	6.0	7.0	8.5	9.5	10.5	12.0	13.0	14.5	15.5	16.5	18.0	19.0	20.5	21.5	22.5	24.0	25.0	26.5	27.0
	4	3.0	3.0	3.5	4.5	5.0	5.5	6.5	7.0	8.0	8.5	9.0	10.0	10.5	11.5	12.0	12.5	13.5	14.0	15.0	15.5	16.0
Peak	1	4.0	5.0	6.0	7.0	7.5	8.5	9.5	10.5	11.5	11.5	13.0	14.5	15.0	16.5	17.0	18.0	19.0	20.0	21.0	21.5	22.5
	2	3.0	3.5	4.0	5.0	5.5	6.0	7.0	7.5	8.5	9.0	10.0	10.5	11.5	12.0	13.0	13.5	14.5	15.0	16.0	16.5	17.0
Race	All	3.0	3.5	4.0	4.5	5.0	5.5	6.0	7.0	7.0	8.0	8.5	9.0	9.5	10.5	11.0	11.5	12.0	13.0	13.0	13.5	14.5
Trans.	All	3.0	3.5	4.5	5.0	5.5	6.5	7.0	8.0	8.5	9.0	10.0	10.5	11.5	12.0	12.5	13.5	14.0	15.0	15.5	16.0	17.0

How to plan weekly training volume.

Once the annual hours are determined and the year divided into periods, you're ready to assign weekly training hours—the volume portion of the season. Find the column heading in Table 7.3 that corresponds with your annual hours at the top of the annual training plan. In that column are weekly hours in half-hour increments. On the left side of the table are all the periods you've written in so far, and the weeks within each. By reading down the appropriate column, determine the number of hours for each week, and write those in the proper rows in the hours column on the annual training plan.

You've now completed the annual training plan with the exception of the workout portion on the right side. That's the task for the next chapter.

REFERENCES

Bompa, T. "Physiological Intensity Values Employed to Plan Endurance Training." *New Studies in Athletics* 3, no. 4 (1988): 37-52.

Bompa, T. *Theory and Methodology of Training.* Dubuque, IA: Kendall/Hunt Publishing, 1994.

Costill, D., et al. "Adaptations to Swimming Training: Influence of Training Volume." *Medicine and Science in Sports and Exercise* 23 (1991): 371-377.

Friel, J. *The Cyclist's Training Bible.* Boulder, CO: VeloPress, 1996.

Martin, D. and P. Coe. *Training Distance Runners.* Champaign, IL: Leisure Press, 1991.

VanHandel, P. J. "The Science of Sport Training for Cycling, Part I." *Conditioning for Cycling* 1, no. 1 (1991): 8-11.

VanHandel, P. J. "The Science of Sport Training for Cycling, Part II." *Conditioning for Cycling* 1, no. 2 (1991): 18-23.

VanHandel, P. J. "Planning a Comprehensive Training Program." *Conditioning for Cycling* 1, no. 3 (1991): 4-12.

PLANNING A WEEK

*Some people are professional trainers and do little racing. But you can make
the greatest gains through competition. I never would have realized my potential
if it weren't for racing. There's nothing like it to push you. It improves fitness and
bike handling. You find yourself at speeds you would never attain in training.*

—NED OVEREND

I'm a strong believer in planning in order to achieve success. Life is too short and time too precious to leave anything that is important to chance. The same may be said of mountain bike racing; it is important to you, or you wouldn't be reading this book, and careful preparation will lead to goal achievement. In the last chapter, you took a big step toward success in racing by planning your season. Now it's time to take a look at the finer details of training—what you do on a daily and weekly basis.

In workout planning, ask one simple question: What is the purpose of this workout? If you can't, or don't, answer that question, there is a high likelihood that the workout is *play* and not *training*. There is nothing wrong with having an occasional playful ride on the trails—if a break from serious riding is the purpose. A weekly schedule of nothing but play, however, does not produce the abilities necessary for mountain bike racing success. To achieve all you're capable of in racing, you must have a purpose for every workout.

The purpose relates to your season goals, training objectives, strengths and limiters. You are either trying to improve or maintain some specific aspect of physical or mental fitness, or the workout's purpose is active recovery. This purpose is often overlooked. Other purposes are ability testing and race simulation. Deciding in advance what benefit the workout will provide and reviewing its purpose before you start, is critical to peaking at the right moments in the season. Of course, this is predicated on first having a well-conceived plan for the season as a whole.

**Purposeful training
produces peak fitness
at the right times.**

This chapter will help you undertand and apply the principles of workout planning. The first task in accomplishing this is the completion of the annual training plan started in Chapter 7. By the end of this chapter, you will have outlined the key workouts for each week of the season on the plan, and have a good understanding of how to blend them into a concrete weekly schedule.

As mentioned before, all work on the annual training plan is done in pencil as changes are usually necessary during the year. Keep the completed annual training plan with your training diary, and review it weekly as your plans for the next training week are determined. Chapter 15 describes how to use the training diary along with your annual training plan to produce a comprehensive daily and weekly schedule.

SCHEDULE WEEKLY WORKOUTS

In Chapter 7, you accomplished the first six steps in designing the blueprint for your season using the annual training plan. By now you should have completed the sections of the plan titled "annual hours," "season goals," "training objectives," "races," "priorities" (pri), "period" and "hours." That brings us to the heart of the plan—the workout categories on the right side of the annual training plan.

Across the top right of the annual training plan are six columns titled with the abilities discussed in previous chapters—endurance, force, speed skills, muscular endurance, anaerobic endurance and power—and a column for testing. In this planning step, you will assign workouts in these categories to each week of the season. Then, when you are ready to start a training week, you can determine which workouts will most benefit each of the abilities.

Appendix B lists some of the possible workouts for each of the abilities. From these you can choose the appropriate one for each day of the week. This workout menu is by no means exhaustive. With a little imagination, you can deign many others specifically to challenge your limiters, maintain your abilities, and take full advantage of the resources available. Workouts may also be combined into a ingle session that challenges more than one ability. More is said about this later in the chapter.

WEIGHTS

Weight training especially benefits those with a force limiter.

Notice that one column has not been mentioned yet—the one titled "weights." In this column, you can note the phases of weight-room strength training for the season. In the past, this has often been a neglected aspect of training, but it seems to be gaining popularity now as more riders become aware of the potential for fitness improvement in weight training. If force or hill climbing is a limiter for you, a winter of strength training is especially likely to result in measurable improvement. Even those who are already good climbers will realize some gains in handling the bike on trails by developing greater total body strength. Weights are a crucial aspect of training for the serious mountain bike racer.

The details of the five strength phases introduced below are discussed in Chapter 13, but with a little information you can complete the weights column now by penciling in the abbreviations for the various phases. Here's how to determine the duration of each phase. (If you are a bit confused about how this may look, flip ahead to Chapter 9 for examples of completed annual training plans.)

Anatomical Adaptation (AA) phase

The AA phase prepares the total body for the more difficult maximum strength (MS) phase. If no strength work has been done in the last four weeks, include four to six weeks of AA at the outset of your training year, preferably during the Preparation period. If there are fewer than four weeks since weight training stopped, assign two to four weeks of AA during Preparation.

Maximum Strength (MS) Phase

In the MS phase, the ability to move great loads is developed. If force is a limiter, schedule the six weeks following AA to MS. Otherwise, schedule just four weeks of MS. This is usually best in the Base 1 period of the season, but it may extend into early Base 2.

Power Endurance (PE) Phase

The PE phase converts the raw strength gains of MS into power for short climbs and long sprints. Schedule four weeks for PE, preferably in Base 2.

Muscular Endurance (ME) Phase

This phase develops the ability to move a relatively heavy load many times. If the weather where you live typically prevents much on-road training in Base 3, schedule four weeks of ME for that period. If bad weather is not generally a problem, omit the ME phase. Muscular endurance is a crucial aspect of fitness for the mountain biker, but I've found it is best developed on a bike. If that is not possible, however, weight-room training can boost it until you can get outside again.

Strength Maintenance (SM) Phase

The purpose of the SM phase is to maintain the strength gains made during the winter months. At this point in the year—about the time high-intensity, Build 1 training is scheduled—many riders in their 20s and into their early 30s may stop weight training. Most masters and women, however, are well advised to maintain their strength gains from the winter months with the SM phase throughout most of the remaining season. Schedule no weight training during the week of A races.

Periodization of Workouts

This selection will help you complete the workouts section of the annual training plan. Let's begin with the rest and recovery (R and R) weeks, since those are often neglected by serious riders, though they are in some ways the most important. If there is any confusion on how to mark this portion of the annual training plan, see the examples in Chapter 9. Masters, novices and elite riders should each read the appropriate part of Chapter 14 before continuing, as there may be some exceptions to what is described here for these groups.

Masters, novices and elites should read Chapter 14 before proceeding.

R and R Weeks

Every fourth week during the Base and Build periods is for rest and recovery from the accumulated fatigue of the previous three weeks. Without such regular unloading of fatigue, fitness won't progress for long. You've already allowed for R and R by reducing the weekly hours during every fourth week of Base and Build (based on Table 7.3. Now let's assign workouts to these weeks).

R and R weeks help prevent overtraining, burnout, illness and injury.

For every low-volume, R and R week in Base and Build, place an X in the endurance and speed skills columns. Also in the Base and Build periods, put an X under the testing column if there is not a race. Other than strength sessions, that's all for those weeks. Their purpose is to allow you to recover in the first few days and feel rested by the weekend. You will also maintain endurance, speed skill, and strength, and test progress once rested. There may be a B- or C-priority race at week's end that serves as a test. Chapter 5 and Appendix B describe tests you may do during R and R weeks.

Now you're ready to complete workout categories for the other, non-R and R weeks by indicating which abilities will be targeted. Later, when you're ready to choose the exact workouts for a given week, Appendix B will help you select the right ones based on the abilities targeted here.

Preparation period

Place an X in the endurance column for each week of the Preparation period. Training during this period concentrates on improving the endurance characteristics of the heart, blood and lungs, referred to collectively as the cardiorespiratory system. Aerobic cross-training should be included during this period, especially when poor weather interferes with riding outdoors. Running is an excellent Preparation period activity. Take care of your legs and feet by avoiding pavement and by always wearing good shoes. Hiking on rugged terrain is also a good cardiorespiratory workout, especially if you tote a backpack. Be careful not to ride indoors too much now, as there will be plenty of time for that later on. Get outside all you can.

The Preparation period is a time of "training to train."

Also place an X under testing in the first and last weeks of the Preparation period.

Base 1 Period

Mark the endurance and speed skills columns for each week of Base 1. During this period, rndurance workouts gradually grow longer and speed skill work is introduced. This is also the time when the weight-training program is typically in the MS phase and takes up a significant amount of training time.

Weather is often the determining factor for on-bike training now. The Base period is a good time to ride your mountain bike on the road, due to better traction on wet or icy roads. You'll also ride slower on a mountain bike than on a road bike while working just as hard, which in cold weather is an advantage for staying warm. Cross-country skiing and snowshoeing are excellent alternatives during this period when the weather makes roadwork difficult. A good indoor bike trainer is also necessary throughout the Base period if you can't get outdoors at all.

Base 1 focuses on endurance, speed skills and weights.

Base 2 Period

Place an X in the endurance, force, speed skill, and muscular endurance columns for each non–R and R week of the Base 2 period. With the exception of one or two weekly speed skills sessions, use your road bike for all rides.

As you can see in the suggested workouts for this period in Appendix B, muscular endurance training is done at moderate intensities and force training is in the initial stages as the strength gained in the just-completed MS phase begins the conversion to bike-specific force. In this and the next period, it's a good idea to stay seated when climbing hills even when on the road, no matter how gradual or steep they are. This will help to develop the power necessary to climb seated off-road in the later periods and in races.

Force and muscular endurance training are introduced in Base 2.

Endurance workouts continue to increase in duration.

Base 3 Period

In Base 3 volume reaches the annual high point.

Mark the endurance, force, speed skill and muscular endurance columns for each week of the Base 3 period, other than the R and R week. Weekly training volume and long-ride duration reach a maximum level during this period. Intensity has also risen slightly with the addition of more force and muscular endurance work.

Build 1 and Build 2 Periods

Mark the schedule for workouts in the endurance, muscular endurance, anaerobic endurance and power columns for each non–R and R week of the Build 1 and Build 2 periods.

In the Build periods, volume is reduced as intensity rises.

This is a lot to accomplish, but the focus will now be on your greatest limiter from this list, and many of the training sessions will combine workout abilities. Force and speed skills will be maintained by the nature of the other workouts scheduled here.

Races count as workouts, too. Each B- or C-priority, cross-country race provides a great muscular endurance, anaerobic endurance and power session. The hillier the race is, the more force is maintained. Races that last longer than two hours keep Endurance high. Early season races in the Build 1 period are best categorized as C-priority. During the weeks of races lasting less than two hours, schedule only endurance and speed skill workouts. Remember that you're training through C-priority races, which means that there is no extensive rest before the race. Schedule each Build 1 and Build 2 period on your Annual Training Plan in this same way.

Peak Period

Place an X in the muscular endurance, anaerobic endurance and power columns. During this period volume is tapering off, as you can see by the gradually reduced volume in the hours column. The workouts are spaced widely to allow for nearly complete recovery, and the intensity of the hard workouts is similar to what is expected in the upcoming A-priority race. Races, especially short ones, may be substituted for these hard workouts. C-priority races in the Peak period are excellent tune-ups for the approaching A-priority races, as they get you back into a racing mode again. There should be a high-intensity workout every 72 hours or so of a Peak period.

In Peak, volume tapers as race-specific intensity is emphasized.

Mark all Peak periods in this way.

Race Period

During each week of this period, either race or, when there is no race, complete a race-effort simulation such as an off-road time trial or a hard group ride. Also mark power for each race week. R and R weeks with a B-priority race at the end may be treated like Race weeks. In Race weeks, the race provides the workout for all higher abilities.

A little power work in the Race period maintains sharpness.

Transition period

Don't mark any of the columns. This is an unstructured period that is meant to recharge your mental and physical batteries. You should, however, stay minimally active, especially in sports other than cycling that you enjoy. These could be team games such as soccer, basketball, volleyball or hockey, or endurance activities including running, swimming, cross-country skiing, snowshoeing, power hiking or in-line skating. Don't become a couch potato, but also don't train seriously. Keep the workouts short and low-effort. Base all intensities on RPE rather than heart rate or power. Work out only when you feel like it. Take several days off, and rest as much as possible.

The Transition period is a time of mental and physical recovery.

BREAKTHROUGH AND RECOVERY WORKOUTS

The only workouts you've scheduled so far are those meant to build or maintain your racing abilities. Those that really challenge you I call "breakthrough," or "BT," workouts. The difficulty of a BT workout will vary by period. For example, a session with lots of 3-zone time challenges your muscular endurance in the Base period. In the Peak period when fitness is higher, however, this same workout would probably not be considered very challenging. In the same way, a long endurance session in Base 1 may really tax you, but later on, once your endurance is well established, such a ride places little demand on the body. BT workouts typically require 36 or more hours to recover from.

BT workouts challenge your fitness.

Recovery workouts that are placed between such difficult BT sessions are not scheduled on the annual training plan, but they are obviously an integral part of any program and should be included frequently. Appendix B offers suggestions for such workouts, and the next section, on weekly training patterns, describes how to incorporate them into a training week.

WEEKLY TRAINING ROUTINES

Now that your annual training plan is complete, the only issues left to decide at the start of each week are the specific workouts to do, the days on which to do them, and how long to make them. Now we're getting down to the really critical decisions. You could have the best possible plan, but if workouts are not blended in such a way as to allow for both recovery and adaptation, then no progress is made—and you may even lose fitness. The problem is that both long- and short-duration workouts must be combined with workouts that are of high- and low-intensity, in addition to possibly lifting weights. This is perhaps the most difficult and complex part of the planning process for self-coaches.

PATTERNS

Figures 8.1 (a–k) provide suggested weekly volume and intensity patterns for each of the training periods. These are examples only as there are too many individual variables, such as different combinations of limiters and daily time available for training, to provide patterns that work for every mountain biker. Use these only as a guide to help you design your own patterns.

FIGURES 8.1A–8.1K
Workout options are selected based on strengths and limiters. See Appendix B for details.

D=Duration
I=Intensity

FIGURE 8.1A
Example of a training week for the preparation period.

PREPARATION		MON		TUE		WED		THU		FRI		SAT		SUN	
		D	I	D	I	D	I	D	I	D	I	D	I	D	I
	HIGH													■	
	MED			■				■				■			
	LOW				■	■			■				■		■
	REC	■					■				■				
	WORKOUT OPTIONS BY CODE (APP. B)	OFF, EI, CROSS-TRAIN?		E2, CROSS-TRAIN?		EI, CROSS-TRAIN?		E2, CROSS-TRAIN?		EI, CROSS-TRAIN?		E2, CROSS-TRAIN?		E2	
	WEIGHTS	AA				AA				AA					

FIGURE 8.1B
Example of a training week for the Base 1 period.

BASE 1		MON		TUE		WED		THU		FRI		SAT		SUN	
		D	I	D	I	D	I	D	I	D	I	D	I	D	I
	HIGH													■	
	MED					■						■			
	LOW			■			■	■		■			■		■
	REC	■						■							
	WORKOUT OPTIONS BY CODE (APP. B)	OFF, EI, CROSS-TRAIN?		S1, S2, S3		E2		E1, CROSS-TRAIN?		S1, S2, S3, S5		E2		E2	
	WEIGHTS	MS						MS							

FIGURE 8.1C
Example of a training week for the Base 2 period.

BASE 2	MON D	MON I	TUE D	TUE I	WED D	WED I	THU D	THU I	FRI D	FRI I	SAT D	SAT I	SUN D	SUN I
HIGH													■	
MED			■		■	■	■				■	■		■
LOW				■				■	■	■				
REC	■	■												
WORKOUT OPTIONS BY CODE (APP. B)	OFF, EI		S1, S2, S3, S4, S5		M1		E2		S1, S2, S3, S4, S5		M1		F1	
WEIGHTS	PE						PE							

FIGURE 8.1D
Example of a training week for the Base 3 period.

BASE 3	MON D	MON I	TUE D	TUE I	WED D	WED I	THU D	THU I	FRI D	FRI I	SAT D	SAT I	SUN D	SUN I
HIGH						■	■						■	
MED			■		■						■	■		■
LOW				■				■	■	■				
REC	■	■												
WORKOUT OPTIONS BY CODE (APP. B)	OFF, EI		S1, S2, S3, S4, S5		F2		E2		S1, S2, S3, S4, S5		M1, M2, M3		F1	
WEIGHTS	ME/SM						(ME)							

FIGURE 8.1E
Example of a R&R week for the Base period.

BASE R&R WEEK	MON D	MON I	TUE D	TUE I	WED D	WED I	THU D	THU I	FRI D	FRI I	SAT D	SAT I	SUN D	SUN I
HIGH												■	■	
MED														
LOW			■		■	■					■			■
REC	■	■		■			■	■	■	■				
WORKOUT OPTIONS BY CODE (APP. B)	OFF		E1		S1, S2, S3, S4, S5		E1		E1		TEST, RACE		E2	
WEIGHTS	MS, PE, ME/SM						MS, PE, (ME)							

FIGURE 8.1F
Example of a training week for the Build 1 period.

BUILD 1

	MON		TUE		WED		THU		FRI		SAT		SUN	
	D	I	D	I	D	I	D	I	D	I	D	I	D	I
HIGH				■	■							■			
MED							■				■				
LOW			■			■									■
REC	■								■						
WORKOUT OPTIONS BY CODE (APP. B)	OFF, EI		P1, P2		E2		F2, M2, M3 (P1-P2 IF B-RACE ON SAT.)		E1		A1, A2, A3, A6, RACE		E2	
WEIGHTS	(SM)													

FIGURE 8.1G
Example of a training week for the Build 2 period.

BUILD 2

	MON		TUE		WED		THU		FRI		SAT		SUN	
	D	I	D	I	D	I	D	I	D	I	D	I	D	I
HIGH				■								■	■		
MED						■	■				■			■	
LOW			■		■										
REC	■								■						
WORKOUT OPTIONS BY CODE (APP. B)	OFF, EI		P1, P2, P3		E2		M2, M3, M4, M5, M6 (P1-P3 IF B-RACE ON SAT.)		E1		A1, A2, A3, A6, RACE		E2	
WEIGHTS	(SM)													

FIGURE 8.1G
Example of a R&R week for the Build period.

BUILD R&R WEEK

	MON		TUE		WED		THU		FRI		SAT		SUN	
	D	I	D	I	D	I	D	I	D	I	D	I	D	I
HIGH												■	■		
MED															
LOW			■	■	■	■					■	■			
REC	■			■			■	■							■
WORKOUT OPTIONS BY CODE (APP. B)	OFF		E1		S1, S2, S3, S4, S5		E1		E1		TEST, RACE		E1	
WEIGHTS	(SM)													

FIGURE 8.1 I
Example of a training week for the Peak period.

PEAK		MON		TUE		WED		THU		FRI		SAT		SUN	
		D	I	D	I	D	I	D	I	D	I	D	I	D	I
	HIGH						■						■		
	MED			■		■						■			
	LOW				■						■				
	REC							■	■	■				■	■
	WORKOUT OPTIONS BY CODE (APP. B)	OFF		E2		M2, M3, M4, M5, M6, A2, A3, A4, A5, A6, A7, P1, P2, P3		E2		E1		RACE, M2, M3, M4, M5, M6, A1, A2, A3, A4, A5, A6, A7, P1, P2, P3		E1	
	WEIGHTS	(SM)													

FIGURE 8.1J
Example of a training week for the Race period.

SATURDAY RACE		MON		TUE		WED		THU		FRI		SAT		SUN	
		D	I	D	I	D	I	D	I	D	I	D	I	D	I
	HIGH				■					■	■		■		
	MED			■								■			
	LOW									■					
	REC	■	■			■	■								■
	WORKOUT OPTIONS BY CODE (APP. B)	OFF		M2, M3, M6, A1, A2, A3, A6, A7, P1, P2, P3		E1		E1		REHEARSE WARM-UP		RACE		F1	
	WEIGHTS														

FIGURE 8.1 K
Example of a training week for the Race period.

SUNDAY RACE		MON		TUE		WED		THU		FRI		SAT		SUN	
		D	I	D	I	D	I	D	I	D	I	D	I	D	I
	HIGH				■				■				■		■
	MED			■				■						■	
	LOW											■			
	REC	■				■	■			■	■				
	WORKOUT OPTIONS BY CODE (APP. B)	OFF		M2, M3, M6, A1, A2, A3, A6, A7, P1, P2, P3		E1		P1, P2, P3		EI, OFF		REHEARSE WARM-UP		RACE	
	WEIGHTS														

In each of these figures, volume and intensity are indicated as high, medium ("med"), low, or recovery ("rec"). Volume levels are meaningful only to you, as high volume for one rider may be low for another. High intensity means anaerobic effort, such as heart rate 5b and 5c zones, or CP30 through CP1 power zones. Medium intensity implies heart rate 3, 4 and 5a zones and power zones CP60 and CP90. Low intensity suggests heart rate 2 and CP180 power zones. Recovery days may be active recovery with heart rate in the 1 zone or power at less than half of CP12. These are also short-duration workouts. Novices usually benefit more from taking these day entirely off. It's also wise for even the experienced rider to take days off from training—even on a regular, weekly basis.

Scheduling BT workouts is a balancing act, with the creation of appropriate levels of stress on one side and recovery on the other. Within a given week there are two commonly accepted ways of doing this. One is the common hard day–easy day approach. With this pattern, a BT day is followed by a recovery day. Another widely used pattern is block training, in which two BT workouts are placed back to back followed by two days of recovery and maintenance. The better pattern for you may be different as the periods change. You may find, for example, that hard-hard-easy-easy works well for Base, but hard-easy-hard-easy is necessary for Build. Individual differences in the capacity to recover will dictate which method you use and how closely the BT sessions are spaced. Figures 8.1 (a–k) illustrate the hard-easy approach.

How to arrange hard and easy training days.

The "workout options by code" portions of Figures 8.1 (a–k) are based on Appendix B. You may want to create other workouts to meet your individual needs. Write these down and assign codes to them. These codes are used as shorthand notations when scheduling workouts in your training diary at the start of the week.

DAILY HOURS

The hours column of your annual training plan lists the volumes for each week of the season. When it comes time to plan a week, it is necessary to decide how those hours are apportioned to each day. Table 8.1 offers a *suggested* breakdown.

In the left-hand column of Table 8.1, find the hours you've scheduled for the first week of the season. Reading across to the right, the weekly hours are divided into daily time (in hours and minutes). For example, find "12:00" in the weekly hours column. To the right are seven daily hours, one for each day of the week, adding up to 12:00. The seven are 3:00, 2:30, 2:00, 2:00, 1:30, 1:00 and off. So the longest ride for one day that week is three hours. The daily hours in Table 8.1 include all the training done in a week— riding, racing, weights and cross-training.

TABLE 8.1

Daily Training Hours

May be two–a–day workouts

Weekly Hours	Longest Ride						
3:00	1:30	0:45	0:45	off	off	off	off
3:30	1:30	1:00	1:00	off	off	off	off
4:00	1:30	1:00	1:00	0:30	off	off	off
4:30	1:45	1:00	1:00	0:45	off	off	off
5:00	2:00	1:00	1:00	1:00	off	off	off
5:30	2:00	1:30	1:00	1:00	off	off	off
6:00	2:00	1:00	1:00	1:00	1:00	off	off
6:30	2:00	1:30	1:00	1:00	1:00	off	off
7:00	2:00	1:30	1:30	1:00	1:00	off	off
7:30	2:30	1:30	1:30	1:00	1:00	off	off
8:00	2:30	1:30	1:30	1:30	1:00	off	off
8:30	2:30	2:00	1:30	1:30	1:00	off	off
9:00	3:00	2:00	1:30	1:30	1:00	off	off
9:30	3:00	2:00	1:30	1:30	1:00	0:30	off
10:00	3:00	2:00	1:30	1:30	1:00	1:00	off
10:30	3:00	2:00	2:00	1:30	1:00	1:00	off
11:00	3:00	2:00	2:00	1:30	1:30	1:00	off
11:30	3:00	2:30	2:00	1:30	1:30	1:00	off
12:00	3:00	2:30	2:00	2:00	1:30	1:00	off
12:30	3:30	2:30	2:00	2:00	1:30	1:00	off
13:00	3:30	3:00	2:00	2:00	1:30	1:00	off
13:30	3:30	3:00	2:30	2:00	1:30	1:00	off
14:00	4:00	3:00	2:30	2:00	1:30	1:00	off
14:30	4:00	3:00	2:30	2:30	1:30	1:00	off
15:00	4:00	3:00	3:00	2:30	1:30	1:00	off
15:30	4:00	3:00	3:00	2:30	2:00	1:00	off
16:00	4:00	3:00	3:00	2:30	2:00	1:00	off
16:30	4:00	3:30	3:00	3:00	2:00	1:00	off
17:00	4:00	3:30	3:00	3:00	2:00	1:30	off
17:30	4:00	4:00	3:00	3:00	2:00	1:30	off
18:00	4:00	4:00	3:00	3:00	2:30	1:30	off
18:30	4:30	4:00	3:00	3:00	2:30	1:30	off
19:00	4:30	4:30	3:00	3:00	2:30	1:30	off
19:30	4:30	4:30	3:30	3:00	2:30	1:30	off
20:00	4:30	4:30	3:30	3:00	2:30	2:00	off
20:30	4:30	4:30	3:30	3:30	2:30	2:00	off
21:00	5:00	4:30	3:30	3:30	2:30	2:00	off
21:30	5:00	4:30	4:00	3:30	2:30	2:00	off
22:00	5:00	4:30	4:00	3:30	3:00	2:00	off
22:30	5:00	4:30	4:00	3:30	3:00	2:30	off
23:00	5:00	5:00	4:00	3:30	3:00	2:30	off
23:30	5:30	5:00	4:00	3:30	3:00	2:30	off
24:00	5:30	5:00	4:30	3:30	3:00	2:30	off
24:30	5:30	5:00	4:30	4:00	3:00	2:30	off
25:00	5:30	5:00	4:30	4:00	3:00	3:00	off
25:30	5:30	5:30	4:30	4:00	3:00	3:00	off
26:00	6:00	5:30	4:30	4:00	3:00	3:00	off
26:30	6:00	5:30	5:00	4:00	3:00	3:00	off
27:00	6:00	6:00	5:00	4:00	3:00	3:00	off
27:30	6:00	6:00	5:00	4:00	3:30	3:00	off
28:00	6:00	6:00	5:00	4:00	3:30	3:30	off
28:30	6:00	6:00	5:00	4:30	3:30	3:30	off
29:00	6:00	6:00	5:30	4:30	3:30	3:30	off
29:30	6:00	6:00	6:00	4:30	3:30	3:30	off
30:00	6:00	6:00	6:00	4:30	4:00	3:30	off
30:30	6:00	6:00	6:00	5:00	4:00	3:30	off
31:00	6:00	6:00	6:00	5:00	4:00	4:00	off
31:30	6:00	6:00	6:00	5:00	4:30	4:00	off
32:00	6:00	6:00	6:00	5:30	4:30	4:00	off
32:30	6:00	6:00	6:00	5:30	4:30	4:30	off
33:00	6:00	6:00	6:00	5:30	5:00	4:30	off
33:30	6:00	6:00	6:00	6:00	5:00	4:30	off
34:00	6:00	6:00	6:00	6:00	5:30	4:30	off
34:30	6:00	6:00	6:00	6:00	5:30	5:00	off
35:00	6:00	6:00	6:00	6:00	6:00	5:00	off

The daily hours may be divided between two workouts in the same day, if your schedule doesn't allow riding so many hours at one time. In fact, there are advantages to working out twice a day, such as the ease of fitting the hours into the work day and an increase in quality for each workout. You may find this to be quite an effective scheduling tool. For example, two hours scheduled for a weekday may be difficult to fit in around work or other commitments. But if you ride one hour of endurance maintenance in the morning and another hour with high intensity in the afternoon, not only might it make daily scheduling easier, but the quality of both sessions also rises since fatigue has less impact on performance.

How to divide weekly hours for each day.

Riders living in more northern latitudes find it difficult to ride outside in the winter due to cold and snow. In more equatorial latitudes, summer heat and humidity also favor indoor training. In addition, work responsibilities may force training into early morning or late evening hours when there is insufficient light for riding outdoors. For these reasons, a quality indoor bike trainer is of great importance. But even with a good trainer, cycling volume will certainly suffer during periods of indoor riding. If you are forced indoors, I suggest riding only half of the duration scheduled. Very long rides indoors can easily lead to burnout. It may be best to switch to an alternate sport, such as cross-country skiing or snowshoeing, when the indoor workout is to be an endurance ride. The flexible rider takes such changes in stride while making training adjustments for these days.

What to do when forced indoors.

When bad weather or other training interruptions force riding indoors or into cross-training modes, weekly training volume also needs to decrease. Knowing in advance what may interfere with riding outside, make changes in your annual hours to allow for this. If you live in Minnesota, for example, you may plan on training at 350 annual hours in the winter when nearly all cycling is indoors, and at 450 hours in the summer when outdoor riding is possible.

Annual hours may be adjusted seasonally.

COMBINED WORKOUTS

On the weekly workouts side of the annual training plan, if you count the abilities scheduled for some weeks, you will see that there are frequently four or five of them, especially in the Build periods. To resolve the problem of too many hard workouts and not enough rest in these weeks, it's necessary to combine workouts in two abilities into one session in the Build periods. Not only does this make better use of available time, but it also more closely simulates the stresses of mountain bike racing.

When combining workouts into one session, a general rule of thumb is to couple either endurance or muscular endurance with force, anaerobic endurance or power. When you do this, the lower-intensity ability of endurance or muscular endurance should follow the higher-intensity ability within the workout. So, for example, a combined workout could start with hill repeats on the road that challenge anaerobic endurance, and then progress to a steady ride at near–lactate threshold for muscular endurance. Such a session is excellent for developing the type of fitness necessary for racing.

Combining abilities within a single workout uses time effectively and simulates race stress.

REFERENCES

Bompa, T. "Physiological Intensity Values Employed to Plan Endurance Training." *New Studies in Athletics* 3, no 4 (1988): 37-52.

Burke, E. *Serious Cycling.* Champaign, IL: Human Kinetics, 1995.

Daniels, J., et al. "Interval Training and Performance." *Sports Medicine 1* (1995): 327-334.

Faris, I. E. "Applied Physiology of Cycling." *Sports Medicine* 1 (1984): 187-204.

Friel, J. *The Cyclist's Training Bible.* Boulder, CO: VeloPress, 1996.

Knuttgen, H. G., et al. "Physical Conditioning Through Interval Training With Young Male Adults." *Medicine and Science in Sports* 5 (1973): 220-226.

VanHandel, P. J. "Specificity of Training: Establishing Pace, Frequency, and Duration of Training Sessions." *Bike Tech* 6, no. 3 (1987): 6-12.

CASE STUDIES

You really don't know why you feel so bad. That's what's so hard about mountain bike racing. You really can't tell. Are you lazy? Undertrained? Overtrained? When you're in the middle of it you can't view yourself objectively, so you don't know what to do.

—Juli Furtado

So far most of what has been written in this book could be called the *science* of training. This is the objective side of preparing to race based on exacting research, methodical planning and precise reasoning. The real world of self-coaching, however, is seldom so neat and tidy. Important races come at the worst possible times, the best week for family vacation conflicts with final race preparations, low-priority races you want to do interfere with systematic training and work clashes with workouts. Then there is the occasional gut feeling that tells you to train a certain way despite what the book says. Add to these challenges a flu bug that takes away a week of workouts, and you may be inclined to just chuck this whole scientific-periodization thing and go back to training by the seat of the pants. Welcome to the real world; this happens to everyone.

The scientific method doesn't solve all problems.

I have never coached anyone who made it through an entire season without something interfering with the logical sequence of training and periodization described in previous chapters. You're human and have a life off the bike—expect training conflicts.

The other, less-precise side of race preparation that deals with such challenges may be called the *art* of training. This is the side that figures out how to cope with problems and still accomplish season goals. It is the often creative and right-brained way of solving the inevitable scheduling problems. I can't teach you this art of training—it must be learned through experience—but I can provide examples so you can see it in action.

Using creativity to solve problems is the art of training.

What this chapter does is show you how I dealt with such problems in developing annual training plans for two athletes in 1999. These are real-world people with real-world issues. Both were successful in their racing, although they failed to accomplish all they set out to do. In fact, achieving all one's goals all the time probably means that the goals aren't high enough.

Notice as you read these athletes' case studies and examine their annual training plans that the rules described thus far are sometimes broken. The art of training occasionally conflicts with the scientific method.

A SEASON ON THE BRINK

In 1990 Jimi Killen won the world cross-country championship in the junior category, and, on turning 18, entered the pro ranks in 1992. I began coaching him in January of that year.

At the time, it was easy to see that Jimi had a great deal of physical talent. Initial testing revealed a high power output at lactate threshold and good muscular endurance—both important criteria for cross-country racing. He could climb like a moun-

Jimi's strengths.

tain goat and his speed skills, including pedaling and bike handling on technical terrain, were exceptional, probably due to many years of racing BMX as a youth. His endurance was also high for a young athlete.

One chink in his racing armor, however, was a low force ability—at least lower than what I would like to see in a cross-country racer. But we never did much with weights, typically just a few weeks of one day per week, because Jimi already climbed so well and

Jimi's limiters.

didn't care for the weight-room environment. Instead, we relied on hill work to build force, at least in the legs. His precise bike handling skills usually made up for his lack of upper body strength. This weakness, however, sometimes came back to haunt him in races when he was tired.

The other fitness challenge we faced had to do with fast starts. Jimi is what I call a patient racer. This is a trait that often served him well. He would let the leaders go at the start, and then gradually reel them back in as two hours of racing progressed. This style grew out of a weakness in the area of anaerobic endurance—his body didn't clear lactate very effectively, nor did he tolerate it well. This limiter often hurt him, though, especially on courses that funneled into single-track early or offered few places to pass. But we became complacent with this limiter—at least for seven seasons.

By the winter of 1998 to 1999 I had been working with Jimi for seven years—longer than any other rider I had ever coached. I knew him well by that point. That winter we talked about how the coming season would be a crucial one. Sponsorship money in the sport was waning, putting pressure on riders to perform or be without a team. Competition was also heating up as we approached an Olympic year in 2000. The 1999 season had to be a good one or his career could be cut short. Consequently, he set some high goals for the season. They are listed at the top of his annual training plan in Figure 9.1.

A season on the brink.

TRAINING OBJECTIVES

I told Jimi that in order for him to reach his goals and have his best year ever, he must achieve four training objectives.

Objective 1: Race Less and Train More

Like most riders, Jimi prefers racing to training alone. His idea of a good workout was to do a C-priority, local road race whenever possible. He'd had a race almost every weekend in previous years. While this did help his fitness sometimes, it was imprecise. We never knew how the race would progress and which of his limiters, if any, would benefit.

Reduce the number of C-priority races.

Racing also has an emotionally dulling effect that is much greater than that of a workout. As a season progressed he became desensitized to the excitement and significance of racing. The emotional investment of starting so many races often brought burnout at the wrong times of the year. And since races tend to be more taxing than workouts, we spent a good bit of time recovering every week instead of training.

At Jimi's level of experience, C-priority races have little benefit. For a novice, they increase the steepness of the learning curve. But Jimi didn't need to learn what racing was all about. I told him to reduce the number of C-priority races, especially road races, and use just a few low-ranked events to build fitness, gauge progress or tune up for an A-priority race. Consequently, the Valley of the Sun Stage Race and the Redlands Stage Race were included for fitness building in the late winter, local road races were done sparingly in the spring, and C-priority races were inserted before several of the A-priority events as final gauges of preparedness.

Making good use of C-priority races.

With a reduced number of races, Jimi could more frequently and more precisely work on the limiters that were holding him back. In previous years, on average, once the

Athlete: Jimmy Killen

Annual Hours: 800

Season Goals

1. Finish in top 5 overall of National Championship Series.
2. Place in top 20 at all World Cup events entered.
3. Win a National Championship Series race.

Training Objectives

1. Race less often (C-pri), train more.
2. Stay with leaders at start in all NCS races.
3. Train consistently—avoid burnout and illness.
4. Improve motivation, confidence, through habits.

FIGURE 9.1
1999 Training Plan

Wk# Mon	Races	Pri	Period	Hours	Weights	Endurance	Force	Speed Skill	Muscular Endurance	Anaerobic Endurance	Power	Testing	Details
01-Nov-02			Tran	?									R&R
02-Nov-09			Prep	12.0		X							X-train, E2
03-Nov-16				13.0		X							X-train, E2
04-Nov-23				13.5	AA	X							X-train, E2
05-Nov-30				13.5		X							X-train, E2
06-Dec-07			Base 1	15.5		X		X					E2, S1, S2
07-Dec-14				19.0		X		X					E2, S1, S2
08-Dec-21				21.5		X		X					E2, S1, S2
09-Dec-28				11.0	MS	X		X				X	E2, S1, S2, CP30
10-Jan-04			Base 2	17.0		X	X	X					F1, S5
11-Jan-11				20.0		X	X	X					F1, S5
12-Jan-18				22.5		X	X	X	X				F1, M1, S5
13-Jan-25				11.5		X		X				X	E2, CP6, CP30, S5
14-Feb-01			Base 3	18.0	PE	X	X	X	X				E2, M1, M2, A6, S5
15-Feb-08				21.5		X	X	X	X				E2, M1, M2, A6, S5
16-Feb-15	Valley of Sun Stage Race	C		17.0			X		X	X	X		P1
17-Feb-22				13.0		X	X				X		E2, S5, P1
18-Mar-01	Redlands Stage Race	C	Build 1	17.0			X		X	X			Race only
19-Mar-08				15.0		X	X		X	X	X		F1, A6, S5, P1
20-Mar-15	Sea Otter	B		10.5				X	X	X	X		Race only
21-Mar-22	Napa World Cup	B		11.5		X	X	X	X	X	X		E2, A4+M5, P1
22-Mar-29			Build 2	15.5		X	X		X	X			E2, M1, A6, A4, S5
23-Apr-05				18.5		X	X	X	X	X			F1, A4, P1, S5
24-Apr-12	Local Road Race	C		18.5		X	X	X	X	X	X		F1, A4, P1, S5
25-Apr-19				11.5		X	X					X	E2, CP6, CP30, S5
26-Apr-26			Peak	14.0		X	X	X	X	X	X		E2, A4+M5, A6, P1
27-May-03	Local Road Race	C		15.0		X	X		X	X	X		F1, A4+M5, P1
28-May-10	Big Bear NCS	A	Race	8.5				X	X	X	X		P1
29-May-17	Redwing NCS	B	Build 1	14.0		X	X	X	X	X	X		E2, A4
30-May-24				17.0		X	X		X	X	X		F1, A6x2, P1
31-May-31				17.0		X	X		X	X	X		E2, A6x2, P1
32-Jun-07	7 Springs NCS	B		11.5		X	X	X	X	X	X		E2, P1
33-Jun-14			Build 2	16.0		X	X		X	X	X		A4, A6, F1, P2
34-Jun-21	Big Bear World Cup	B		10.5		X	X	X	X	X	X		E2, A6, P2
35-Jun-28	Canada World Cup	B	Peak	12.5		X	X	X	X	X	X		E2, M3, P1
36-Jul-05				15.0		X	X		X	X	X		E2, A4+M5, A6, P2
37-Jul-12	Mammoth NCS	A	Race	10.0				X	X	X	X		P1
38-Jul-19	Utah NCS	A		10.0				X	X	X	X		P1
39-Jul-26			Build 2	13.5		X	X		X	X			E2, F1, M1, A4
40-Aug-02				12.5		X	X	X	X	X	X		E2, A6, M5, F1, P1
41-Aug-09	King of the Rockies	C	Peak	11.5				X	X	X	X		A4, P1
42-Aug-16	Mt. Snow NCS Finals	A	Race	10.0				X	X	X	X		P2
43-Aug-23	Mercury Tour	B		10.0				X	X	X	X		Race only
44-Aug-30	Snake River	C	Peak	11.0		X	X	X	X	X	X		E2, P1
45-Sep-06				14.5		X	X	X	X	X	X		E2, A6, A7
46-Sep-13	Worlds	A	Race	10.0				X	X	X	X		P1
47-Sep-20			Tran	?									R&R
48-Sep-27				?									R&R
49-Oct-04				?									R&R
50-Oct-11				?									R&R
51-Oct-18				?									R&R
52-Oct-25				?									R&R

race season began, he had just seven weeks without racing. In 1999, he would have 13 nonracing weeks. More importantly, most of those quality training weeks would come in April as we prepared for his first A-priority event of the year—the National Cup Series opener at Big Bear, California. At this time, we used local road races to check his progress and maintain his race focus. Late in the season, when limiters should be well developed, we included more off-road, C-priority races.

Objective 2: Stay With the Leaders at the Start in All National Cup Series Races

It was time for a change in Jimi's typical, patient race strategy. To be competitive he had to ride with the leaders from the start. This would be his greatest training challenge over the next few months. In past years, when we worked on the anaerobic endurance necessary for fast starts, he would often fail to finish these grueling workouts. Now they would be an integral part of his regular training.

Preparing for fast starts.

As shown on his training plan, A4 workouts—lactate tolerance reps—were regularly scheduled in the spring as we built up to Big Bear NCS. After that, they were included less often, as the more frequent races would help to maintain this capability.

We also used a variation of this basic workout: a combination of lactate tolerance reps and threshold ride (A4 + M5). After completing the last recovery of the repetitions, he would immediately go into a 20- to 30-minute ride at near lactate threshold. This simulated the stresses of a fast start followed by a long, steady-state effort. This workout could be done on the pavement with a road bike or on a mountain bike riding a fireroad.

Using a combined workout.

Objective 3: Train Consistently—Avoid Burnout and Illness

In past years, burnout had been a problem for Jimi. It was not a sign of weakness, but rather an indicator of too much racing and training stress. I believed we could take one big step toward accomplishing this objective by paring back the race schedule.

One thing we didn't do that would have helped was taking a break from training for a week after his first peak of the season—a Transition period. But unfortunately, the schedule of National Cup and World Cup events didn't allow for that. Instead, we reduced the volume for the second half of the season by dropping down from 800 annual hours to about a 650-hour basis by May, and then to even lower levels by late July and August. Combined with a few endurance workouts (E2) and frequent high-priority racing, I felt this would keep burnout under control.

Manipulating volume to prevent burnout.

Illness is a different matter. We talked about how a head cold at the wrong time could be devastating to his season, and how to avoid catching colds. Much of what we talked about is described in Chapter 11.

Objective 4: Improve Motivation, Confidence and Thought Habits

Mental skills are crucial to success, and even more so in the higher race categories.

After seven years of coaching Jimi, it became apparent to me that physical fitness wasn't the only factor holding him back. A greater challenge was mental skills. This is often the case with athletes in the highest racing categories, as the riders' abilities are very close to each others'.

While I might help him a little bit with this area, it was so crucial that I believed we needed to include a sports psychologist on his support team. He interviewed two local counselors and by early summer settled on one, Scott Tate, to work with. This was a critical decision, as this person had to be someone he could trust and feel comfortable with when discussing deep feelings. Scott worked with Jimi on maintaining high levels of focus throughout races and on eliminating self-defeating thoughts and behaviors that were holding him back.

THE SEASON

We weren't concerned about the early season, C-priority results—whatever happened was okay so long as he got good workouts focused on improving limiters. At Redlands, however, a head cold in the last three days put him in survival mode. The cold was short lived and he went to Sea Otter to work on fast starts. We didn't get them, but we weren't concerned as we had only just started working on anaerobic endurance.

Results don't always tell the whole story.

The first World Cup race results in Napa didn't turn out well, despite Jimi's having his best base fitness in years. He was seeded in 88th position at the start line, flatted, and crashed to finish in 65th place. Our confidence was buoyed, however, as he felt good throughout the race and rode well.

Now with time to prepare for Big Bear NCS—and no other races to prepare for—we went to work on cross-country–specific training. This seven-week period needed to go well, as we were establishing most of the fitness necessary for the remainder of the season. After Big Bear, there were never more than two consecutive weeks without racing. We had to make the most of it.

Confidence is as important as fitness.

Despite another illness, a death in the family, and some marginal weather in northern Colorado, we accomplished a lot in these few weeks. By early May Jimi reported that he felt the best he had in years and was convinced the rest of the season would go well.

At Big Bear he was eighth, and the following week in Redwing took tenth. Not what we had hoped for, but he had good starts and climbed well. Jimi even led at the start in Redwing—a new experience for him that further boosted his confidence. In the Seven Springs NCS race he took fifth in the cross-country, and was now ranked third overall in the series, due to a major reshuffling of the leaders.

From this point on, we could see improvement with nearly every race—not only in race fitness, but also in confidence. Despite muscle cramps, he finished fourth in Mammoth NCS, another A-priority race. The following week, in the Deer Valley, Utah, NCS race, he was in second place but flatted twice, dropping to eleventh. He was still in the National Cup Series top five overall, however.

All of this was great for his confidence and positive thought habits as we approached the NCS finals in Mount Snow, Vermont. Having won King of the Rockies in Winter Park, Colorado, the week was an added bonus—as was narrowly beating Lance Armstrong, fresh off of a Tour de France victory.

Both of us knew that barring mechanical problems, he would race well in the all-important NCS Finals. His race strategy worked well as he placed fifth in the race clinching his fifth-place overall position in the series and qualifying him for the World Championship team.

While we could place a checkmark next to goal number one, the others eluded us. In three World Cup races, we managed just one top 20, in Big Bear. But we also didn't give these races an A-priority. A few days' rest before them was not enough to prepare Jimi to race competitively with the best mountain bikers in the world. But ranking these races as B-priorities was a decision we made early in the season based on what was most important—a top five in the National Cup Series. We didn't waver from that decision throughout the season.

Make hard decisions and then stay with them.

Nor did he win a National Cup Series race, although he came close a couple of times. But all told, it was Jimi's best season in his eight as a pro. Making it even sweeter, he received the Richard Long Sportsmanship award at the end of the season. The previous winners were some of the sport's most respected riders—Susan DeMattei, Ned Overend, John Tomac and Dave Wiens. Sometimes it takes a season on the brink to bring out the best in us.

FINE-TUNING FOR BETTER RESULTS

If you work or go to school full time and have about 10 to 15 hours per week to train, the case study described here should be instructive for you. The race schedule it is based on may also be close to yours, with 12 regional and 2 national-caliber races in 19 weeks.

The athlete described here is Neal Burton, age 21, an industrial cook in Wolcott, Connecticut. Neal had been racing for six years when he contacted me about coaching in 1998. I began working with him in the fall of that year.

Neal is an excellent example of a dedicated rider who needed just a little fine-tuning of his training program to improve his race results. The program we followed that season brought noticeable growth.

Experienced athletes typically only need to fine-tune their training—not make major changes.

In four years, he had moved up the ranks to the expert category and had seen steadily improving results at this level for the past two seasons. When I looked over his race résumé for those two years, the first thing that stood out was a significant variability in results—he had both good and bad races. This is often indicative of someone who is coming into races tired or is making training mistakes, particularly during the week of a race. In the 1998 season, there was noticeable progress in this area, especially near the end of the racing year. He was learning, I could tell. But in two of his most important races that season—the National Cup Series events in Pennsylvania and Vermont—his performances were lacking. This unevenness was an area he especially wanted to improve on and was part of the reason he contacted me.

The closer you get to a race, the more critical everything becomes.

ASSESSMENT

In assessing his abilities, I found that Neal had good endurance, could climb well, and had good speed skill on technical courses. This is an excellent foundation for mountain bike racing fitness. I knew he would do well with a carefully prepared training plan that peaked him for the A-priority races.

At 74 inches (188cm) of height and weighing 168 pounds (77kg), his weight-to-height ratio was 2.27 (0.41 in metric), well above the 2.0 (0.35) typical of the top climbers. That he could climb well with such a body mass indicated that he must have sound anaerobic endurance. Mountain bikers of his size have a lot to lift as they ride up

Big riders can climb.

a hill and must go deeply anaerobic to climb as fast as the smaller riders.

But he didn't own a CompuTrainer or a power meter, nor did he have access to a testing facility, so I had no way of assessing other aspects of his fitness, such as maximal power, power at lactate threshold and power at VO_2 max. While not critical, this is very helpful information in gauging progress, especially in the Base period of training.

We could, however, determine his heart rate training zones. Initially, I did this by examining his average heart rates from past off-road races, as these are usually quite close to the lactate threshold heart rate. He had averaged around 173 beats per minute in races, and later testing on the road with 30-minute time trials (as described in Chapter 4) confirmed this estimate of his lactate threshold heart rate.

His force ability was good, judged by his climbing, but we both agreed that he could improve in this area—particularly in the upper body strength that is critical for controlling the bike on rough terrain. Greater hip-extension strength should also make him a better climber and increase his overall power.

Our main focus, however, would be on muscular endurance. This is the basis for racing well in off-road events in which drafting and team tactics play only a small role in race outcomes. Success in individual events that last between 12 minutes and three hours depends heavily on the power one can put out when at lactate threshold. The only ways we would have to judge Neal's progress in this area would be time trials, both on- and off-road, and finishing times in spring races as compared with previous years. If these got faster, we could be fairly certain that power at lactate threshold had improved. But this is a far from accurate measure, as there are many factors that affect such performances. Without a reliable power-measuring system, we were left to do some subjective evaluation. Neal proved to be good at this.

Muscular endurance is critical for mountain bike race success.

I also believed we needed to make some slight adjustments in Neal's diet. He was taking in plenty of carbohydrate, but much of it was from one source—wheat. I suggested shifting some of these calories towards animal protein while increasing his vegetable intake and reducing dairy consumption. (Chapter 16 discusses my recommendations in the area of diet.)

Where Neal lives in Connecticut, there are plenty of trails to ride nearby, and the area is quite hilly. These are nearly perfect conditions for mountain bike training. The major drawbacks are that there are few flat roads for recovery rides, winter weather can be harsh, and Neal has no other riders to train with regularly. This last point is sometimes an advantage, however. Riders who prefer to do their workouts with groups often wind up burned out early in the year. Overtraining is common when group workouts are

Group rides offer both advantages and disadvantages—have a purpose for them.

common, and riding frequently with others also usually makes training somewhat haphazard, also. But not having others to ride with meant that Neal would have to be highly motivated—there would be no shared enthusiasm for riding to keep him going.

This latter concern turned out to be a nonissue for Neal. His mental skills profile (see Chapter 5) indicated that his motivation was excellent, as were most of his other mental skills. After a few weeks of coaching him, it was apparent to me that he had exceptional psychological qualities. I never had to give him a pep talk or be concerned that he would simply skip a workout because he didn't feel like doing it. My only concern in this area was that he might push himself too hard. My job would be to keep him reined in.

Successful athletes often must be held back by someone such as a coach.

GOALS AND PLANNING

The top priority on Neal's list of goals for the season was to upgrade to the semipro category. He also wanted to finish in a podium position in cumulative standings in the two big race series in his region—the Trail 66 Series and the New England Series.

To accomplish these goals, he would need to ride consistently well in the series races. Because of this, and with only 14 events on his schedule, most races were ranked as B-priority. The A-priority races needed to have added significance for upgrading and for overall series placement. They turned out to be nearly perfectly grouped, with two A-priority races back-to-back in June and a final pairing of A-priorities nine weeks later. That allowed us to maintain peak form for two weeks and then rebuild fitness for the second peak. Notice in Figure 9.2 that after the first pair of A-priority races we returned to Base training for three weeks.

It's often necessary to return to Base training in the summer.

EARLY SEASON RACING

The only race-scheduling issue that concerned me was the absence of a race to peak for in the spring. After a long winter of training, we didn't want to delay testing what we had accomplished any longer. And I wanted to experiment with peaking to see what worked best for Neal. So we decided to call the first New England Series race of the season (week 26) a B+ priority and peak for it. While this violated the "four A-priority races per season rule," the other A races were grouped and spaced so nicely that a fifth would not cause any problem.

It's okay to break rules when it offers an advantage.

This decision worked out well, as I discovered that Neal could handle a lot of stress in training when the hard workouts were separated by about 96 hours. This was apparent in the C-priority race at the end of the second Peak week as he rode strongly on the climbs, feeling as strong as he ever had, he said, and handled the technical sections quite well.

Athlete: Neal Burton

Annual Hours: 550

Season Goals

1. Upgrade to semi-pro
2. Top 3 overall in Trail 66 Series.
3. Top 5 overall in New England Series

Training Objectives

1. Leg press 420 pounds 6 times by 12/6/99.
2. Increase lactate threshold power--faster spring races.
3. Train consistently--avoid burnout and illness.
4.
5.

FIGURE 9.2
1999 Training Plan

Workouts

Wk# Mon	Races	Pri	Period	Hours	WEIGHTS	ENDURANCE	FORCE	SPEED SKILL	MUSCULAR ENDURANCE	ANAEROBIC ENDURANCE	POWER	TESTING	Details
01-Nov-02			Prep	12.0	AA	X							E2
02-Nov-09					MS	X							E2
03-Nov-16						X							E2
04-Nov-23			Base 1	14.0		X	X						E2, S1, S2
05-Nov-30				15.0		X	X						E2, S1, S2
06-Dec-07				15.5	PE	X	X	X					F1, S5
07-Dec-14				10.0		X	X					X	E2, S5, CP6, CP30
08-Dec-21			Base 2	14.0		X	X	X	X				F1, S5, M1
09-Dec-28				15.5		X	X	X	X				F1, S5, M1
10-Jan-04				15.5		X	X	X	X				F1, S5, M1
11-Jan-11				10.0	ME	X	X					X	E2, S5, CP6, CP30
12-Jan-18			Base 3	15.5		X	X	X	X				F1, F2, S5, M2
13-Jan-25				15.5		X	X	X	X				F1, F2, S5, M2
14-Feb-01				15.5		X	X	X	X				F1, F2, S5, M2
15-Feb-08				10.0		X	X					X	E2, S5, CP6, CP30
16-Feb-15			Build 1	13.5		X	X	X	X	X			E2, F1, S5, M3, A2
17-Feb-22						X	X	X	X	X			E2, F1, S5, M3, A2
18-Mar-01						X	X	X	X	X			E2, F1, S5, M3, A2
19-Mar-08				10.0		X	X				X	X	E2, S5, P1, CP6, CP30
20-Mar-15			Build 2	11.5		X	X	X	X	X			E2, S5, M4, A4
21-Mar-22						X	X	X	X	X			E2, S5, M4, A4
22-Mar-29						X	X	X	X	X	X		E2, S5, M4, A4, P1
23-Apr-05				10.0		X	X				X	X	E2, S5, P2, CP6, CP30
24-Apr-12			Peak	11.5		X	X		X	X	X		E2, S5, A4+M5, A5+M5
25-Apr-19	Fat Tire Classic	C		9.5		X	X	X	X	X	X		E2, A5+M5, P1
26-Apr-26	New England #1	B+	Race	8.5			X	X	X	X	X		M2, P1
27-May-03			Build 2	13.0		X	X	X	X	X	X		E2, F1, S5, M5, P1
28-May-10	New England #2	B		11.5		X	X	X	X	X	X		E2, F1, P2
29-May-17				13.0		X	X	X	X	X	X		E2, F1, S5, A4, P1
30-May-24	New York	C		8.5		X	X	X	X	X	X		E2, A7, P1
31-May-31			Peak	11.5		X	X	X	X	X	X		E2, M2+M5, A5+M5, P1
32-Jun-07	7 Springs NCS	A	Race	8.5			X	X	X	X	X		P1
33-Jun-14	Trail 66 #1	A		8.5			X	X	X	X	X		A4+M5, P1
34-Jun-21	Northfield	B	Base 3	14.0		X	X	X					E2, M5
35-Jun-28				15.0		X	X	X					E2, F1 x 2, S5
36-Jul-05	New England Finals	B		10.0		X	X	X	X	X	X		E2, A5, P1
37-Jul-12			Build 1	12.5		X	X	X	X	X	X		E2, F1, S5, M2, A4
38-Jul-19	Trail 66 #2	B		11.0		X	X	X	X	X	X		E2, M2, M5, P1
39-Jul-26	Trail 66 #3	B		11.0		X	X	X	X	X	X		E2, M2+M5, P1
40-Aug-02	Trail 66 #4	B	Peak	9.0		X	X	X	X	X	X		E2, M2+M5, P1
41-Aug-09	Trail 66 #5	B		11.0		X	X	X	X	X	X		E2, M2+M5, P1
42-Aug-16	Mt. Snow NCS	A	Race	10.5			X	X	X	X	X		P1
43-Aug-23	Trail 66 Finals	A		8.5			X	X	X	X	X		A5, P1
44-Aug-30			Tran	?									
45-Sep-06				?									
46-Sep-13				?									
47-Sep-20				?									
48-Sep-27			Prep	10.0	AA	X							E2
49-Oct-04				12.0		X							E2
50-Oct-11				12.0		X							E2
51-Oct-18				11.5		X							E2
52-Oct-25				10.0	MS	X							E2

But we also learned in this race that he wasn't ready for fast starts. This didn't surprise me since it was so early in the season. But we would have to go to work on this as soon as possible. In addition, he had muscle cramps in the race, which he had experienced in previous years. I felt these might be related to the sports drink he was using and suggested trying a different one. This turned out to be a positive change, or at least something worked, as he only cramped up in one other race that season. That episode, occurring on the last lap, was undoubtedly due to dehydration, as he didn't drink enough on a hot day.

Early season races offer clues about changes that may be needed.

Besides learning a lot about him with two weeks of peaking and one race, it looked like we were on our way to a good B+-priority event the following weekend. And, indeed, the race did go well—at least for a while. Two pinch flats put him in the DNF (did not finish) column. In typical fashion, Neal remained positive despite dropping out and was excited about preparing for the next A-priority races.

THE SECOND AND THIRD PEAKS

For the most part, Neal came on strong the remainder of the season. One of the reasons for this involved the changes we made after the first spring races. But there was one setback that caused concern about our direction.

In the second Peak period of the season, building up to the National Cup Series race in Seven Springs, Pennsylvania, he didn't recover well. I was concerned that we may have done too much anaerobic endurance training prior to this second taper of the year. His starting position at the back of the field with so many to try to pass made it difficult to gauge how fit he was. Another DNF for a mechanical breakdown, this time in the Trail 66 Series opener, had us scratching our heads. Then a lackluster 17th-place finish the following week in a B-priority race really made us wonder. Through it all, Neal remained positive and focused.

After a setback, analyze and make necessary changes, but remain confident.

Once we dropped out the highest intensity work and focused on the basic abilities—and Neal got some much-needed rest—he came on strong the remainder of the season. A 10th place in the National Cup Series Championship at Mount Snow, Vermont, and taking third in the Trail 66 Series confirmed that we were doing things right late in the year.

Although he didn't get the semipro upgrade he was after this year, he came very close and will probably be able to accomplish it before the end of the next season. Following a Transition period in September, Neal began the next year's campaign with renewed focus and enthusiasm in October.

CASE STUDIES WRAP-UP

Notice in both of the case studies described here that the annual training plans followed most of the guidelines presented in the previous two chapters—but not all of them. The rules were broken in each case to match each athlete's training needs to his unique situation. Just as with Jimi and Neal, it's unlikely that you'll be able to design a perfect annual training plan and follow it without change for an entire year.

As I mentioned earlier, it's not possible for me to describe how to work your way around the many planning obstacles that are going to appear—there are just too many possibilities. That is the art of self-coaching. It will take a lot of thought and maybe even some trial and error to find workable solutions. Don't let this discourage you; it is necessary for reaching your mountain bike racing goals.

Rules are meant to be broken—but only when there is a good reason.

RACING AND RECOVERY

In this part we examine two extremes—racing and recovery. They are on opposite ends of the mountain bike training spectrum.

Competition brings out the best in an athlete. If it weren't for the other competitors, you would never push that hard and learn so much about yourself in the process. In fact, the word "compete" is derived from the Latin word competere, meaning "to meet or come together." When racing, you come together with the other athletes, striving to achieve the highest level of performance possible. The better the competition, the better you will do. At its most basic level, racing is a cooperative venture requiring you to give your best effort to help others achieve their peak performances. They do the same for you. We don't compete against other riders—we compete with them.

On the contrary, recovery places no demands on the athlete to perform. It's just the opposite. This is a time when there are no physical or mental challenges—or at least there shouldn't be. Sometimes obsessive-compulsive riders find that down time is mentally challenging. They feel guilty training at low workload levels, and (heaven forbid!) taking days off. But without recovery there can be no peak of fitness, and these athletes' ability to carry a share of the competitivenes in races is diminished.

Illness, injury, burnout and overtraining are often the results of not allowing enough recovery time. When one of these forces downtime, it's time to question if your training plan is allowing your body adequate time to recover from races and hard workouts.

RACING

I'm not one of those guys who rides a road bike all week and then races a mountain bike on the weekend. I don't enjoy riding road bikes. I wish I could do nothing but epic mountain bike rides and race on the weekend, but I can't.

—DAVE WIENS

The week of your first A-priority race of the season has finally arrived. It's been a long time coming. In the winter you got in the long rides, high volume, hill work, and weights despite cold, wet weather and short days. In the late winter and early spring you suffered through several weeks of intervals, hill repeats and threshold efforts. You even competed in a couple of low-priority races. Now is the time to see what you've accomplished with all of this.

Wouldn't it be a shame to make a major training mistake now? All of the preceding weeks and months of building fitness would be for naught. Unfortunately, it happens to even the best of riders. Blunders made the week of the race and on race day can lead to a poor performance. In this chapter we examine the details of last-minute race preparation.

PEAKING

Previous chapters have briefly discussed the peaking process by describing how workload is reduced, primarily by a reduction in volume, and race intensity is maintained. Race week continues that pattern. Let's review the periodization concepts of the Peak period to see how to continue them seamlessly into an A-priority race week.

Volume is low and intensity high in the Race period.

Most athletes believe that peaking is as simple as taking a few days of rest before a big race. There's more to it than that. In fact, as scientific studies have shown, such a "taper" will not produce a true fitness peak: The athlete is likely to be rested, but not at the apex of his or her potential.

You'll know it when a true peak of fitness is achieved. Astonishing physiological changes occur, including increased leg power, reduced lactic acid production, increased blood volume, greater red blood cell concentration and increased fuel storage. You will also experience sharper mental skills, such as concentration, confidence and motivation. All this is achieved without illegal drugs.

Peaking produces dramatic changes in physiology.

In the 1980s and 1990s there were numerous scientific studies of the peaking process using runners, swimmers, triathletes and cyclists as subjects. The following concepts emerged from this research and are applicable to peaking for any endurance event.

TAPER LENGTH

The length of the volume taper depends on two elements: how fit you are coming into the Peak period, and the nature of the race for which you're peaking. If you have a great base of fitness, meaning endurance, force, speed skill and muscular endurance are at high levels, taper longer than if your fitness level is low. The more unfit you are, the more important it is to continue training and creating higher levels of fitness until perhaps as little as seven to ten days before the big race. Since it takes several days to realize the full benefits of a given workout, training with a high workload beyond about a week prior to the event will produce no additional fitness.

Taper duration depends on fitness and race length.

Deciding how fit you are is a difficult decision. If you err, make it on the side of tapering too long.

The longer the race is for which you're tapering, the longer the taper should be. An off-road, hundred-mile race needs a longer taper than a dirt criterium. This, in part, is to allow time for accumulated fatigue and possible muscle damage to completely improve.

TAPER VOLUME

If you're tapering for three weeks (two-week Peak period and one-week Race period), reduce each week's volume by about 20 percent of that of the previous week. A two-week taper (one-week Peak period and one-week Race period) involves cutting back on volume by about 30 percent each week. For a seven- to 10-day taper, cut volume by 50 percent for the entire period. The first week's reductions are determined by the average volume of the non–R and R weeks in the most recent training period. The Peak and Race periods in Table 7.3 are based on weekly 20-percent cutbacks.

Tapering involves cutting volume 20 to 50 percent, depending on the length of the taper.

WORKOUT FREQUENCY

In reducing volume, you're better off cutting back on the number of hours you train each day rather than the number of weekly workouts. Some studies have shown that reducing how often you ride could result in a loss of fitness. Swimmers have an interesting way of describing this phenomenon; they call it "losing feel for the water." They are probably describing a loss of economy. Greatly cutting back on the frequency of your workouts by spacing them far apart in a taper period could cause a loss of "feel for the bike." You may not seem as smooth and comfortable in pedaling and handling movements as you normally do. It's probably best to decrease the number of workouts by no more than one or two in a week during the Peak and Race periods.

Be careful not to reduce workout frequency too much.

WORKOUT INTENSITY

High-intensity training is the most potent stimulus for both improving and maintaining fitness. A race-intensity workout every 72 hours is all the stimulus needed at this point in the season to peak your fitness. One of these could be a tune-up race on the weekend or an off-road workout that simulates the race conditions anticipated. The others should focus on your greatest weakness for the targeted race. For example, if climbing is what you're most worried about, do some hill workouts during the taper. The intensity of these key workouts should closely simulate the effort you expect in the race. It does not need to exceed expected race intensity, and, in fact, this may prove detrimental.

A few workouts should be at race intensity.

EASY WORKOUTS

All other workouts are easy enough to allow for recovery. Ride in the small chain ring at low intensities, such as heart rate 1 and 2 or CP180 zones and lower. By taking it easy you'll come into the race-effort workouts every 72 hours fully rested. This will allow you to accomplish more in the race-intensity sessions. Rest is the key to greater fitness at this time, both because it allows the body to adapt to the stress you've been placing on it, and because it results in more intense workouts.

Rest between hard workouts is the key.

Such a peaking process should only be done two or three times in a season. The shorter the race season, the fewer peaks are possible without losing too much fitness loss. Each of these combined Peak and Race periods could last three to four weeks. Eventually, aerobic fitness will erode, necessitating a return to Base 3 or Build 1. At that point the preparation for the next A-priority race begins.

RACE WEEK

The week of an important race is a critical time. Too much or too little stress will leave you either "flat" or tired on race day. When done right, a week of tapering finishes off the Peak period by boosting physical abilities and sharpening mental skills. Let's examine how to plan for a peak performance by counting down the days leading to an A-priority race.

SIX DAYS BEFORE RACE

Take it easy today.

For a Sunday race, today is Monday. This is a good day for an active-recovery ride or day off since the day before was probably a race-effort simulation at the end of a Peak period week. Don't lift weights today, or any day this week. Now is not the time to tear down muscle tissue or attempt to maintain strength. If you find yourself exceptionally tired from the previous day's workout, a day off is wise.

Make your bike race-ready today.

This is a good day to get your bike ready for the race by cleaning it, ensuring bolts are tight, lubricating all moving parts and truing the wheels. Most of the rides this week are done on a road bike, but at least one at race effort, although short, should be off-road. On these rides, make sure that everything is working properly. Race day is not the time to discover a mechanical problem. The one exception is race tires. These are best saved until the day before the race to protect them from cuts and tiny slivers that could go unnoticed. When installing your race tires later this week, check them for potential problems.

Match eating to activity level.

Today and every day this week, be cautious about how much and what you eat. Due to the decreased workload, fewer calories are needed, but the tendency is to eat normally or even reward yourself by overeating. By the end of the week you may have gained an extra pound or so primarily due to the storage of water. That's okay, but avoid adding body fat.

THREE TO FIVE DAYS BEFORE RACE

If the race is on a Sunday, this period consists of Tuesday, Wednesday and Thursday. Rest is still the most important ingredient, but some intense effort is also necessary. Feeling flat on race day may result from not riding hard a few times this week.

Several university studies have demonstrated that a moderate and decreasing amount of high intensity during a taper week produces better endurance performances than either total rest or easy, slow training. The reason for this is that rest allows glycogen stores to rebuild, increases aerobic enzyme levels, boosts blood volume and allows for repair of damaged tissues. Well-spaced high-intensity training maintains or even improves muscle-recruitment patterns. Not doing any high intensity in this week is likely to leave you feeling a bit weak on short climbs and a little awkward on the bike at high cadence. The speed skill and power abilities are lost first when workload is reduced, so maintenance of these must be paramount in race week.

Combine low volume with brief, high intensity efforts on these days.

Brief bursts of intense movement with long recoveries, such as those described in the power workouts in Appendix B, are effective for these days. Another workout I sometimes have riders complete at this time is 90-second repetitions at race intensity or just slightly harder. They do one of these repetitions for every day remaining until race day. So if it's Tuesday and the race is on Sunday—five days away—they will do 5 reps of 90 seconds. Wednesday would have four of these reps, Thursday three. With a three-minute recovery after each rep and only a few of them done each day, this workout is not stressful. A full recovery is certain by the next day. Yet they are long and intense enough to maintain and even sharpen race-specific fitness. At least one of these workouts should be off-road.

Thursday is the best day to preride the course. Pay special attention to technical sections, places where you might be able to pass other riders, corners in fast descents and landmarks approaching the finish line. Because it's off-road, this workout will be hard enough without adding any repetitions or power work. Be careful not to make it long, however. One or two laps at the most, if you're paying close attention, is enough. This is best done at the time of day you will race, if possible. Stay off your legs the rest of the day.

TWO DAYS BEFORE RACE

This is Friday for a Sunday race. The emphasis today is on making sure you are rested for the race. If you arrive at the race site today, it's still better to take the day off and ride the course tomorrow. It's important that you get one last day of full recovery.

This is the best day to rest.

If traveling to the race today, the night before is the time to pack your bike. Travel is quite stressful, so anything you can do to reduce its psychological and physical impact is beneficial. A travel checklist that includes everything you might want to take reduces your fear of forgetting something. Another stress reliever is traveling with a nonracing friend or spouse who can deal with the inevitable hassles as they arise.

Besides staying as calm and relaxed as you can today, eat food that you're accustomed to (you may need to carry some), drink plenty of water (not sports drinks) throughout the day and go to bed at a time that is normal for you.

DAY BEFORE RACE

Today is the last time to work out before the race. If you arrived at the race venue

If you haven't already, check out the course today.

yesterday, it's also the time to check out the course. If it is possible, the best time to do this is at the hour you are supposed to race tomorrow. That way, shadows, wind and air temperature are likely to be much as they will be tomorrow. Keep this course preview mostly as easy as possible, but attack a few short hills at race effort.

Of course, it's better to have done this earlier in the week, leaving today free to practice your warm-up routine. Rehearsing all the details of the warm-up today—including when, where, how and how long—will make the real thing easier tomorrow. The warm-up should have enough intensity to maintain race fitness and keep you from feeling flat tomorrow.

Avoid rushing through the prerace administrative process. Keep everything in perspective today by minimizing the significance of the inevitable day-before-the-race hassles. Remain calm and collected and don't let anything frazzle you. Neither physical nor psychological energy should be wasted today.

Rest and get your mind off the race.

After all race activities are taken care of, get your mind off the race, avoid crowds of nervous athletes, and stay off of your legs and out the sun. Some possible activities include going to a movie, renting a videotape, watching television and reading. Throughout the day, continue to sip from a bottle of water (not a sports drink), and don't allow hunger to set in. But also don't overeat today. Have dinner a bit on the early side, avoiding caffeine, alcohol and roughage. Eat foods that are normal for you the day before the race.

RACE DAY

If you've carefully prepared during the week, there is little that can go wrong today. Now it's simply a matter of following a procedure or ritual that, hopefully, you've done scores of times before. The day of an A-priority race is not the time to experiment with new pre-race rituals; stick with what you know works.

Race-day rituals are important because they let you operate without making decisions, allowing you to think only about what is important for the coming race. There is a confident, focused and businesslike manner about the successful athlete's prerace ritual from the moment of waking until the race starts. If you don't have a ritual established for race-day waking, eating and traveling, use C-priority races and hard workouts to develop one that exactly fits your needs and personality. This will allow you to prepare calmly and confidently prepare for an important race.

STARTING-LINE STRESS

That your bladder is becoming difficult to control as your body attempts to shed water is one sure sign of the anxiety known as "starting-line stress." This anxiety triggers the ancient "fight or flight" preparation the human body goes through whenever it senses a threat. Only now the threat is not a saber-toothed cat, but rather a race.

The level of arousal you sense at this time can have a beneficial or detrimental effect on your performance. High arousal is beneficial for power movements requiring only gross motor skills, such as at the moment of the start. However, low arousal is helpful for the finesse moves needed on very technical sections of the course. Also, if arousal is too great, energy is wasted and your pacing strategy may fall apart early in the race. Low arousal results in a lethargic and unmotivated performance. Figure 10.1 illustrates the "inverted-U" relationship between arousal and performance, and the indicators of the extremes of arousal.

For most athletes, the greater concern is overly high arousal. Reducing it to optimal levels requires the development of coping skills. The refinement of such skills is one of the reasons for the inexperienced athlete to participate in many C-priority races. Those

The body is preparing to fight or flee.

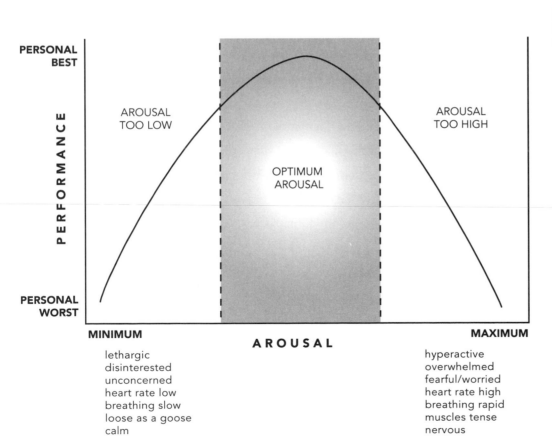

FIGURE 10.1
The relationship between arousal and performance.

who have been around the sport for years will have already mastered them, which is apparent in their "another day at the office" demeanor. Some examples of arousal-lowering skills include:

- Physically slow down your movements and relax muscles by "shaking out" the tension. Breathe slower and use your heart rate monitor as a biofeedback device to slow your pulse.
- Mentally slow down by replacing negative, fearful thoughts with positive ones that emphasize recent successes.
- Allow your body to operate on autopilot throughout the warm-up as your mind dissociates and plays with other stimuli such as music, conversation, hobbies, scenery or anything else that interests you.
- Learn to trust that your training and racing experience will allow you to perform at near maximal ability without undue effort or pain. Know that when the race starts, you'll simply "flip a switch" and race as you always have.
- Mentally separate yourself from thoughts of winning and losing. Race like a child by simply enjoying the challenge and the event.
- Don't be overly concerned with the actions of other racers; you have no control over them. You can only control your effort and skill.
- Forget about race outcomes. Think only about here and now.
- Act as if you were calm. Look at others who appear relaxed and emulate their appearance.
- Pretend this is merely another workout with friends.
- Remind yourself that no matter what happens, only positive things will come from the race. If it's a good performance, you'll be happy with the results. If it's not, you'll learn something from the experience that will make you better next time. The difference between winning and losing is that when you lose, you learn something.

WARM-UP

Warm-up has several benefits for race performance. It increases the flow of fatty acids to the muscles for use as fuel, while simultaneously reducing dependence on your limited stores of carbohydrate-based glycogen. It raises the temperature of the working muscles. The capacity of the body to produce energy rises by 13 percent for every degree Celsius of temperature rise. Heart stroke volume and lung capacity increase with warm-up. The production of lactate is reduced following a warm-up, meaning that you're less likely to go anaerobic at the start. It opens capillaries to allow more oxygen into the muscles. Warm-up sensitizes the nervous system for smoother movements so that you waste less energy at the start of the race. And finally, perceived exertion is lower following warm-up.

Scientific studies have supported the value of warm-up when it duplicates the movements of the sport and doesn't cause undue fatigue. A few studies have even shown that passive warm-up, such as a hot bath or massage, may have some benefit, but not nearly as much as active warm-up.

On race day, start warming up early enough so that you can take care of minor problems that may arise at the last minute, such as the gears not shifting smoothly. For a race of about two hours duration or less, this might mean beginning some 45 to 60 minutes before your start time. For longer races, shorten the warm-up. Most competitors should do little or no warm-up before an ultraendurance event.

Plan warm-up time according to race duration.

Other factors that influence warm-up duration are your fitness level and the weather. The more endurance base you have built up, the longer your warm-up may be. For example, if your longest recent workout is two hours and the race will probably take three hours, a warm-up is not advised. Under such conditions, you would be wise to conserve energy and start slower to allow for warm-up within the race. In cool weather, more warm-up may be needed. In hot weather, decrease the length of the warm-up.

Weather and fitness also determine warm-up duration.

It would be perfect if you could stop the warm-up five minutes or less before the start. This is almost never possible in a mountain bike race, however. Standing around in the start area for 10 minutes or more is more common. There's nothing you can do about this except to stay calm and use the time to rehearse race strategy.

Whatever warm-up procedure you use, practice the various portions of it weekly before your most intense workouts in the Build, Peak and Race periods of your season. It should become so natural that you warm up without even thinking about it. Here is a warm-up routine I suggest for the mountain bikers I coach. It involves dividing the warm-up into two phases.

Suggested warm-up routine.

Phase 1

Phase 1 may take about half the total warm-up period, perhaps 10 to 30 minutes, and can be done on a stationary trainer to keep you close to fluids, clothing, shade, music, friends, family, and anything else that may provide relaxation and comfort before a race. Gradually raise your cadence and effort by bringing your heart rate up to the 1 and 2 zones. In the last few minutes, include a few spin-ups to high cadence to get the legs ready for the second phase.

	TABLE 10.1

Phase 2 suggested warm-up routine

Time	Activity
5 minutes	Ride to a hill, gradually raising the intensity with brief jumps.
6–12 minutes	Climb the hill three to five times for 20 to 30 seconds each with 1.5- to 2-minute recoveries. Stay seated on the first two climbs and stand on the others. Make each effort harder than the previous one.
5 minutes	Ride to the starting area. Keep moving as long as possible.

Phase 2

In Phase 2, the second half of the warm-up, strip off excess clothes, take your bike off the trainer, replace the rear wheel if necessary, and get away from the crowd. This could be done with a teammate or alone. Decide ahead of time which works better for you. Follow the guidelines suggested in Table 10.1.

Phase 2 of the warm-up is a good time to clear your mind of daily concerns and begin concentrating on the task at hand. During the routine, and while standing in the starting chute, review race strategy, technique concerns and process goals, such as staying in tune with your body or maintaining fluid levels. Don't think about how the race could come out or what your results might be. Concerns about how you will do are worse than a waste of time; such thoughts tend to produce negative, or, at best, nonconfident thinking. What you want now is mental focus and positive thought patterns.

STRATEGY

Most riders go into a race without ever thinking about how they intend to perform. They race strictly based on tactics—immediate reactions to the course, what others do and how they feel at the time. While tactics are an important aspect of racing, they should not be based on whim, but rather on a strategy, which is nothing more than a predetermined plan for how to achieve race goals.

Questions to ask in formulating a strategy.

A strategy may have several aspects, but for a mountain bike race, it generally comes down to answering three questions:

- How will I start?
- How will I manage hills and technical sections?
- How will I regulate energy expenditure and intake?

For the advanced racer there is also a strategy decision to be made regarding the competition. Who must you watch? Is there a rider you must stay with throughout the race? Based on experience, who can you let go early on knowing they will fade as the race progresses? What are the strengths and weaknesses of other competitors? While race strategy cannot be entirely based on what others do, it must take them into account if a high placement is to be attained.

In addition, a well-conceived strategy should have contingencies based on likely changes in conditions, such as mud, cold weather, hot weather, and competitors who do or do not show up.

Be prepared to change a strategy at the last minute.

START STRATEGY

In the last five minutes or so before the race begins, review start strategy. This usually has to do with pacing and comes down to two options—race all-out from the gun or hold back to prepare for a race of attrition in which you will slowly work your way through the field. This strategy is determined based on current levels of anaerobic fitness, course characteristics, weather and the competition. Don't wait until the last minute to make this decision. Begin thinking about it in the week leading up to the race and finalize the strategy after previewing the course, seeing the start list and hearing the weather forecast for race day. Then, assuming nothing has changed, stick with your strategy when the race begins. Don't make last minute changes based on what others do. Trust yourself.

Develop and stick with a start strategy.

Course-Management Strategy

Just as with start strategy, course-management strategy is determined by how this race fits into your season goals, the race priority, your limiters, your current level of fitness, and the type of course. With C-priority races, you may want to take some risks by trying a previously untried strategy. For B-priority events, work on refining strategies. A-priority races demand that you employ tried-and-true strategies based on the unique mix of characteristics described above.

Race priority helps to determine course-management strategy.

ENERGY-MANAGEMENT SRATEGY

The longer the race is, the more important it is to determine how to pace yourself, when and what you will eat and drink, and how you will get hand-ups in the feed zone. For A- and B-priority races the solutions should be based on what you know works from previous experience. C-priority events are a good time to experiment.

Pacing strategy is determined by how your recent long and hard workouts have gone. In the race, perceived exertion or RPE (see Chapter 4 for details) is the best indicator of intensity. While you may want to wear a heart rate monitor for later data scruti-

Pacing strategy depends on perceived exertion.

ny, it's unlikely to help you during a typical cross-country mountain bike race. Cross-country requires constant attention to the course, and the terrain changes so frequently that heart rate is often lagging behind what your body is actually experiencing.

The type of fuel you use is an individual matter. Certainly you should carry a sports drink and use it liberally throughout the event. Plan on consuming 16 to 24 ounces of sports drinks every hour. This is all that is really necessary for a race of about two hours. For longer races, gel packets are also convenient since they can be carried in the back pocket and accessed easily. Getting bottles handed up in the feed zone requires making arrangements well before race day with a teammate, friend or family member.

HIGH-ALTITUDE RACES

Cross-country mountain bike races are often held at altitudes above 7500 feet, such as at Big Bear and Mammoth in California, Steamboat Springs in Colorado, and Park City in Utah. For the rider who lives at lower altitudes, this presents a unique challenge. When should you arrive at altitude for the race? Is there any way to prepare for a high altitude race? Should you race differently?

Racing at such altitudes means there is less oxygen getting into the blood for delivery to the muscles than at low altitude. This results in a lowered aerobic capacity (VO_2 max), not only for you, but for everyone else in the race. For each 1000 feet of increase in altitude above 5000 feet there is a 3- to 4-percent drop in VO_2 max. So at 7500 feet, the sea-level rider can expect to see a loss of 7.5 to 10 percent of aerobic function from what is experienced at home. That's a hefty loss. Not only that, but there is an increased production of lactic acid when racing at altitude, which effectively lowers the lactate threshold. All of this means slower race times.

The effects of high altitude result in slower racing.

Such a double whammy can be somewhat lessened if the athlete adapts to the altitude before the race. For example, moving to the race venue for three to four weeks before the race enables the body to produce more erythropoietin (EPO), resulting in increased red blood cell volumn and boosting VO_2 max. The downside here, besides the obvious financial cost of such a stay, is that training at altitude causes some loss of muscular fitness—you just can't train as hard at altitude. It's possible, however, that by moving to someplace where you can sleep at night above 7000 feet and then go down to 5000 feet or lower to ride, you can have the best of both worlds. Such a training camp is possible in places like Albuquerque, New Mexico; Flagstaff, Arizona; and Salt Lake City, Utah. But again, that's not very practical.

Another unlikely solution is to buy a Gamow (*gam-off*) hypobaric chamber for several thousand dollars and sleep in it nightly. This boosts EPO just like living in the Rocky Mountains. Even less likely is the conversion of your home into a high-altitude house, as the Finnish cross-country skiers did successfully before the 1998 Winter Olympics.

Cycling is already expensive enough, so let's look at some less costly solutions involving training, diet, ergogenic aids and, especially, travel plans.

TRAINING

Going someplace to ride that has high elevations, such as a nearby mountain, won't do you any good. Riding at high altitudes is not what you want to do to physically prepare. You'll simply ride slower and get less fitness from it. You may even lose fitness from riding slower. The only benefit of such excursions is to get a sense of what racing at high altitude will feel like. One or two such trips are all that's necessary for this, however.

The best you can hope to accomplish in the last three to four weeks before an A-priority race at high altitude is to boost your aerobic capacity and lactate threshold to the highest possible levels. This will improve your hematocrit—the number of cells, especially red blood cells, in the blood—and your ability to tolerate and process the higher levels of lactate expected in the race due to the altitude. The best way to accomplish such fitness upswings in a short time is with anaerobic endurance intervals as described in Appendix B. Doing these once or twice a week with at least 48 hours between sessions will peak your anaerobic fitness within six to 10 weeks.

How to train for high altitude races.

Diet

At high altitudes, your body may use more carbohydrate-derived glycogen to power the muscles, while sparing fat. This makes your limited glycogen stores extremely important for the race, so it's a good idea to carbohydrate-load the last three days before the event. It also means that you need to keep the carbohydrates coming in throughout the race, as the bonk will occur sooner than at sea level.

Keep the carbohydrates coming in during the race.

The other challenge you need to prepare for is dehydration. The air is drier at high altitude, so you're more likely to lose body fluids, making your blood into a thick sludge that slows you down. Starting the day before the race, increase your fluid intake. If you're sleeping at altitude, place a bottle of water by your bed and sip from it every time you wake up during the night.

Stay well hydrated before the race.

Supplementation with 400 milligrams of vitamin E daily for 10 weeks has been shown in research to preserve VO_2 max in high-altitude mountain climbers. In another study, 1200 IU of vitamin E every day caused athletes to maintain a higher percentage of their VO_2 max at altitude compared with subjects who took a placebo. If you've never taken such large doses of vitamin E, it's a good idea to talk with your doctor before starting. Certain conditions and medications when combined with vitamin E may cause health complications. Chapter 16 offers more information on vitamin E supplementation.

Vitamin E may help maintain VO2 max.

Ergogenic Aids

There is no research to support this, but loading with sodium phosphate may help when racing at high altitude. This substance has been repeatedly shown in research to boost VO_2 max and reduce lactate levels in the blood, but I'm not aware of any such studies at high altitude.

Sodium phosphate may help.

Sodium phosphate is discussed in greater detail in Chapter 16. Read that section before trying it, as there are some potential complications.

Travel Plans

The timing of your arrival at altitude may have the greatest single effect on how well you subsequently race. About 15 percent of those who come to a higher altitude suffer from altitude sickness, with flu-like symptoms such as headache, nausea, loss of appetite and lethargy. These symptoms often show up after about 24 to 48 hours of exposure to the thin air. Also common at high altitudes is a loss of sleep due to frequent waking. And VO_2 max declines are most likely to occur after a day or so of being at high altitude.

When you arrive is the single most important aspect of high altitude racing.

This means that there is a small window of opportunity to race without feeling drained. So the trick in going to altitude is to time it so that you arrive the day before the race, if possible. While this limits your opportunity to check out the course, you may nevertheless race better. The worst time to arrive is between 48 hours and up to 10 days prior to the race, as that's when the nausea, headaches, lethargy and changing blood chemistry are likely to be the worst.

If you must arrive two or more days before the race, arrange to stay in a hotel at a lower altitude and drive up on race day. This may allow you to avoid some of the negative consequences of being in the thin air for too long.

Preparing for a high-altitude race requires some planning to make sure that training, diet, ergogenic aids and travel all merge properly, allowing you to produce a peak performance despite the obstacles.

REFERENCES

Anderson, O. "Things Your Parents Forgot To Tell You About Tapering." *Running Research News* 11, no. 7 (1995): 1–8.

Astrand, P. O. and K. Rohdahl. *Textbook of Work Physiology.* New York: McGraw-Hill, 1977.

Banister, E. W., et al. "Training Theory and Taper: Validation in Triathlon Athletes." *European Journal of Applied Physiology* 79, no. 2 (1999): 182–191.

Bonen, A. and A. Belcastro. "Comparison of Self-Selected Recovery Methods on Lactic Acid Removal Rates." *Medicine and Science in Sports and Exercise* 8 (1976): 176–178.

deVries, H. A. "Effects of Various Warm-Up Procedures on 100-Yard Times of Competitive Swimmers." *Research Quarterly* 30 (1959): 11–20.

Dimsdale, J. et al. "Postexercise Peril: Plasma Catecholamines and Exercise." *Journal of the American Medical Association* 251 (1984): 630–632.

Hemmert, M. K., et al. "Effect of Plasma Volume on Exercise Stroke Volume in Normally Active and Endurance-Trained Men." Paper presented at the American College of Sports Medicine annual meeting, 1985.

Hermiston, R. T. and M.E. O'Brien. "The Effects of Three Types of Warm-Up on the Total Oxygen Cost of A Short Treadmill Run." In A.W. Taylor (ed.), *Training: Scientific Basis and Application.* Springfield, IL: Charles C. Thomas, 1972.

Houmard, J., et al. "The Effect of Warm-Up on Responses to Intense Exercise." *International Journal of Sports Medicine* 12, no. 5 (1991): 400–403.

Houmard, J. A. "Impact of Reduced Training on Performance in Endurance Athletes." *Sports Medicine* 12, no. 6 (1991): 380–393.

Houmard, J., et al. "The Effects of Taper on Performance in Distance Runners." *Medicine and Science in Sports and Exercise* 26, no. 5 (1994): 624–631.

Houmard, J. A. and R. A. Johns. "Effects of Taper on Swim Performance. Practical Applications." *Sports Medicine* 17, no. 4 (1994): 224–232.

Ingjer F, Myhre K. "Physiological Effects of Altitude Training on Elite Male Cross-Country Skiers." *Journal of Sports Science* 10, no. 1 (1992): 37–47.

Karvonen, J. "Importance of Warm-Up and Cool Down on Exercise Performance." In J. Karvonen (ed.), *Medicine in Sports Training and Coaching.* Dasel, Germany: Karger, 1992.

Kreider, R. B., et al. "Effects of Phosphate Loading on Oxygen Uptake, Ventilatory Anaerobic Threshold, and Run Performance." *Medicine and Science in Sports and*

Exercise 22, no. 2 (1990): 250–256.

Levine, B., and D. Stray-Gundersen J. "A Practical Approach to Altitude Training: Where to Live and Train for Optimal Performance Enhancement." .*International Journal of Sports Medicine* 13 (S1) (1992): S209–212.

McArdle, W. D., F. Katch and V. Katch. *Exercise Physiology.* Baltimore, MD: Williams & Wilkins, 1996.

Neary, J. P., et al. "The Effects of a Reduced Exercise Duration Taper Program on Performance and Muscle Enzymes of Endurance Cyclists." *European Journal of Applied Physiology* 65, no. 1 (1992): 30–36.

Rushall, B. *Psyching in Sport. The Psychological Preparation for Serious Competition in Sport.* London: Pelham Books, 1979.

Shepley, B., et al. "Physiological Effects of Tapering in Highly Trained Athletes." *Journal of Applied Physiology* 72, no. 2 (1992): 706–711.

Simon-Schnass I and H. Pabst. "Influence of Vitamin E on Physical Performance." *International Journal of Vitamin and Nutritional Research* 58, no. 1 (1988): 49–54.

Stine, T. A., et al. "Quantification of Altitude Training in the Field." *Medicine and Science in Sports and Exercise* 24 (S5) (1992): S103.

Velikorodnih, Y., et al. "The Marathon (Pre-Competitive Preparation)." *Soviet Sport Review* 22, no. 3 (1986): 125–128.

Zarkadas, P. C., et al. "Modeling the Effects of Taper on Performance, Maximal Oxygen Uptake, and the Anaerobic Threshold in Endurance Triathletes." *Advanced Experiments in Medical Biology* 393 (1995): 179–186.

RECOVERY

You've got to rest as hard as you train.

—ROGER YOUNG

The need for the body's cells to restore themselves is grossly underrated by some athletes who believe they have discovered a training secret based on minimal or no recovery. Such a strategy is doomed to failure. Fatigue, which is a natural result of a hard workout, is the body's way of saying that rest is needed. Ignoring this message only increases the burden of fatigue. It soon becomes chronic, and if still ignored, inevitably leads to overtraining or illness, which interrupt training consistency and produce a loss of fitness.

As strange as it may seem, there are athletes who believe that fatigue is the reason for training. They have come to view this natural side effect of hard work as a marker of improved fitness. Short-term increases in fatigue are normal as the volume or intensity of training rises, but it must be unloaded frequently to maintain fitness growth. Failure to do so is a training mistake.

Chronic fatigue is a training mistake.

For serious competitors who train with a relatively high workload, the focus of training should be as much on recovery as on working out. Speeding up the recovery process means that more high-quality workouts are possible in a given number of days. Quick recovery from fatigue is the key to excellent fitness. To those who master this concept, who moderate motivation with patience, and who balance intensity with intelligence, go the medals.

This chapter examines two subjects related to recovery. The first is what happens when we deny the body the opportunity to recover. The second involves methods that reduce the time needed for recovery. For the rider who inevitably winds up overtrained, sick or injured every season, this may be the most important chapter in the book.

RECOVERY-RELATED PROBLEMS

The setbacks riders experience in training are often of their own making. Among highly motivated athletes with overly aggressive training programs, desire to excel may be exceeded only by inability to listen to their bodies. The result is often overtraining, illness or injury.

OVERTRAINING

Overtraining is a decreased capacity for work that slowly develops from an imbalance between stress and rest. The overtrained athlete experiences declining performance and a nagging exhaustion that no longer responds to a few days of rest. These are the best indicators of overtraining, or what is sometimes called "staleness." When faced with the onset of this condition, serious athletes are as likely to train harder as to take time off. That is how they've always dealt with fitness declines. They may put in more miles, or do more intervals, or both. It's a rare athlete who rests more when things aren't going well.

Overtraining is marked by poor performance and exhaustion.

Of course, poor performance and exhaustion don't only result from too much training. The cause may not be overtraining, but rather "overliving," in which the stress of training is magnified by a lifestyle in which we try to accomplish too much in too little time. A 50-hour-per-week job, two kids to raise, a home to maintain and other responsibilities all take their toll on physical and psychological energy. Combine this with a high training workload and the result is often the kind of decreased performance and chronic exhaustion that overtraining causes.

When an athlete is faced with this dilemma, training is the stress that must be reduced, no matter how low the athlete thinks his or her workload is. Calling the boss to ask for the day off is probably not an option. Nor can the kids be told to get themselves to the soccer game. The grass still needs to be cut and the house painted. At such times, the only option is to train less and rest more.

"Overliving" may also contribute to an overtrained state.

Figure 11.1 shows the consequences of denying recovery despite an ever-increasing workload on the bike. Notice that constant increases in the training load produce fitness improvement—for a while. At some critical level of training, fitness declines despite an increasing workload. Training beyond your current workload capacity results in a loss of fitness. Notice that the previous sentence says "current." The workload that produces overtraining is a moving target determined by one's present level of fitness and lifestyle stress.

Overtraining that results strictly from riding-related stress and not from lifestyle stress is produced by one or more of three common training excesses: 1) workouts are too long (excess duration); 2) exertion is too high too often (excess intensity); and 3) too

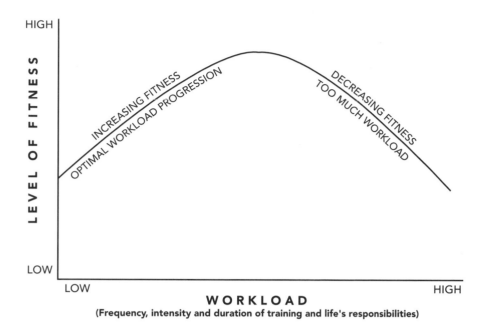

FIGURE 11.1
The overtraining curve.

many workouts are done in too little time (excess frequency). Probably the most common cause in competitive athletes is excess intensity. Either the rider starts anaerobic endurance training too soon in the season and tries to keep it going for several months, or spaces the hard workouts too close together. Depending on the duration, cross-country events are about 90-percent aerobic and 10-percent anaerobic. That's roughly the same mix necessary for optimal training. An excessive emphasis on anaerobic effort week after week without adequate recovery ultimately leads to overtraining.

Excessive intensity is the most common cause of overtraining.

Overtraining Indicators

When overtraining is imminent, the body issues warnings. Table 11.1, "Overtraining Indicators," lists the most common ones. The markers of overtraining are not the same for all athletes, nor are they consistent for any given athlete. Furthermore, any single indicator, such as an elevated heart rate, is not a reliable predictor of overtraining when taken by itself. Some unique mix of several indicators is almost always present in the overtrained athlete.

Overtraining is the body's fail-safe system.

Many elite athletes have blood chemistry testing done in the Preparation or early Base periods of training. This establishes a healthy baseline for later comparison, should training go awry. When they aren't responding normally to training during other periods of the season, they have blood drawn and tested again to see if there are significant differences, such as changes in serum iron (a common cause of lagging power and endurance). Blood testing may also help to rule out health-related causes of poor performance, such as infectious mononucleosis. Your doctor will interpret the meaning of blood test results.

Blood testing may confirm a health-related nutritional cause for overtraining.

Such testing may help serious mountain bike racers of all abilities determine the

	TABLE 11.1

Overtraining indicators.

Physical	**Behavioral**
Reduced performance	Apathy
Constant fatigue	Lethargy
Weight change	Depression
Increased thirst	Poor concentration
Morning heart rate change	Changes in sleep pattern
Muscle soreness	Irritability
Swollen lymph glands	Decreased libido
Diarrhea	Clumsiness
Injury	Sluggishness
Infection	Craving for sugar
Amenorrhea	
Decreased exercise heart rate	
Slow healing of cuts	

cause of poor performance, and perhaps even a cause, such as poor nutrition. But regardless of the cause, if the condition is suspected to be overtraining, the first stage of treatment is rest.

None of the items listed in Table 11.1, or even those deduced from blood testing, is a certain indicator of overtraining. Unusual blood parameters may exist in perfectly healthy athletes who are in top shape and obviously not experiencing any decrement in performance. In dealing with overtraining, there are no absolutes. You're looking for a preponderance of evidence to confirm what you already suspect.

Stages of Overtraining

To become overtrained, you must pass through three overlapping and indistinct stages. The first stage is "overload," a normal part of the process of increasing the training workload in order to cause adaptation. If the load is appropriate, it results in over-compensation, as described in Chapter 3. It's typical to have short-term fatigue when experiencing overload. At this stage, fatigue easily decreases with 48 to 72 hours of rest, depending on the individual. But it's also common during this stage to feel you are invincible. That feeling often leads to the next stage.

In "overreaching," the second stage of progressing toward overtraining, the workload

Overloading the body is a normal part of training.

may rise slightly for a period of two weeks or more. Extending the Build period without a rest week is another common cause of overreaching. After two or more weeks of this, performance begins to decline. This may be apparent only in workouts at this time, as high motivation often maintains race performance. Fatigue lasts longer than in the overload stage, but with a few consecutive days of rest it is still reversible. What often happens, however, is that the athlete decides to increase the workload or continue without a rest break in order to improve what appears to be lagging performance. This brings on the third stage.

Overreaching is necessary, but risky.

The third and final stage is a full-blown overtraining syndrome. Fatigue is now chronic. You wake up tired and remain so all day, and yet have trouble sleeping normally at night. Your body is exhausted. Neither decreased training nor even a few days of rest make any difference. You're overtrained.

Overtraining is marked by exhaustion that does not go away with a few days of rest.

The Geography of Overtraining

The challenge for the serious rider is that the trip to the "peak of fitness" passes through the "valley of fatigue" and dangerously close to the "edge of overtraining." Figure 11.2 shows how excessively increasing the training load causes a decline in fitness as marked by performance, pushing you to the edge.

The idea is to go the edge infrequently, once every four weeks or so, and then rest. Since it takes about three weeks of increasing the training workload to overtrain, you need to allow for recovery after no more than 21 days. Riders of about age 40 or older and novices may need to recover more frequently, perhaps after only two weeks of training increases. To go beyond occasional overreaching is to fall over the edge and start the downward spiral to overtraining.

Go to the edge cautiously and then recover.

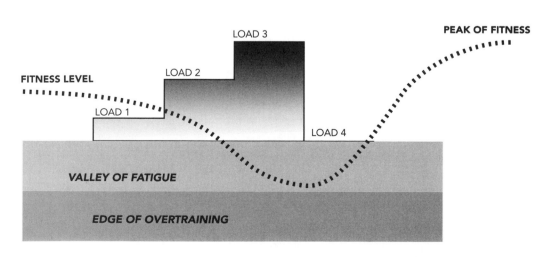

FITNESS LEVEL

LOAD 1

LOAD 2

LOAD 3

LOAD 4

PEAK OF FITNESS

VALLEY OF FATIGUE

EDGE OF OVERTRAINING

FIGURE 11.2
Valley of Fatigue

When you enter the valley of fatigue, overtraining indicators appear. You will continually experience excessive fatigue and perhaps poor sleep quality, as well as muscle soreness or other markers in Table 11.1. The athlete who has just gone over the edge is often confused about what is wrong, since the overtraining indicators may be few in number and not very severe. When you suspect even a hint of overtraining, there is but one course of action to take—rest. Take 48 hours of complete rest—meaning no training of any sort—and then try a short recovery workout in the heart rate 1 zone or less than half the power zone CP12. If still fatigued, take another 48 hours off and repeat the easy workout. It could take five to eight weeks of this to recover fully from overtraining. All the while, a great deal of fitness is lost.

Recovering from overtraining requires extended rest.

The Art of Training

The art of training is knowing where the edge of overtraining is for you. This can only be determined by cautious experience. Highly motivated riders are unlikely to realize when they have gone over the edge until it's too late. That's one reason why serious athletes are advised to train under a coach's supervision.

The art of training depends on regular and frequent assessment of the body's capacity for work. Chapter 15 provides a training diary format to help you do this, with suggested daily indicators to rate. There may be other indicator you have discovered that work better for you. If so, watch them daily. Carefully monitoring such indicators will help you pay close attention to your body's daily signals about its status. By paying close attention you will become good at safely overreaching and going to the edge but not over it.

Listen to your body.

There is no certain way of knowing when you've overreached too much and need to back off. What causes overtraining at one time of the season may not at another. Frequent recovery and constant status monitoring is the best prevention. If you make a mistake, make it on the side of doing too little training. It's much better to be undertrained than overtrained. When in doubt—leave it out.

ILLNESS

The athlete who trains at a high level is a prime candidate for an upper respiratory infection. As the workload increases, so does the risk of catching a cold or the flu. A few years ago a study of entrants in the Los Angeles Marathon found that those who ran more than 60 miles per week had twice as many illnesses as those who ran less than 20 miles weekly. Runners who completed the marathon were six times as likely to be ill in the week following the race as those who trained hard for the race but for some reason did not run it.

High-volume training is associated with illness.

The Critical Time

The six hours following a high-intensity or very long workout or race is a critical phase for remaining healthy. During this brief window of time, the immune system is depressed and less capable of fighting off disease. This six-hour period is a good time to avoid people and public places if at all possible. Washing your hands frequently after having contact with others or with public facilities during this time is also a good idea for staying healthy. Develop the habit of touching your face only with your left hand and touching objects, such as doors and telephones, with your right. Take extra care of yourself at this time. Some athletes have even been known to wear a surgical mask when around others following races.

Be cautious for the six hours after a race.

Neck Check

What should you do when, after all these precautions, you feel a cold coming on—continue riding as normal, reduce training, or simply rest? A "neck check" will help you decide. If you have above-the-neck symptoms, such as a runny nose or a scratchy throat, start your workout, but reduce the intensity to low levels and keep the duration shorter than usual. You may begin to feel better once warmed up, but if you feel worse after the first few minutes, stop. If the symptoms are below the neck, such as chest congestion, chills, coughing up matter, achy muscles or a fever, don't even start the workout. These are symptoms of a flu virus. Exercising with such a condition will make it worse.

Don't train with symptoms below the neck.

Recuperating

Even after full health has apparently returned, you're likely to experience a decrease in performance for some time. How long depends on the type and severity of the illness. One study found a 15-percent reduction in muscle strength that lasted up to a month following a viral infection. Other negative effects may linger. Aerobic capacity may need up to three months to return to previous levels. During this time, muscles may produce more lactic acid at lower levels of intensity than before the illness. Even though the acute stage is past, you may feel weak for some time. So it's probably wise, following a below-the-neck illness, to return to the Base period of training for two days for every day you had symptoms. That means an emphasis on re-establishing endurance, force, speed skill, and muscular endurance, while avoiding anaerobic endurance training. Limited power work may also be included.

Return to Base training following a serious illness.

Training with the flu will not bring an improvement in fitness. It will only make the condition worse and delay the return of health and normal training. Complete rest is needed. Try to get rid of the bug as soon as possible by allowing your body's limited energy reserves to fight the disease, rather than forcing it to deal with the stresses of training.

OVERUSE INJURIES

The most likely cause of an injury in mountain biking is a crash. These can be devastating and must be avoided by developing handling skills and always riding within one's limits. Overuse injuries in cycling are also common, but not as likely as in a sport such as running.

The knee is often injured in cycling.

The most common overuse injuries for cyclists are to the knee, especially patella tracking problems and iliotibial band inflammations. When pain initially appears in the knee from one of these, it is seldom intense enough to interrupt training. Most riders notice that the knee doesn't feel right and continue training as normal. After a few days the pain increases to the point that the pedal stroke is slightly modified to protect the joint. At this point it is usually obvious that there is a problem and something must be done.

There are four courses of action to take simultaneously at this time.

Treatment

If the pain doesn't subside within a few days, see your doctor.

The first is to see your family doctor, or, better yet, a sports medicine doctor. Don't delay, as injuries are easier to mend in the early stages than when they become chronic. The doctor will probably prescribe an over-the-counter nonsteroidal, anti-inflammatory drug, such as aspirin, ibuprofen or naproxen, to get the inflammation under control. Or he or she may write a prescription for a drug. If the pain continues and the injury is to a tendon, the doctor is likely to suggest a cortisone injection. Before going that route, however, you might ask about a treatment called *iontophoresis*, a noninvasive method that I've found to be quite effective. This treatment will probably require going to an orthopedic or sports medicine clinic. Family doctors are unlikely to have the equipment.

Rest

Rest the injured area.

The second course of action you must take is to cut back on training until the injury is gone. As medical treatments begin, it's best to rest the injured area. This probably means no riding for a few days to give the treatment a good chance to reduce the inflammation. While rest is the least desirable medicine for serious riders to take, it is also the strongest. Continuing to ride may keep the injured area sore and prolong the healing process. Ask for your doctor's advice on complete rest at this initial stage of treatment. If he or she is unsure, take the more conservative route by taking a few days off the bike.

During this time, stay active in ways that don't aggravate the injury. Swimming and some exercise machines may be good choices and will maintain your cardiovascular fitness. So long as the activity doesn't irritate the injured area, you can exercise quite intensely.

Eliminate Mechanical Causes

While medical treatment and rest of the injured area is proceeding, you must determine what caused it and eliminate that cause so the injury doesn't return when training resumes. Overuse injuries in cycling commonly occur because the bike is setup incorrectly, or not enough time was allowed for a gradual change to a new position, such as a lower saddle. Have your position checked by a knowledgeable rider, bike shop or coach. Make sure that your road and mountain bikes are set up similarly.

Determine and eliminate the cause of the injury.

In some cases, injury may result from riding a bike that just doesn't fit. Women are especially prone to this cause, as they often ride bikes designed for men's body proportions. For riders shorter than about 63 inches (160 cm) or taller than 74 inches (188 cm), or who have arms or legs disproportionately long or short for their height, a custom bike may be necessary.

There may also be biomechanical causes of an injury. In some riders, an injury, especially to the knee, may develop from having an unstable foot. Orthotics may correct such a cause. These are shoe inserts made by a podiatrist that support the foot so pedaling forces are properly directed. In other athletes, a leg-length discrepancy may lead to injury. It's not unusual for the legs to be of slightly different lengths, but the knee or hip may not tolerate an extreme difference. To get a rough idea of how close your legs are to the same length, try this. Sit on a level floor with your back against a wall and knees bent so that your feet are near your butt. Then place a carpenter's level across the tops of your knees. If the bubble stays centered, your legs are the same length. If the bubble moves well to the right or left, you probably have one leg much shorter than the other and should have this checked out. Cleat shims or cleat repositioning may be necessary to correct this problem.

Improve Strength and Flexibility

It's also possible that the injury is due to a lack of strength or flexibility. If you have not been doing resistance work or stretching, begin developing sound muscle tone and range of motion in the recently injured area *once the injury is healed*. Be aware that strength or stretching movements may worsen an injury if done before healing is complete. Also, excessive strength development or stretching itself is sometimes the cause of injury. Know

Strength and flexibility may help in preventing a recurrence.

what you are doing before you start and maintain a moderate approach in both these areas.

RECOVERY TIMING AND METHODS

Intense exercise damages muscle cells.

Muscle damage following a hard workout or race can be extreme, with cell walls torn and fluids leaking. The session has also depleted the muscles and liver of glycogen. Before normal training proceeds, these conditions must be resolved.

Quick recovery is advantageous to building fitness.

How long it takes to repair the damage and restock glycogen stores determines how great your workload is. Athletes who recover slowly are forced to space breakthrough workouts far apart, while those who recover quickly may space them closely. The rate of recovery is an individual matter affected by such variables as age, experience, fitness level, nutrition and psychological stress.

How long does it take to recover? One university study using young, well-trained weight lifters found that the average recovery time from a maximal exertion strength-training session was 36 hours. Researchers found that it took this much time for protein synthesis to repair the damaged muscle cells. A similar study using untrained subjects in weight lifting found that 48 hours was not quite enough time for muscle-damage repair to be complete. Now weight lifting is not mountain bike riding, but the results are probably not too far off what may be expected in our sport.

RECOVERY PHASES

What can you do to speed up the recovery process so that more workouts can be done in a short time span? To answer that question, let's look at the recovery process as three distinct phases relative to the workout or race—before and during, immediately following, and long-term. By manipulating the factors that are key to rejuvenation during each phase, it is possible to increase your rate of recovery.

Recovery Before and During

Warm-up speeds recovery.

Recovery actually starts before the workout or race, not after. The warm-up is one of the keys to a speedy return to form. A good warm-up, as described in Chapter 10, before the start of intense training or a race helps limit damage early in the session by:

- Thinning body fluids to allow easier muscle contractions
- Opening capillaries to bring more oxygen to muscles
- Raising muscle temperature so that contractions take less effort
- Conserving carbohydrate and releasing fat for fuel

What you do during the session or race, especially what you eat and drink, also determines how quickly the body comes back afterward. Recall that another part of recovery besides muscle damage repair is glycogen replenishment. If these fuel stores are allowed to become extremely low, it will take longer to restock them afterward. For a workout or race of less than about three hours, all that's needed to accomplish this is a good sports drink. Gels and water may also be used, but solid food is not necessary for a session of this duration.

Refueling during workouts speeds recovery.

Take in 18 to 24 ounces of a sports drink every hour during periods of high exertion. There are individual differences in how well carbohydrate drinks are tolerated and emptied from the stomach. Some riders, for example, don't tolerate fructose well, often experiencing upset stomachs or even cramping. Many sports drinks contain fructose. Find a sports drink that tastes good and doesn't cause you any problems when you are working intensely. It may take some experimentation to discover the one right one for you.

Before a race, have plenty of what works for you on your bike, and have bottles prepared for hand-ups at feed zones. It's best if the bottles in the feed zone are kept chilled. Be careful not to make a drink more concentrated than on the label recommends unless you've tried it that way and know it works for you. High concentrations of sugar may cause you to dehydrate during a race as body fluids are shunted to the gut to digest it. Races and workouts that take longer than one hour will benefit from a sports drink. In sessions lasting longer than about three hours, solid food is also recommended. Sports bars are a good choice. Again, avoid using fruit during rides unless you know it works well for you.

Recovery after the race or workout continues with a brief cool-down. The cool-down should be an easy effort of only a few minutes. When breathing has returned to a normal resting rate, it is time to stop the cool-down. Long cool-downs have been shown to delay recovery by further depleting glycogen stores. All you really want to accomplish at this time is to gradually return the body's systems to their resting levels. With a few minutes of easy spinning, lactate is cleared from the blood, heart rate drops, and energy production shifts toward dependence on fat instead of glycogen.

Recovery Immediately Following

Upon finishing, the most important thing you can do to speed recovery is to start replenishing fuel stores. Besides burning glycogen, a very hard session also expends some protein. This must be replaced or the body may break down tissue in little-used muscle to get what is needed.

Protein is also beneficial in another way at this time. One study shows that combining protein with carbohydrate after hard training causes the carbohydrate to be absorbed

Use a carbohydrate-protein drink immediately following a race or hard workout.

40 percent faster than carbohydrate alone. So combining carbohydrate and protein will speed recovery because immediately after intense exertion, your body is several times more capable of absorbing these nutrients than at any other time. Waiting to take in food at a later time may greatly detract from how quickly you spring back.

Most athletes find that post-ride recovery food is best taken in fluid rather than solid form. Liquids are easier on the stomach and also help to replace low fluid levels. It's best to use something other than the same sports drink used during the ride, which is rather weak in carbohydrate concentration and doesn't include protein. There are several commercial products available to meet this need. As long as you like the taste and, depending on your size, can get about 15 to 20 grams of protein and 80 grams or so of carbohydrate from one of them, it will meet your recovery needs. Dr. Owen Anderson in *Running Research News* suggests making a recovery "home-brew" by adding five tablespoons of table sugar to 16 ounces of skim milk. The sugar provides the carbohydrate and the milk furnishes the type of protein needed by the body. Use skim milk, as it is low in fat, which has been shown to slow absorption.

Down the recovery drink within 30 minutes of finishing.

It may be best not to use a high–glycemic index carbohydrate, such as a sugary drink without also including protein (see Chapter 16 for the glycemic index). Some scientists believe this may reduce the body's release of growth hormone, further slowing the recovery process. Whatever you use, try to drink all of it within the first 30 minutes after finishing.

Long-Term Recovery

Long-term recovery goes well beyond merely resting. You can speed it up considerably by taking the right course of action during a critical window of opportunity lasting six to nine hours after a breakthrough workout or race. During this time, actively seeking recovery by using one or more recovery-enhancing methods will have you ready to go again quickly. The most effective is sleep, since growth hormone is released in pulses from the pituitary gland at the base of the brain starting about 30 minutes into slumber. Growth hormone stimulates protein synthesis for the rebuilding of tissues damaged by training and promotes the use of fat as fuel. In addition to a 30- to 60-minute nap, seven to nine hours of sleep are needed that night.

Sleep provides the best form of recovery.

Other recovery methods are unique to each individual. Experiment with several to find the ones that work best for you. The accompanying sidebar, "Recovery Methods," offers several suggestions. By employing some of the specific methods described here, you can accelerate the recovery process and return to action sooner. Figure 11.3 illustrates how this happens.

Recovery methods

Engaging in certain activities following a race or hard workout may enhance recovery. Most of the methods listed below speed recovery by slightly increasing the heart rate, increasing blood flow to the muscles, accelerating the inflow of nutrients, reducing soreness, lowering blood pressure, and relaxing the nervous system. Experiment to find which work best for you.

Hot Shower or Bath

Immediately following the cool-down and recovery drink, take a hot shower or bath for 10 to 15 minutes. Do not linger, especially in the bathtub, as you will dehydrate even more.

Active Recovery

For the experienced athlete, one of the best recovery methods is to pedal easily for 15 to 30 minutes several hours after the workout and before going to bed. The intensity should be extremely light, with heart rate well below the 1 zone. Light exercise in water is also effective. If you're at a race, swim or merely paddle about in the hotel pool for several minutes late in the day before retiring. Novice riders are better off resting.

Massage

Other than sleep, most riders find a massage by a professional massage therapist is the most effective recovery method. A post-race massage should employ long, flushing strokes to speed the removal of the waste products of exercise. Deep massage at this time may increase muscle trauma. After about 36 hours, the therapist may apply greater point pressure, working more deeply.

Due to the expense of massage, some athletes prefer self-massage. Following a hot bath or shower, stroke the muscles for 20 to 30 minutes, working away from the extremities and toward the heart.

Sauna

Several hours following a workout or race, you may find that a dry sauna speeds recovery. Do not use a steam room, as it will have the opposite effect. Stay in the sauna for no more than 10 minutes, drinking fluids while there.

Relax and Stretch

Kick back and be lazy for several hours. Your body wants quality rest. Stay off your feet whenever possible. Never stand when you can lean against something. Sit down whenever possible. Better yet, lay on the floor with your feet elevated against a wall or furniture. Sit on the floor and stretch gently. Overused muscles tighten and can't seem to relax on their own. This is best right after a hot bath or sauna and just before going to bed.

Walk in a Park or Forest

A few hours after finishing the workout or race, a short, slow walk in a heavily vegetated area such as a park or forest seems to speed recovery for some. Abundant oxygen and the aroma of grass, trees and other plants are soothing.

Other Methods

The sports program of the former Soviet Union made a science of recovery and employed several methods with their athletes that may or may not be available to you. Many are also unproven in the scientific literature. They included electromuscular stimulation, ultrasound, barometric chambers, sport psychology, and pharmacological supplements including vitamins, minerals, and adaptogens such as ginseng. These require expert guidance.

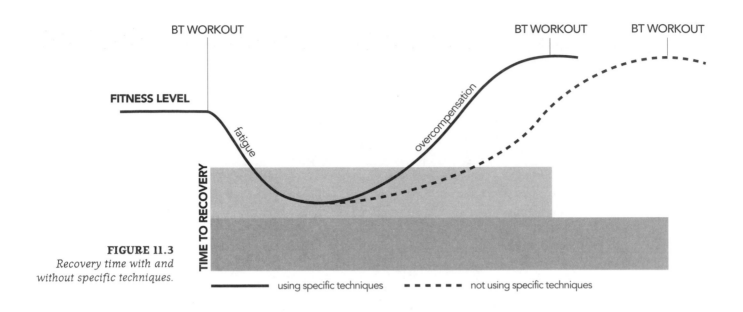

BT WORKOUT   BT WORKOUT   BT WORKOUT

FITNESS LEVEL

fatigue

overcompensation

TIME TO RECOVERY

——— using specific techniques   - - - - - not using specific techniques

FIGURE 11.3
*Recovery time with and
without specific techniques.*

INDIVIDUALIZATION OF RECOVERY

The rate at which athletes recover from hard training sessions varies considerably. Different recovery methods are most effective for individual athletes based on age, experience, gender, current level of fitness, climate, diet and psychological stress. It's even likely that the body will respond in a different way following various types of workouts. All of this has to do with the principle of individualization discussed in Chapter 3. While there are many physiological similarities between athletes, each is unique and responds in his or her own way to any given set of circumstances. Experimentation will help you discover the best recovery methods for you.

**Optimal recovery
techniques vary with
the individual.**

What signs indicate that recovery is progressing well? The best is performance in races and hard workouts, but this is often too late. It's far better to have a handle on how recovery is progressing on a daily basis. Good indicators are a positive attitude, feelings of health, a desire to train intensely again, high-quality sleep, normal resting and exercising heart rates and balanced emotions. If any of these are lacking, continue the recovery process and be careful with stress of any sort. Monitoring these signs should help you determine not only the best methods, but also the time required to recover from different types of workouts and races.

Look for signs of recovery.

RECOVERY IN THE REAL WORLD

Utilizing a periodization program as suggested in Part IV will often result in weeks when you experience an increasing load of fatigue. Despite doing everything possible to relieve this fatigue, you will still go into some hard workouts feeling a bit leg-weary and lacking power. This is normal, and, in fact, may boost fitness due to something called "supercompensation"—an increased level of overcompensation, which was described earlier. But this should not occur more often than about every third or fourth week. How much lingering fatigue is tolerated depends on your ability to avoid overtraining, illness and injury. As always, if you are unsure what to do, do less. A rest and recovery week should immediately follow a period in which fatigue played a major role in training.

Be careful with the "creative" use of fatigue.

REFERENCES

Baker, A. *Bicycling Medicine*. San Diego, CA: Argo Publishing, 1995.

Bompa, T. *Theory and Methodology of Training*. Dubuque, IA: Kendall/Hunt, 1994.

Bonen, A., et al. "Mild Exercise Impedes Glycogen Repletion in Muscle." *Journal of Applied Physiology* 58, no. 5 (1985): 1622–1629.

Brenner, I.K.M. "Infection in Athletes." *Sports Medicine* 17, no. 2 (1994): 86–107.

Brunner, R. and B. Tabachnik. *Soviet Training and Recovery Methods*. Sport Focus Publishing, 1990.

Burke, L.M., et al. "Muscle Glycogen Storage After Prolonged Exercise: Effect of the Glycemic Index of Carbohydrate Feedings." *Journal of Applied Physiology* 75, no. 2 (1993): 1019–1023.

Cade, J.R., et al. "Dietary Intervention and Training in Swimmers." *European Journal of Applied Physiology* 63 (1991): 210–215.

David, A.S., et al. "Post-Viral Fatigue Syndrome: Time For a New Approach." *British Medical Journal* 296 (1988): 696–699.

Dragan, I. and I. Stonescu. *Organism recovery following training*. Bucharest: Sport-Turism, 1978.

Driver, H.S., et al. "Prolonged Endurance Exercise and Sleep Disruption." *Medicine and Science in Sports and Exercise* 26, no. 7 (1994): 903–907.

Fallowfield, J.L. and C. Williams. "Carbohydrate Intake and Recovery From Prolonged Exercise." *International Journal of Sport Nutrition* 3, no. 2 (1993): 150–164.

Fitzgerald, L. "Exercise and the Immune System." *Immunology Today* , 9, no. 11 (1988): 337–339.

Fry, R.W. and D. Keast. "Overtraining in Athletes." *Sports Medicine* 12, no. 1 (1991): 32–65.

Heath, G.W., et al. "Exercise and Upper Respiratory Tract Infections: Is There a Relationship?" *Sports Medicine* 14, no. 6 (1992): 353–365.

Hoffman-Goetz, L. and B.K. Peterson. "Exercise and the Immune System: A Model of the Stress Response?" *Immunology Today* 15, no. 8 (1994): 382–387.

Hooper, S.L. and L.T. MacKinnon. "Monitoring Overtraining in Athletes: Recommendations." *Sports Medicine* 20, no. 5 (1995): 321–327.

Hooper, S.L., et al. "Markers for Monitoring Overtraining and Recovery." *Medicine and Science in Sports and Exercise* 27, no. 1 (1995): 106–112.

Ivy, J.L., et al. "Muscle Glycogen Synthesis After Exercise: Effect of Time of Carbohydrate Ingestion." *Journal of Applied Physiology* 64, no. 4 (1988): 1480–1485.

Keast, D., et al. "Exercise and the Immune Response." *Sports Medicine* 5 (1988): 248–267.

Kuipers, H. and H.A. Keizer. "Overtraining in Elite Athletes: Review and Directions For the Future." *Sports Medicine* 6 (1988): 79–92.

Lehmann, M., et al. "Overtraining in Endurance Athletes: A Brief Review." *Medicine and Science in Sports and Exercise* 25, no. 7 (1993): 854–862.

MacDougal, J.D., et al. "The Time Course For Elevated Muscle Protein Synthesis Following Heavy Resistance Exercise." *Canadian Journal of Applied Physiology* 20, no. 4 (1995): 480–486.

Masten, et al. "Different Short-Term Effects of Protein and Carbohydrate Intake on TSH, GH, Insulin and Glucagon." *Scandinavian Journal of Clinical and Laboratory Investigation* 50, no. 11 (1990): 801–805.

Milne, C. "The Tired Athlete." *New Zealand Journal of Sports Medicine* 19, no. 3 (1991): 42–44.

Newham, D.J., et al. "Muscle Pain and Tenderness After Exercise." *Australian Journal of Sports Medicine and Exercise Science* 14 (1982): 129–131.

Nieman, D.C., et al. "Infectious Episodes in Runners Before and After the Los Angeles Marathon." *Journal of Sports Medicine and Physical Fitness* 30 (1990): 316–328.

Phillips, S.M., et al. "Mixed Muscle Protein Synthesis and Breakdown After Resistance Exercise in Humans." *American Journal of Physiology* 273, no. 1 (1997): E99–107.

Roy, B.D., et al. "Effect of Glucose Supplementation Timing on Protein Metabolism After Resistance Training." *Journal of Applied Physiology* 82 (1997): 1882–1888.

Sharp, N.C.C. and Y. Koutedakis. "Sport and the Overtraining Syndrome." *British Medical Journal* 48, no. 3 (1992): 518–533.

Sherman, W.M. "Recovery From Endurance Exercise." *Medicine and Science in Sports and Exercise* 24 (9S) (1992): S336–S339.

Stone, M., et al. "Overtraining: A Review of the Signs, Symptoms, and Possible Causes." *Journal of Applied Sport Sciences* 5, no. 1 (1991): 35–50.

Tipton, C.M., et al. "The Influence of Physical Activity on Ligaments and Tendons." *Medicine and Science in Sports and Exercise* 7 (1975): 165–175.

Urhausen, A., et al. "Blood Hormones As Markers of Training Stress and Overtraining." *Sports Medicine* 20 (1995): 251–276.

Zawadzki, K.M., et al. "Carbohydrate-Protein Complex Increases the Rate of Muscle Glycogen Storage After Exercise." *Journal of Applied Physiology* 72, no. 5 (1992): 1854–1859.

THE COMPETITIVE
EDGE

In the previous 11 chapters we looked at the "big picture" of preparation for racing: training philosophy, the science of fitness, purposeful training, methodical planning, and readiness for and recovery from peak performances. I believe that by understanding and applying the principles and guidelines described thus far your race results will improve. I've seen it happen time after time with riders I've coached.

In this part of the book we examine several other aspects of training. Chapter 12, discusses dealing problems presented by winter. In Chapter 13, I present the strength and flexibility program the athletes I train follow. The unique needs of several subgroups of mountain bikers are looked at in Chapter 14. Making effective use of a training diary is examined in Chapter 15. And finally, Chapter 16 discusses diet and ergogenic aids. Combining these with what you learned in the first five parts will give you a competitive edge.

WINTER

You have to be flexible relative to the environment. The training is sport-specific in that your sport, mountain biking, is never specific—there are so many variables.

—DAVID FARMER

Training for mountain bike cross-country racing isn't for wimps. There are challenges demanding personal sacrifice almost daily. One of the greatest challenges is winter, with its short days, bone-chilling cold, and wet and snowy weather. This is the time of the year when riders find out how serious they really are about training.

In the winter, when "normal" people come home from a tough day at work, they light the fireplace, pour a glass of wine, and get warm and comfy in front of the television. Not the serious rider. You have a workout to do. If riding outside, you must hurry because the sun is about to go down. Getting dressed is like preparing for a Polar expedition—several layers of warm clothes, leg and arm covers, booties, hood, jacket and gloves. Then top off the tires, make sure the lights are working, and, finally, start riding.

Winter is the cruelest season for the serious rider.

Now the real challenge begins. You must dodge potholes while watching for icy patches on the road and contending with drivers who are reluctant to share it. Your fingers and face are cold before you've even gone a mile—and the sun is just setting, so it will get worse.

Some how you get through this frigid, 90-minute ride safely and return home. The next day will be the same, unless really foul weather forces you inside onto a trainer, where the challenge is boredom. This goes on day after day for three to five months, depending on where you live. It's enough to make you want to quit or at least move nearer to the equator where all there is to deal with is the stifling heat of summer.

Some improve by making the most of what winter has to offer.

When it comes to winter training, you're not the Lone Ranger. Faced with the same wintry challenges, some riders are not just surviving—they're thriving.

Take Ned Overend, for example. During his world-class racing career he lived in the high mountains of Durango, Colorado, where the winter is *really* harsh. Yet, when it came time for early summer's big races, Ned was always a contender. His secret to winter-training success was attitude. He simply stayed flexible and learned to make the most of winter. When he couldn't ride outside, which was common in snow-packed Durango, he would ski, snowshoe, run, swim, lift weights, or put in some time on an indoor trainer. In fact, all of this winter cross-training made Ned into one of the country's top off-road triathletes.

You can learn a lesson from Ned: Treat winter like an old friend, be flexible, and improvise when it comes time to train. But most of all, make it fun. Mountain bike cross-country racing is a sport with varying challenges. You must be able to get off and run up a muddy hill with a bike on your shoulder, instinctively choose the best line through a technical descent, and avoid crashes with expert balancing and handling skills. Winter is a great time to develop and refine all of these abilities with cross-training. Let's take a look at how.

TRAINING ALTERNATIVES

By now you've developed a detailed annual training plan. Every week until, perhaps, the first A-priority race, or even until the end of the season, is mapped out. Right now, your dedication to your plan is high; you're determined to stick to it. Winter isn't going to allow that to happen. If you try to put in all of those Base-period hours regardless of winter weather and indoor boredom, you'll be flying by February, but ready to quit in June. There are limits to how much sacrifice one person can endure.

Train consistently, but stay flexible.

I know this may sound like the opposite of what I was telling you just a few chapters back when I was preaching consistency. But the message hasn't changed—you still need to train with dedication on a regular basis. It doesn't have to all be on the bike, however. Some of it may come in the form of cross-training with alternative outdoor activities. How much of what kinds of training you do depends largely on what the winter weather is like where you live. Flexibility is the key.

Cross-training in the Preparation and Base 1 periods.

Another key is knowing what the purpose of training is in each of the season's periods. Early in the season, during the Preparation and Base 1 periods, one of the most important objectives is the development of cardiovascular fitness. The heart, blood vessels, blood and lungs don't know the difference between riding a bike and running. It's all the same to them. Feel free at these times in the season to cross-train as much as you want or have to. Keep indoor riding to a minimum.

In Base 2 you can continue to cross-train, but indoor training begins to take on greater significance. Now is a good time to set some limits on how much indoor training you'll do. I discuss this issue and offer some suggestions in the "Riding Inside" section of this chapter.

Cross-training in the Base 2 period.

By Base 3 you need to be on the bike almost daily. There may be some cross-training, but it is minimal. You and your indoor trainer may get to know each other quite well, since developing bike-specific fitness is now critical to moving on to the next period.

Cross-training in Base 3.

The Build period is a time when training must be as specific as you can make it to the demands of cross-country racing. This requires riding a bike. There is now little or no cross-training.

Cross-training in the Build period.

CYCLO-CROSS?

Will training for and racing cyclo-cross make you more fit for mountain bike racing? The answer depends on when your first A-priority race is scheduled. If it is planned for January, then cyclo-cross is a great way to prepare. Your muscular endurance and anaerobic endurance will be peaked and ready to go. But if your first important event isn't until spring, the fitness gained from cyclo-cross will be long gone, or you will be totally spent from trying to maintain it all winter. By June or July you'll be thinking about quitting.

Whether or not you race cyclo-cross depends on when your first A-priority race is.

Following a stressful cyclo-cross season, especially one that started immediately on the heels of a long year of mountain bike racing, most riders need a Transition period. During this break any fitness gained from cyclo-cross will soon disappear. And since there is a need to rebuild fitness from the ground up, it will take at least 14 weeks to come to a full race peak again. Assuming the month of January was spent in a Transition period, that puts you at mid-May for the first A-priority race of the mountain bike season— at the earliest. Some riders need more time than this to prepare for a peak of fitness, putting the first peak in June or even July. Of course, you could go straight from cyclo-cross to mountain bike training and racing, but that's a surefire way to be toast by June.

Don't get me wrong—cyclo-cross has much to offer. It will improve your bike-handling skills, and provide motivation for training, and it is a lot of fun. These are great reasons to participate. Just don't delude yourself into thinking that the anaerobic fitness gained in the fall and early winter is still going to be there in the spring. If it is, you're a candidate for a short mountain bike season.

If you decide to race cyclo-cross, some careful thought should go into the process of planning a year of racing that includes it. All events you plan to enter—including cyclo-cross, road and mountain bike—need to be considered as part of your race schedule. They should all be prioritized into A, B and C categories as described in Chapter 7. As you may recall, that means only three or four A-priorities in a season and eight to 12 B-priority races. The rest are the low-priority, C kind. Let's look at how this planning scheme helps with the cyclo-cross racing decision.

If one or more cyclo-cross races are on the A-priority list, then you must build to a fall peak by following a periodization plan as you would for any other important race. Then include a Transition period of two to four weeks following the last cyclo-cross race before returning to the Preparation or Base periods. Base work would typically be at least six weeks and as much as 12 weeks. Its length depends on the levels of your endurance, force, speed skill and muscular endurance abilities. Baseline testing with follow-ups, or even a long, early season race or group ride, will tell you if you need more Base training development.

If you follow this route and decide to make some cyclo-cross races A-priority, then training correctly for them is just as important as training for your mountain bike season. In this case, I'd highly recommend reading *Cyclo-Cross* by Simon Burney (VeloPress, 1996) to learn how to develop the necessary fitness, refine skills and set up your bike correctly.

If cyclo-cross races are B-priority, then there is no attempt to peak, but fitness still needs to be at a high level. Training in this case includes weekly cyclo-cross–specific workouts mixed with your normal mountain bike Base training. These cyclo-cross workouts might be hill run-ups, mounting and dismounting drills and off-road rides. But most of the training in the late fall and early winter months for the B-priority cyclo-cross racer is focused on preparing for the upcoming mountain bike season.

If C-priority is what you plan for the cyclo-cross season, then you train only for your "main" sport—mountain biking—and go to a few cyclo-cross races just for fun. The focus is now on the mountain bike season. But if you go this route, don't expect podium results. Race to finish and have a good time regardless of the outcome.

CROSS-TRAINING WORKOUTS

The following cross-training workouts are ones I typically use with the riders I coach. There are other possibilities, such as aerobics classes and exercise machines found in health clubs. When cross-training, do only what you enjoy. For example, many mountain bikers run, but if you hate running, do something else. You may also combine one or more of these workouts to produce a longer session with variety.

All races—including cyclo-cross—need to be prioritized.

If cyclo-cross is A-priority, then train seriously for it.

If cyclo-cross is B-priority, then include some weekly workouts specifically for it.

If cyclo-cross is C-priority, race it for fun while keeping your focus on mountain bike training.

Cross-training provides a break from riding a bike while building cardiovascular fitness.

Hike

Hiking is one of the favorites with the riders I coach, especially those who live near the mountains. One of the reasons it is so popular, I believe, is because it can be done with a spouse or friend who is not a mountain biker. No particular skills are needed. Just pick a trail and start walking briskly. Don't dawdle; you must move along at a good pace, especially on the uphills. To increase the workload, wear a loaded backpack.

Run

Running is one of the most basic human movements, so this is also a good choice. The problem with it is that the risk of injury is high. To keep the risk low, start into running with very conservative workout durations, such as 15 to 20 minutes. Every week add a few minutes, up to about 45 to 60 minutes. Also, don't run on back-to-back days. Spread them out to allow time for damaged muscles and tendons to heal. Running on softer surfaces such as trails, grass or dirt roads will also help keep you injury-free.

Brick

"Brick" is a term used by multisport athletes to describe a combined bike-run workout. This is also a perfect session for mountain bikers, especially when they are just getting back into running at the start of the season. There are many ways to combine the two sports. For example, every week you can increase the distance run within a 90-minute workout. Initially, there might be a 75-minute ride followed by a 15-minute run. Every week decrease the bike time while increasing the run time so that you build up to something like 30 minutes of riding and 60 of running. The bike portion can be done on an indoor trainer when the weather stops you from riding outside. Following the bike portion, quickly change into dry clothes and running shoes before starting the run. The first few times this workout is done, your legs will feel wobbly at the start of the run. After a few of these bricks this will no longer be a problem.

Cross-Country Ski

Cross-country skiing is another popular workout in the winter months in snowy regions. It is one of the best activities for developing cardiovascular fitness, and it also works the upper body—an area in which most mountain bikers are lacking. If you're new to the sport, it will take a few of these workouts to develop the skills. One of the added benefits is that you can do long workouts without the risk of injury running. The cost of equipment is the major obstacle.

Snowshoe

Snowshoeing is similar to running and hiking. The skills can be picked up quickly and it can be done any time there is enough snow covering the ground. As with cross-country skiing, the cost of equipment is an issue. Using ski poles will also work the upper body.

Swim

Swimming is a good choice because the risk of injury is low, weather is not a concern, the upper body gets a good workout, and pools are plentiful. If you aren't an experienced swimmer, however, you'll be surprised and exasperated by how quickly you fatigue. While riding for hours is no problem, after just a few minutes of low-effort swimming you'll be ready for a breather. It will take weeks to refine the skills necessary to do continuous workouts. Since your intent is not to become a swimmer, but to get a cardiovascular workout, it's best to do swim workouts as interval sets. Swim a length or two, recover until breathing quiets, and repeat. You can also swim with a masters team, which will provide a group workout and technique tips from a coach on deck.

Weights

During the winter months, I have all riders lift weights. I've found this to be one of the best ways to develop total-body muscular fitness. If you don't have the equipment available, improvise. Squats or step-ups can be done with a loaded backpack. Almost any exercise done with weights can also be done with a rubber stretch cord. These are available in sporting goods stores and catalogs. Or you can make your own from heavy-duty surgical tubing. Don't just lift weights for cross-training—include an aerobic exercise from the above list as well. The next chapter goes into detail on weights.

RIDING INSIDE

In some places, riding inside on a trainer is the only riding there is in the winter. Athletes who live in these cold, snowy regions soon learn that the trainer is their best friend when it comes to developing the fitness necessary for spring races. After all, skiing and running are not the same as cycling. (Remember the principle of specificity?)

REASONS AND GUIDELINES

Trainers make good use of time.

The trainer can be a great way to train regardless of the conditions outside. They make for efficient training: When there is little time to ride, you can get a quick and purposeful workout on a trainer without dealing with stoplights, traffic, and traveling to the best outdoor locations. Often, in the time it takes to ride to the hill or flat time trial course, an indoor trainer workout can be completed. This is especially beneficial in the winter when days are short.

For far less money than joining a health club, a trainer allows you to get in a great workout. There is also no waiting for equipment, and the bike will always fit you just right.

Trainers also allow for very precise workouts. On the road, there are always confounding circumstances, such as a hill that isn't quite long enough, a "flat" course that has rolling hills in it, or an intersection to slow down for when doing intervals. None of this is a concern on the trainer. You can do the workout just as it was intended. For this reason alone, there are riders who even do some of their summer training indoors.

Trainers produce precise workouts.

But there is quite a bit of difference in how much indoor-trainer work individual athletes can handle. There are some who ride inside day after day in the winter and even include weekly three- and four-hour rides on a trainer with little difficulty. Others dread getting on a trainer and have a hard time making it through an hour. It's best to pay attention to these signs of your tolerance for monotony and train accordingly. If you are unsure of your tolerance but often find yourself burned out and ready to quit by early summer, it's probably best to ride less in the winter.

To be on the safe side, I generally advise riders to train inside no more than three days in a row. If you are kept from riding outside on the fourth day, select an outdoor alternative. Also, I limit indoor workouts to 90 minutes, regardless of what the schedule calls for. I make slight exceptions to these rules for riders who have a great tolerance for indoor training, but this is rare.

Suggested guidelines for indoor training.

TYPES OF TRAINERS

There are four types of indoor trainers to choose from. The one that has been around the longest is still one of the most effective. It has small fans that produce the resistance. These "wind" trainers are good in that the resistance increases exponentially as speed increases linearly, just as it does on the road with aerodynamic drag. These are not as sophisticated as the other options, but are also among the least expensive trainers available. One disadvantage is the noise. If you live in an apartment, a wind trainer will definitely disturb your neighbors. But if you can use it in a garage or basement, the noise will bother no one but you.

Wind trainers offer several advantages.

Magnetic trainers are quiet compared with wind trainers, but the resistance increase with a linear rise in speed is also linear. On the road, the load goes up at a higher rate of change than does the speed. This means the workouts don't have as realistic a feeling on

Magnetic trainers produce a less realistic feel than wind trainers.

a "mag" trainer as on a wind trainer.

Another option is using rollers when training indoors. These are excellent for developing a fluid pedal stroke, but are not as good as wind or mag trainers when it comes to developing other fitness abilities. If you use rollers, and I recommend it, also purchase a wind or mag trainer.

Rollers will refine your pedaling skills.

The top end of indoor training devices is clearly the CompuTrainer. If you find indoor trainers boring, this will help. You may even find yourself looking forward to riding indoors. Besides making training into an interactive experience, the CompuTrainer also allows you to complete self-tests, determine lactate threshold heart rates, and train indoors with power. Cost is the major challenge, with a CompuTrainer price about the same as that of a decent bike frame. But if indoor riding is a big part of your winter, or you simply want more accurate training data, this is the way to go.

A CompuTrainer makes indoor training fun.

INDOOR SESSION DESIGN

Some riders leave an old bike set up on an indoor trainer all winter. That way, if forced inside by bad weather or working late, they can start the workout quickly—before they get out of the mood. That's easy to do when it's cold, snow is falling, and you've had a long day at work or it's early in the morning.

While you're setting up a near-permanent indoor workout spot, be sure to include one or more fans. Even in an unheated garage or basement a fan is needed. Without some way to cool off, heat buildup will increase the perceived effort of any workout and heart rate will be higher than normal.

Staying cool is critical for indoor riding.

Since sweat production is prodigious with indoor training, fluids and a towel are also necessary. Be sure to protect your bike from sweat damage, especially the headset and seat post.

Indoor training sessions should be organized just as they are on the road or trail. This means a warm-up, one or more workouts with each focusing on an ability, and a cool down. The warm-up should consist of at least 10 minutes of slowly increasing effort. Don't leave it out in an attempt to get the session over with quickly.

More than likely, your indoor training sessions will seem harder than they do when you are outside. Almost everyone reports this. That may result from heat build-up or the greater psychological stress of going nowhere fast. Because of this, I'd recommend doing more intervals and fewer steady-state workouts when indoors.

Because indoor sessions seem harder than outdoor sessions, include more intervals.

Nearly all the workouts described in Appendix B can be done on an indoor trainer. Especially effective indoors are speed skill workouts such as spin-ups and isolated leg training. Raising the front wheel five to six inches may help to simulate hill climbing position.

Indoor trainers are also very effective for recovery workouts any time of year. Easy spinning sessions done on a trainer are especially important if you live in a hilly or mountainous area where flat courses are not available.

Consider using a trainer for recovery rides year-round.

SKILLS

Bike handling skills often determine who gets on the podium and who goes home early. If your skills could stand improvement, and most everyone's could, winter is a good time to refine them.

Let's think of handling skills as falling into two broad categories—basic and advanced. Advanced skills are the creative combination of basic skills into an intricate "dance" that get you through a technical section of a race course in the least amount of time. At the highest levels of competition, these moves are made subconsciously. Just as Michael Jordan doesn't contemplate the complex mechanics of making a 20-foot jump shot during a game, the highly skilled mountain biker doesn't think about riding a tough stretch of the course. It just happens. He or she sees a line and takes it, makes subtle weight shifts, lifts the front wheel at just the right time, turns, brakes, accelerates, stands and sits, all without making conscious decisions.

Technical riding is a "dance" of refined basic handling skills.

Trying to think your way through a challenging section causes you to handle the bike mechanically and slows your reactions. This is a stage all riders go through on the way to becoming experienced. Those who have spent a lot of time in other sports where balance and agility are prerequisites for success, such as downhill skiing, generally pick up advanced mountain bike skills rapidly.

Regardless of your ability, winter is a good time to go back to the basics. The most basic skill to work on at this time of the year is balance. Watching observed trials competitions will give you some pointers. Balance is what this part of the sport is all about.

Balance is the most basic of handling skills.

On your mountain bike, practice track stands, picking up water bottles while riding, wheelies, hopping sideways, jumping obstacles and slalom. Make it into a game by riding with a friend. This can be done in a park or parking lot, or even in a garage or basement when the weather forces you inside. Those new to mountain biking should continue to work on these skills year-round.

The other basic skill to refine in the winter is pedaling. Research at the Olympic Training Center in Colorado Springs, Colorado, found that elite mountain bikers pedaled more efficiently than did elite road cyclists. There's a good reason for that. Riding off-road, often on loose terrain, requires applying relatively even pressure throughout

Mountain bikers must pedal economically.

the pedal stroke to prevent the back wheel from slipping. This is not a problem for road racers, so they can afford to be a bit more sloppy with their pedaling. It also tells us that working on pedaling skills is critical for success in mountain biking.

In Appendix B, several speed skill workouts are listed that can be done on an indoor trainer to enhance pedaling ability. Winter is the time to do these workouts and to think frequently about applying even force to the pedals, whether on the trainer, road or trail. By the time you get to the Base 3 period, pedaling skill must be well-honed and second nature. You can't think about it then.

REFERENCES

Baker, A. *Smart Cycling*. San Diego, CA: Argo Publishing, 1995.

Burke, E. *Off-Season Training for Cyclists*. Boulder, CO: VeloPress, 1997.

Burney, S. *Cyclo-Cross Training and Technique*. Boulder, CO: VeloPress, 1996.

Howard, J. *Dirt!* New York: Lyons Press, 1997.

Marsh, A. P. and P. E. Martin. "Effects of Cycling Experience, Aerobic Power, and Power Output on Preferred and Most Economical Cycling Cadences." *Medicine and Science in Sport and Exercise* 29, no. 9 (1997): 1225-1232.

Overend, N. and E. Pavelka. *Ned Overend. Mountain Bike Like a Champion*. Emmaus, PA: Rodale Press, 1999.

Skilbeck, P. *Single-Track Mind*. Boulder, CO: VeloPress, 1996.

van der Plas, R. *The Mountain Bike Book*. San Francisco: Bicycle Books, 1995.

STRENGTH AND STRETCHING

*I don't need to win by three or four minutes. I just want to
make it across the finish line first—three minutes, three seconds,
three one-hundredths-of-a-second, it's all the same, really.*

—TINKER JUAREZ

There are many factors that go into determining who gets to the finish line first, not
the least of which is the condition of the athlete's connective tissues—
muscles and tendons.

The human body has more than 660 muscles, making up some 35 to 40 percent of
its mass. How strong and flexible these muscles are contributes immensely to the athlete's race performance. Developing the ability to produce great forces while maintaining a wide range of motion means greater racing speeds and a reduced risk of injury. If
the muscles are even a bit weak or inflexible, the rider never realizes his or her full potential, as power for climbing and handling the bike is too low and muscle pulls and strains
are likely. And crashes are more likely to have devastating effects on well-being.
Developing the muscles has the potential to improve significantly racing at all levels.
Every successful athlete I have trained has lifted weights for at least part of the season.

STRENGTH

What is there about lifting weights that produces improved racing performance?
Studies using cyclists as subjects have found improved endurance following a strength-
building program, although there was no change in aerobic capacity (VO_2 max). One possible reason for this apparent contradiction is that the greater strength of the slow-twitch,

endurance muscles allows them to carry more of the burden of powering the bike, thus relying less on the fast-twitch muscles. Since the fast-twitch muscles fatigue rather quickly, reducing their contribution to the total force created means greater endurance.

One study done at the University of Maryland showed that improved strength from weight lifting was associated with a higher lactate threshold. Since lactate threshold is a major determiner of performance in an event such as mountain bike cross-country racing, anything that elevates it is beneficial. This finding may have resulted from the athletes' using more slow-twitch and less fast-twitch muscle to power the bike. Since fast-twitch produces abundant amounts of lactic acid, using them to provide less of the pedaling force means less lactate in the blood at any given power output, thus raising lactate threshold.

Lifting weights also has the potential to increase the total amount of force that can be applied to the pedal in every stroke. As you may recall from Chapter 4, as force rises at any given cadence, power increases. Greater power outputs are always associated with faster times.

Improving the power of the upper body, especially the pulling power, enhances bike handling on technical courses. This is most evident in attempts to lift the front wheel over obstacles. Riders with weak upper bodies will find technical courses all that much more challenging.

Strong and flexible muscles are less prone to injury than weak and stiff muscles. A real concern for mountain bikers is a crash that injures the shoulder. Improving the soundness of the connective tissue around this joint provides an extra measure of protection in a fall.

The weakest point in a muscle is where it attaches to the tendon. Most muscle tears occur at this point. Increasing the load capacity of these muscle-tendon unions reduces the risk of pulled muscles during a sudden change in power, as when accelerating quickly or climbing a short hill.

Strength training also has the potential to improve muscle imbalances. These may be gross imbalances, such as a weak upper body and a strong lower body, or they may be relative imbalances between muscle groups that have opposing effects on a joint. Again, such enhancements reduce the chances of an injury.

There are riders who don't lift out of fear that pumping iron may cause an increase in body weight and thus slow them on climbs. While there are some who have a tendency to increase muscle mass, few who excel at endurance sports such as mountain biking are genetically inclined to gain significant bulk, especially on an endurance-based program such as that described in this chapter.

CHOOSING A PROGRAM

There are as many different weight-training programs as there are coaches, it seems. Everyone has a lifting program they swear by. There are two problems I see with most of them.

The first is that they are usually unrealistic in the number of exercises to complete, often listing a dozen or even more. Most riders don't have enough time to even ride as much as they would like, let alone spend hours in a gym, much of it spent waiting for stations to open. The designers of these programs are well intentioned, and list all the exercises that should help the rider get stronger. With adequate time, many of these programs are good. But if finding enough time is always a challenge for you, then fewer exercises are needed so you can concentrate on the depth of your strength development, rather than on its breadth. The program presented here is pared down to what is necessary. If you have more time and enjoy the weight room, do more exercises.

Time and equipment availability is a concern in weight training.

The second problem I see with many programs intended for mountain bikers is that they are designed on the bodybuilding model. The purpose of a bodybuilder's weight workout is to alter muscle shape and body symmetry. They do this by emphasizing muscle hypertrophy and working muscle groups in isolation. Mountain bikers lift weights to improve function; few care about how it makes them look. The following program's only purpose is to improve how you ride a bike. It will not give you bulging muscles and a beautiful physique.

Function, not form, is the goal of the mountain biker.

WEIGHT-TRAINING GUIDELINES

How can you ensure that your weight-training program develops function and not simply form? The following guidelines will help regardless of what program you choose to pursue.

Focus on Prime Movers

Prime movers are the big muscle groups that do most of the work. For example, a prime mover for riding a bike is the quadriceps muscle group on the front of the thigh. Other prime movers for cycling are the hamstrings and gluteals (butt). The mountain biker must also be able to lift the bike, so upper body pulling exercises should be included.

Prevent Muscle Imbalances

Some of the injuries common to riders result from an imbalance between muscles that must work in harmony to produce a movement. For example, if the lateral quadriceps on the outside of the thigh is overly developed relative to the medial quadriceps above and inside the knee, a knee injury is possible.

Use Multijoint Exercises Whenever Possible

Biceps curls are a single-joint exercise since only the elbow joint is involved. This is the type of muscle-isolation exercise bodybuilders do. On the contrary, squats, a basic cycling exercise, includes three joints—the hip, knee and ankle. Such exercises more closely simulate the dynamic movement patterns of the sport, and also limit time in the gym. However, exercises done for muscular balance are single-joint by nature. For example, the limited-range knee extension exercise, a movement involving only one joint, maintains quadriceps balance for healthy knees.

Mimic the Positions and Movements of Riding

Position your hands and feet so they are in similar positions to when you are on the bike. When doing leg presses on a leg-press sled, for example, the feet should be placed about the same width as the pedals. You don't ride with your feet spread 18 inches (45 cm) and your toes turned out at 45 degrees. Another example: When grasping the bar for seated rows, place your hands as if holding you were on to handlebars.

Include the "Core"

When you ride a bike, the forces applied by your arms and legs must pass through the abdomen and low back. If these areas are weak, much of the force is lost. Your body transfers energy like an accordion instead of a crow bar. A strong core means, for example, that when climbing out of the saddle, more of the force generated by pulling against the handlebars is transferred to the pedals.

Limit the Number of Exercises

As mentioned earlier, focus more on the number of sets than the number of exercises. This will give your workouts greater depth than breadth, yet still yield significant improvement. As the season progresses, reduce the number of exercises, retaining only those that will provide the greatest gain for the least time invested.

Periodize Strength Training

Weight training should come before bike training. For example, the Maximum Strength (MS) phase described below is intended to develop strength for climbing. This phase should be included just before starting hill training on the bike. That generally means the MS phase is included in the Base 1 period, since hill work starts in Base 2. Once the high-intensity riding begins in the Build period, strength training is de-emphasized and takes on a maintenance role.

The strength program presented in this chapter follows the above guidelines and was designed specifically for the competitive mountain biker. I believe it will improve your riding if force has been a limiter and hills are your greatest challenge. This doesn't mean that other weight programs aren't effective. If the program you already use generally adheres to the above guidelines and has produced good results, then by all means continue to use it. Or consider making slight modifications in your current program to match the guidelines.

TABLE 13.1	

Anatomical Adaptation (AA) phase

Total sessions/phase	8–12
Sessions/week	2–3
Load (% 1RM)	40–60
Sets/session	2–5
Reps/set	20–30
Speed of lift	Slow
Recovery (in minutes)	1–1.5

Exercises (in order of completion):
1. Hip extension (squat, leg press or step-up)
2. Lat pull-down
3. Hip extension (use a different exercise than in #1)
4. Chest press or push-ups
5. Seated row
6. Personal weakness (hamstring curl, knee extension or heel raise)
7. Standing row
8. Abdominal with twist

PERIODIZATION OF STRENGTH

The program I use with the athletes I coach has five distinct phases. Not all phases are used for every athlete, but the order presented here is always followed. The following is an explanation of each of those phases and their periodization.

Anatomical Adaptation (AA)

AA is the first phase of strength training, and is usually started during the Preparation period in the late fall or early winter. Also, return to it whenever there has been a significant gap in weight training, regardless of time of year or period. The purpose is to prepare the muscles and tendons for the greater loads of the ensuing Maximum Strength phase. The purpose of this phase is improved general body strength, so more exercises are done at this time of year than at any other. Due to the greater number of exercises, the workouts in this phase generally take

Preparation period.

more time than those in the other phases. This shouldn't be a problem, since other forms of training are minimal and cross-training is employed. Machines can be used in this period, but free-weight training is beneficial, as it enhances the strength of smaller, support muscles. If your weight room is not too busy, circuit training adds an aerobic component to this phase.

In this phase, as in most others, increase the loads by about 5 percent every four or five workouts. Table 13.1 provides the details of the AA phase.

Maximum Strength (MS)

The purpose of the MS phase is to improve the ability to lift heavy loads. This is done by gradually increasing resistance and decreasing repetitions. This phase, which is **Base 1.** usually included during the Base 1 period, is necessary to teach the central nervous system to easily recruit high numbers of muscle fibers. There are fewer exercises included in MS than in the AA phase.

Care must be taken not to cause injury in this phase, especially with free-weight exercises such as the squat. Select loads conservatively at the start of this phase, and in the first set of each workout. Loads are gradually increased throughout MS up to certain goal levels based on body weight (BW). These are summarized in Table 13.2. Generally, women will aim for the lower ends of the ranges and men the upper ends. Those new

TABLE 13.2

MS phase load goals based on body weight (BW)

The goal is to complete three sets of six repetitions each at these loads by the end of the MS phase. If a goal is achieved early, maintain the load and increase the repetitions beyond six for the remainder of the MS phase.

Freebar squat	1.3–1.7 x BW
Leg press (sled)	2.5–2.9 x BW
Step-up	0.7–0.9 x BW
Seated row	0.5–0.8 x BW
Standing row	0.4–0.7 x BW

to weight training should also set goals in this phase at the lower ends of these ranges.

Only the exercises listed in Table 13.2 are done following the MS phase routine. All other exercises, such as abdominals and personal weakness areas, continue with the AA phase routine of light weights and 20 to 30 repetitions per set.

Once these goals are achieved, repetitions are increased and loads remain constant. For example, a 150-pound (68kg) male rider doing the leg press has a goal of 435 pounds (197kg), or 150 x 2.9. Once he can lift this weight six times, he will increase the repetitions beyond six in subsequent workouts while keeping the load at 435 pounds (197kg) for the remainder of the phase. Also, once all the goal weights are achieved, there is no reason to go beyond eight MS workouts. On the other hand, if the goal loads are not achieved even though 12 MS workouts have been completed, end the phase and go onto the next.

When to end the MS phase.

Some athletes will be tempted to do more than one hip-extension exercise, or to increase the loads beyond the goals listed above. Others will want to extend this phase beyond the recommended number of workouts in Table 13.3. Doing so is likely to result in muscle imbalances, especially in the upper leg, which may contribute to hip or knee injuries. During the early part of the MS phase, endurance performance will suffer as the legs and arms may feel "heavy." As a result, your rating of perceived exertion and breathing will be noticeably harder for any given power output. This is a temporary setback that will fade away as you adapt to heavier loads.

Excess MS phase training may cause injury.

Either the Power Endurance (PE) or Muscular Endurance (ME) phase follows the MS phase depending on the rider's limiters. If explosive power is needed, go to the PE phase. If muscular endurance is a limiter, the next phase is ME. These are typically included in the Base 2 period of the season.

Base 2.

Power Endurance (PE)

The purpose of this phase is to convert the raw strength developed in the MS phase into the ability to quickly recruit many muscle fibers, and to briefly sustain their use at a high power output. Examples of this in a race situation might be attacking short, steep hills or long sprints.

High power results from producing the greatest possible force in the shortest possible time. It may be expressed as power = force ¥ velocity. This means that speed of

TABLE 13.3	
Maximum Strength (MS) phase	
Total sessions/phase	8–12
Sessions/week	2–3
Load (% 1RM)	BW goals*
Sets/session	2–6
Reps/set	3–6+*
Speed of lift	Slow to moderate
Recovery (in minutes)	2–4*

*Note: Only **bold** exercises listed below follow this guideline. All others continue AA guidelines.

Exercises (in order of completion):
1. **Hip extension (squat, leg press or step-up)**
2. **Seated row**
3. Abdominal with twist
4. Upper body choice (chest press or lat pull-down)
5. Personal weakness (hamstring curl, knee extension or heel raise)
6. **Standing row**

Explosive movement is necessary in the PE phase.

movement is critical to improving power, so the lifting portions of all exercises are done with an explosive movement. Be careful not to move so quickly that you risk injury. Do not "throw" the weight, but rather move quickly with the load completely under control. The weight is always lowered slowly. When the ability to move quickly diminishes, the exercise is stopped, regardless of the number of repetitions completed. A proper warm-up is critical before a PE workout.

The PE phase generally starts in the Base 2 period, and may extend into Base 3 depending on how long the MS phase lasted. Depending on how great your need for power development is, this phase may last from three to six weeks, with one or two sessions per week. Table 13.4 provides the details.

Muscular Endurance (ME)

Muscular endurance is at the heart of training for endurance sports, and ME phase lifting greatly benefits riders whose race endurance is a limiter. This phase follows on the heels of the MS phase for these riders. The purpose is to extend the ability to manage fatigue at high load levels by increasing capillary density and the number and size of mitochondria—the energy production sites within the muscles. Circuit training may be used during this phase, if preferred.

As with the PE phase, in the ME phase the number of sessions per week may be reduced to one since riding the bike is becoming increasingly important. This phase may last from four to eight weeks. The loads are light, but the repetitions are quite high in order to adequately stress the aerobic system. The routine of the ME phase is detailed in Table 13.5.

Muscular Endurance is slow to develop.

TABLE 13.4

Power Endurance (PE) phase

Total sessions/phase	6–8
Sessions/week	1–2
Load (% 1RM)	40–60*
Sets/session	2–3
Reps/set	8–15*
Speed of lift	Fast*
Recovery (in minutes)	3–5*

*Note: Only **bold** exercises listed below follow this guideline. All others continue AA guidelines.

Exercises (in order of completion):
1. **Hip extension (squat, leg press or step-up)**
2. **Seated row**
3. Abdominal with twist
4. Upper body choice (chest press or lat pull-down)
5. Personal weakness (hamstring curl, knee extension or heel raise)
6. **Standing row**

TABLE 13.4

Muscular Endurance (ME) phase

Total sessions/phase	4–8
Sessions/week	1
Load (% 1RM)	30–50*
Sets/session	1–3
Reps/set	40–60*
Speed of lift	Moderate
Recovery (in minutes)	1–2*

*Note: Only **bold** exercises listed below follow this guideline. All others continue AA guidelines.

__Exercises (in order of completion):__

1. **Hip extension (squat, leg press or step-up)**

2. **Seated row**

3. Abdominal with twist

4. Upper body choice (chest press or lat pull-down)

5. Personal weakness (hamstring curl, knee extension or heel raise)

6. **Standing row**

TABLE 13.5

Strength Maintenance (SM) phase

Total sessions/phase	Indefinite
Sessions/week	1
Load (% 1RM)	60, 80 (last set)*
Sets/session	2–3
Reps/set	6–12*
Speed of lift	Moderate
Recovery (in minutes)	1–2*

*Note: Only **bold** exercises listed below follow this guideline. All others continue AA guidelines.

__Exercises (in order of completion):__

1. **Hip extension (squat, leg press or step-up)**

2. **Seated row**

3. Abdominal with twist

4. Upper body choice (chest press or lat pull-down)

5. Personal weakness (hamstring curl, knee extension or heel raise)

6. **Standing row**

Strength Maintenance (SM)

This phase maintains the basic strength established in the MS phase while hills, intervals, and steady-state efforts maintain power and muscular endurance. Stopping all resistance training at this point may cause a gradual loss of strength throughout the season. Maintenance of strength is particularly important for women and masters. Some athletes, particularly males in their twenties, seem capable of maintaining adequate levels of strength, and may not need to continue weight training throughout the Build, Peak and Race periods.

In the SM phase, only the last set of each exercise stresses the muscles. This set is done at about 80 percent of your one-repetition maximum (1RM). The one or two sets that provide warm-up for this last set are accomplished at about 60 percent of 1RM. The details of the SM phase are shown in Table 13.6.

Build, Peak and Race periods.

Hip-extension training (squats, step-ups and leg presses) is optional during the maintenance phase. If you find hip-extension exercises help your racing, continue doing them. If, however, working the legs only deepens your fatigue level and makes recovery difficult, eliminate them. Continuing to work on core muscles, shoulder strength, and personal weakness areas will maintain your basic muscular needs. Starting seven days before A-priority races, eliminate all strength training to allow for peaking.

Should you work the legs in the SM phase?

DETERMINING LOAD

The preceding tables suggest loads based on a percentage of 1RM. While that's a traditional method for arriving at how much weight to use, it presents some possible problems. Attempting to find your 1RM for each exercise increases the risk of injury, especially for an exercise such as the squat. It may also leave you very sore for two or three days afterward, eliminating most, if not all, training. This is not the best method.

A simpler and safer method is to estimate the load initially based on experience, and then make adjustments as the phase progresses. The estimate should be conservative. Always start with less than you think is possible for the goal number of repetitions, and increase it gradually and cautiously.

Estimate loads based on experience.

You can also estimate 1RM from several repetitions with a lighter load continued to failure. Start with a warm-up set of 10 repetitions with a light weight. Based on the warm-up set, estimate a load you can lift at least four times, but no more than 10. It may take a couple of experimental sets to discover this load. Recover for at least five minutes between these experimental attempts. Once you've found a load for a given exercise that you can only lift four to 10 times, divide that weight by the factor that corresponds with the number of repetitions completed. These factors are listed in Table 13.7. This provides an estimate of 1RM. For example, if you were able to complete six repetitions of the leg press with 350 pounds (158kg), dividing 350 by 0.85 produces an estimated 1RM of 412 pounds (185kg).

Estimate loads based on multiple reps.

	TABLE 13.7

Estimating 1RM from a multiple repetition set

To estimate 1 RM, divide the weight lifted by the factor below that corresponds to the number of repetitions completed in a set done to failure to estimate 1RM.

Repetitions	Factor
4	0.9
5	0.875
6	0.85
7	0.825
8	0.8
9	0.775
10	0.75

MISCELLANEOUS

Other than load, there are many other concerns to address in starting a strength-building program.

Machines or Freeweights

Either exercise machines or free weights may be used in all phases. Most athletes employ both, depending on the exercise. During the MS, PE and ME phases, free weights are likely to produce greater results than machines, since barbells and dumbbells are better for developing the small muscles that aid balance. If you use free weights in these phases, also include them in the latter sessions of the AA phase. Again, be cautious whenever using barbells and dumbbells, especially with rapid movement. Never "throw" the weight, but always keep it under control. Injury is likely when lifting weights, especially in the MS and PE phases. If you're taller than 72 inches or shorter than 63 inches, you may find it difficult to use some exercise machines; in this case, free weights are again preferable.

Should you use free weights or machines?

Experience Level

If you're in the first year of strength training, stay in the AA phase the entire season. Concentrate on perfecting movement patterns and strengthening connective tissue. Do not attempt to find your 1RM for any exercise. Those who have experience with weight training are less likely to sustain injury during the high-risk MS and PE phases than are novices. Still, caution must guide all weight workouts, even for the seasoned athlete.

Warm-up and Cool Down

Before a weight workout, warm up with five to 10 minutes of easy aerobic activity. Running, rowing, stair-climbing and cycling may be done for this. Afterward, spin on a bike in a low gear or with a light resistance at a comfortably high cadence, such as 90 rpm, for five to 10 minutes. Use little effort and allow your body to relax. Do not run immediately following a strength workout, as this raises your risk of injury.

Starting a New Phase

As you move into a new phase of strength training, blend the prior and new phases for a week. This is especially critical when going from the AA to the MS phase. For example, when going from AA to MS, the transition week may have one AA workout and one MS workout. Or half of each workout in the first week of MS could include AA and the other half MS. For example, do one or two sets of MS training following one or two sets of AA exercise for a week. This will help you adjust to the new stresses more gradually, thus limiting soreness and lost training time.

Recovery Intervals

In the tables, notice that the recovery time between sets is specified. During this time the muscle burn fades away, your heart rate drops and breathing returns to a resting level as lactate is cleared and energy stores are rebuilt in preparation for the next set. In the AA and ME phases, this recovery period is quite short, while in the other phases it is relatively long. Some phases require longer breaks than others due to the increased need for system recovery. Don't shorten these recoveries as this may compromise the fitness gains sought. During the recovery time, stretch the muscles just exercised. Later in this chapter, illustrations of stretches are provided.

Stretch during the recovery intervals.

Exercise Order

The preceding tables listed exercises in the order of completion to allow for a progression from big to small muscle groups, and for muscle-group recovery. In the AA and ME phases, you may circuit train by completing the first set of all exercises before starting the second sets. For example, in AA you might do the first set of hip extensions followed by the first set of the next exercise, and then go on to the third station for one set. If the weight room is crowded, of course, this routine won't work. In that case, simply complete all the sets of one exercise before going to the next. In the other phases, all sets of each exercise are done to completion before progressing to the next exercise. If time is tight, two exercises may be done as a "superset" in any phase by alternating sets between the two exercises to completion. Supersetting makes better use of your time in the gym, since you spend less time waiting for recovery of a specific neuromuscular group. This does not eliminate the need to stretch following each set, however.

Supersetting uses time efficiently.

Recovery Weeks

Every third or fourth week is a time of reduced training volume coinciding with your recovery weeks scheduled on the annual training plan. Reduce the number of strength workouts that week, or reduce the number of sets within workouts. Keep the loads the same as in the previous week. An exception to this may come at the end of the week that finishes off the MS phase: After several days of rest, see if you can attain the goals listed in Table 13.2.

STRENGTH EXERCISES

The mountain bikers I coach do the following exercises. Should a rider have an exercise he or she prefers that has proven beneficial in the past, we include it. Each exercise is accompanied by recommended stretches. If you have any question about one of these, meet with a certified personal trainer or an experienced athlete or coach for a demonstration.

HIP EXTENSION—SQUAT
(Quadriceps, Gluteus, Hamstrings)

The squat improves force delivery to the pedals. For the novice, the squat is one of the most dangerous exercise options in this routine. Great care is necessary to protect the back and knees.

1. Wear a weight belt during the Maximum Strength (MS) phase.
2. Stand with the feet pedal-width apart, about 10 inches, center to center, with the toes pointed straight ahead.
3. Keep the head up and the back straight.
4. Squat until the upper thighs are just short of parallel to floor—about the same knee bend as at the top of the pedal stroke.
5. Point the knees straight ahead, maintaining their position over the feet at all times.
6. Return to the start position.
7. Stretches: Stork Stand and Triangle

FIGURE 13.1
Squat

HIP EXTENSION—STEP-UP
(Quadriceps, Gluteus, Hamstrings)

Improves force delivery to the pedals. The step-up closely mimics the movement of pedaling, but the exercise takes more time than the squat or leg press, since each leg is worked individually. Caution is necessary to ensure a stable platform and overhead clearance. The platform should be a height equal to twice the length of your cranks. That's approximately 14 inches (35cm). A higher platform puts great stress on the knee and raises the possibility of injury.

1. Use either a barbell on the shoulders or dumbbells in the hands. Use wrist straps with dumbbells.
2. Place the left foot fully on a sturdy platform with the toes pointing straight ahead.
3. With the back straight and the head erect, step up with the right foot, touching the top of the platform, and immediately return to the start position.
4. Complete all left-leg reps before repeating with the right leg.
5. Stretches: Stork Stand and Triangle

FIGURE 13.2
Step Up

HIP EXTENSION—LEG PRESS
(Quadriceps, Gluteus, Hamstrings)

Improves force delivery to the pedals. It is probably the safest of the hip-extension exercises, and generally takes the least time. In the PE phase, be careful not to "throw" the platform, since it may damage knee cartilage when it drops back down and lands on legs with locked knees.

1. Center the feet on the middle portion of platform about 10 inches (25cm) apart, center to center. The feet are parallel, not angled out. The higher the feet are placed on the platform, the more the gluteus and hamstrings are involved.

2. Press the platform up until the legs are almost straight, but with the knees short of locking.

3. Lower the platform until the knees are about 8 inches (20cm) from the chest. Going lower places unnecessary stress on the knees.

4. The knees remain in line with the feet throughout the movement.

5. Return to the start position.

6. Stretches: Stork Stand and Triangle.

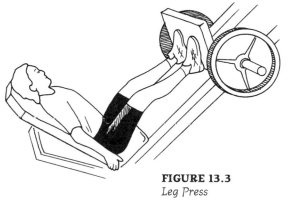

FIGURE 13.3
Leg Press

SEATED ROW

(Upper and Lower Back, Lower Lats, Biceps)

This simulates the movement of pulling on the handlebars while climbing a hill in a seated position. Strengthens the core—the lower back.

1. Grasp the bar with the arms fully extended and the hands about the same width as when gripping the mountain bike handlebar.

2. Pull the bar toward the stomach, keeping the elbows close to the body.

3. Keep movement at the waist to a minimum, using the back muscles to stabilize the position.

4. Return to the start position.

5. Stretch: Pull-down and Squat Stretch.

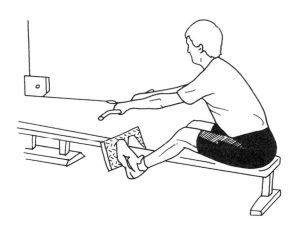

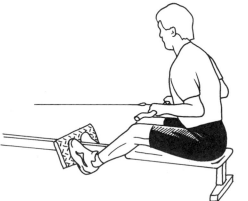

FIGURE 13.4
Seated Row

FIGURE 13.5
Chest Press

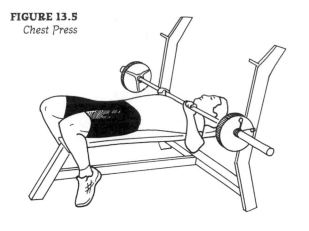

CHEST PRESS
(Pectorals and Triceps)

The chest press, along with the lat pull-down and the standing row, helps support the shoulder in the event of a (heaven forbid!) crash. The chest press also produces arm and shoulder stability for riding on rough and bumpy terrain. With free weights, a spotter is necessary in the MS phase.

1. Grasp the bar with the hands above the shoulders and about as wide apart as when holding the handlebars.
2. Lower the bar to the chest, keeping the elbows close to the body.
3. Return to the start position without raising the butt off the bench.
4. Stretch: Pull-down

PUSH-UP
(Pectorals and Triceps)

The push-up provides the same benefits as the chest press. The advantage is that no equipment is necessary, so it can be done anywhere.

1. Place the hands slightly wider than the shoulders.
2. Keep the back straight and the head up.
3. Maintaining a straight-line, rigid body position, lower the body until the chest is within about 4 inches (10cm) of the floor. This may be done with the knees on the floor as strength is developing.
4. Return to the start position.
5. Stretch: Twister

FIGURE 13.6
Push-up

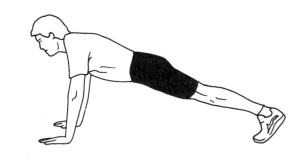

HEEL RAISE

(Gastrocnemius)

This is a "personal weakness" exercise for athletes who experience calf and Achilles tendon problems. The heel raise may reduce susceptibility to such injuries, but be careful to use very light weights when starting, as it may also cause some calf or Achilles tendon problems initially. Progress slowly with this exercise. Never attempt a 1RM test with this exercise if the lower leg is a personal weakness area.

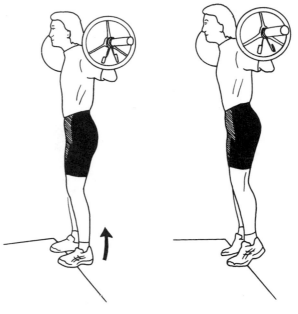

FIGURE 13.7
Heel Raise

1. Stand with the balls of the feet on a 1- to 2-inch (2.5 to 5cm) riser, with the heels on the floor.
2. The feet are parallel and pedal-width apart.
3. With straight knees, rise up onto the toes.
4. Return to the start position.
5. Stretch: Wall Lean.

KNEE EXTENSION

(Medial Quadriceps)

If you are plagued by a kneecap tracking injury, this exercise may help by improving balance between the lateral and medial quadriceps, keeping the injury under control.

FIGURE 13.8
Knee Extension

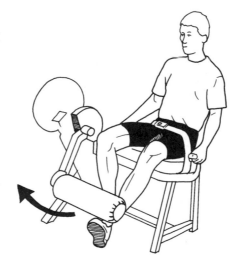

1. Start with the knee fully extended and the toes pointing slightly to the outside. Work one leg at a time.
2. Lower the ankle pad only about 8 inches (20cm)—do not go all the way down, as this may increase internal knee pressure, making the underside of the kneecap sore.
3. Return to the start position.
4. Stretch: Stork Stand

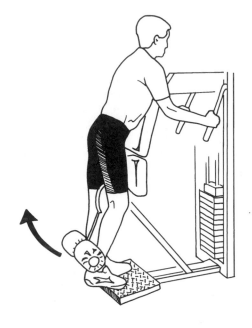

FIGURE 13.9
Leg Curl

LEG CURL
(Hamstrings)

Hamstring injuries may result from an imbalance between the quadriceps and hamstrings. By strengthening the hamstrings, the strength ratio between these two major movers is improved. Leg curls are done on either prone or standing machines.

1. Bend the leg to about a 90-degree angle at the knee.
2. Return to the start position.
3. Stretch: Triangle.

FIGURE 13.10
Abdominal with twist

ABDOMINAL WITH TWIST
(Rectus Abdominus, External Oblique)

This is a core exercise to improve the transfer of energy from the upper to the lower body.

1. Sit on a decline board with the knees bent at about 90 degrees and the ankles held firmly in place.
2. The arms are crossed over the chest and may hold a weight plate.
3. Lower the upper body to about a 45-degree angle from parallel with the floor.
4. Return to the start position with a twist. With each repetition, alternate looking over the right and left shoulders as the torso twists to the right and left.
5. Stretch: Arch the back and extend the arms and legs.

LAT PULL-DOWN

(Latissimus Dorsi, Biceps)

Just as with the chest press, the lat pull-down stabilizes the shoulder.

1. Grasp a straight bar with the arms fully extended and the hands placed about as wide as they would be on the handlebars.
2. Pull the bar toward the upper chest (not behind the head).
3. Minimize both movement at the waist and rocking back and forth to start the weight moving. Keep the body still, using the back muscles to stabilize this position.
4. Return to the start position.
5. Stretch: Pull-down.

FIGURE 13.11
Lat Pull Down

STANDING ROW

(Deltoids, Trapezius, Biceps)

The standing row stabilizes the shoulder and improves the ability to lift the front wheel when clearing obstacles.

1. At the low-pulley station, or with a barbell or dumbbells, grasp the bar at thigh height with the hands handlebar grip–width apart.
2. Pull the bar to the chest.
3. Return to the start position.
4. Stretch: Grasp a stationary object, such as a pole, behind your lower back with the hands as high up as possible. Lean away from the pole, allowing your body to sag while relaxing.

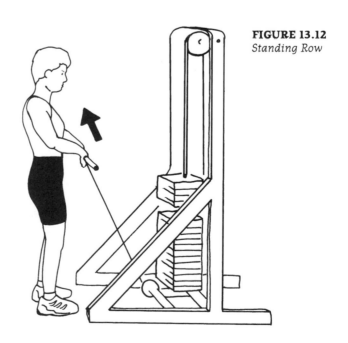

FIGURE 13.12
Standing Row

STRETCHING

Aerobic exercise and weight lifting are repetitive activities. The same muscle groups are used over and over. This promotes a shortening and tightening of the muscles and a loss of elasticity. Eventually, the joints lose some of their original range of motion. The aging process also produces this restricted movement. Tight muscle-tendon units and stiff joints are prime candidates for injury.

Inflexible muscles also detract from cycling performance. Banjo string–tight hamstring and calf muscles pull on the back of the leg on the downstroke. During a long ride, this produces enough discomfort in the legs, hips and lower back that the aching rider may lower his or her saddle to accommodate the tightness. Now with a saddle set too low, the force applied to the pedal declines—as does performance.

A tight lower back plagues many riders, such as pro Jimi Killen, who was described in Chapter 9. Not only does it impede training progress, low-back tightness may become low-back pain, when not riding requiring medical attention. A consistent and effective program of stretching may prevent such problems from occurring. Prevention is always preferable to treatment.

Loss of flexibility detracts from performance.

Low-back tightness is a "pain."

THE SCIENCE OF STRETCHING

Besides improving performance, one study found that stretching following workouts also aided recovery by improving muscle cells' uptake of amino acids, promoting protein synthesis within muscle cells, and maintaining the integrity of muscle cell walls.

Stretching may hasten recovery.

In addition, stretching's injury-reducing reputation among athletes is well established, and has garnered some support in the scientific literature, although it's not universally acclaimed by research. Many years ago, a study of runners in the Honolulu Marathon discovered that those who stretched regularly following workouts had fewer injuries than those who didn't.

Stretching may reduce injury risk, especially in men.

In a study conducted by the New Jersey Medical School, flexibility was found to have a direct relationship to the risk of injury, especially for men. At their preseason physical examinations, more than 200 college athletes were graded on a 10-point scale for flexibility of the hip and leg muscles and ligaments. Their progress was then followed throughout their competitive seasons. For men, as their muscle tightness increased by 1 point on the 10-point flexibility scale, their risk of injury increased by 23 percent. There was no relationship, however, between the women's grade on the flexibility scale and their risk of injury.

Don't get the idea, however, that stretching is a way to prevent all injuries and make you into an elite rider. Some riders already have plenty of flexibility. Trying to increase it with excessive stretching may produce slack muscles and excessive range of motion in joints.

One study has even shown that highly elastic muscles reduce economy in runners by decreasing the stored-energy return. When a joint is extended during an activity such as running or pedaling a bike, muscles are stretched. Just as with a stretched rubber band, these stretched muscles have a potential elastic energy that helps provide locomotion without effort on the athlete's part. If this potential energy is reduced because muscles are excessively slack, more effort is needed to produce the work.

Too much stretching may reduce economy of movement.

Nevertheless, stretching plays a role in injury prevention and in improved performance in some athletes. Do you need to stretch more? If you are often tight on the back side of your torso and legs, uncomfortable when riding no matter how the bike is adjusted, and prone to muscle or tendon strains, you may need to stretch more frequently—especially right after getting off the bike. For others, moderation in stretching, as in most other aspects of life, is best.

Besides stretching for a few minutes after a ride, another good time is during strength workouts. Weight lifting produces extreme tightness. By lightly stretching the exercised muscles during the rest time between sets, range of motion is maintained. Notice that each of the weight-lifting exercises described earlier in this chapter is accompanied by the stretches to be performed during recovery.

Also stretch during weight-lifting workouts.

If lack of flexibility is a problem for you, stretching a little bit throughout the day is also beneficial. While sitting at a desk, working or reading, you can gently stretch muscle groups such as the low back, hamstrings and calves. Stretch gently while watching television, standing in line and talking on the telephone, and first thing in the morning while you are still in bed. A little stretching done often and regularly is preferable to infrequent and prolonged sessions devoted strictly to stretching.

STRETCHING MODELS

Stretching didn't become an accepted aspect of fitness training until after World War II. In the last 40 years, four major stretching methods have been popular.

Popular stretching methods.

Ballistic

In the 1960s, ballistic stretching was common. Bouncing movements were thought to be the best way to make muscles limber. Later it was learned that this technique had just the opposite effect: Muscles resisted lengthening and could even be damaged by overly motivated stretchers. Today almost no one stretches this way.

Static

In the 1970s, Californian Bob Anderson popularized a new stretching method and in 1980 released a book called *Stretching*. This book is still widely read and is available in bookstores and catalogs. Anderson's approach was just the opposite of ballistic stretching, involving little or no movement. A position is assumed as the targeted muscles are stretched to a level of slight strain, and then held in that position for several seconds. Static stretching remains the most popularly used method some 20 years after the book came out.

PNF

About the same time static stretching was being popularized by Anderson, another method also developed, but it never received much exposure or support until the 1990s. This method, proprioceptive neuromuscular facilitation, or PNF, has been supported by research going back to the early 1970s. Some studies have shown it to be 10 to 15 percent more effective than static stretching.

There are many variations on PNF stretching. Some are quite complex. Here is one version:

1. Static-stretch the muscle for about 8 seconds.
2. Contract the same muscle for about 8 seconds.
3. Static-stretch the muscle again for about 8 seconds.
4. Continue alternating contractions with stretches until you have done four to eight static stretches. Always finish with a static stretch.

The static stretches should become greater with each repeat as the muscles relax. Using this PNF method, a stretch takes one to two minutes.

ACTIVE ISOLATED

A relatively new arrival on the fitness scene, active-isolated stretching involves brief, assisted stretches that are repeated several times. Here is a typical routine:

1. Contract the opposing muscle group as you move into a stretching position.
2. Use your hands, a rope or a towel to enhance the stretch.
3. Stretch to the point of light tension.
4. Hold for two seconds and then release.
5. Return to the starting position and relax for two seconds.
6. Do one or two sets of eight to 12 repetitions of each two-second stretch.

STRETCHING EXERCISES

The following are a few of the many possible stretches for mountain bikers. You may find that some are more important for you than others, or that you need to include stretches not illustrated here.

TWISTER

(Pectoralis)

Weights: chest press and push-up

1. With your back facing a wall, grasp a stationary object at shoulder height.
2. Look away from the arm being stretched and twist your body away from it, also.

FIGURE 13.13
Twister

STORK STAND

(Quadriceps and Hip Flexors)

Weights: hip extension and seated knee extension

1. While balancing against your bike or a wall, grasp your right foot behind your back with your left hand.
2. Hold this position as you move the knee backward—don't pull up on the foot.
3. Keep your head up and stand erect—do not bend over at the waist.

FIGURE 13.14
Stork Stand

FIGURE 13.15
Triangle

TRIANGLE

(Hamstring)

Weights: hip extension and leg curl

1. Bend over at the waist while leaning on your bike or a wall.
2. Place the leg to be stretched forward with the foot about 18 inches (4.5cm) from the support.
3. The other leg is directly behind the first. The farther back this leg is placed the greater the stretch.
4. With your weight on the front foot, sag your upper body toward the floor. You should feel the stretch in the hamstring of the forward leg.

FIGURE 13.16
Pull-down

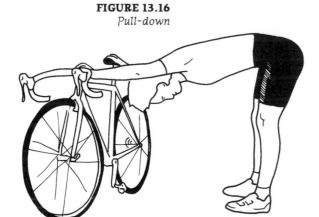

PULL-DOWN

(Latissimus Dorsi, Trapezius, Pectoralis, Triceps)

Weights: lat pull-down and seated rows

1. Hold onto your bike or a railing for balance with your upper-body weight resting on your arms.
2. Allow your head to sag deeply between outstretched arms to create a stretch in your lats.

SQUAT

(Low Back, Soleus, Quadriceps, Gluteus)

Weights: seated row

FIGURE 13.17
Squat

1. Holding onto something for balance, squat down, keeping your heels on the floor (this is easier with cycling shoes off).
2. Allow your butt to sag close to your heels as you rock forward.

WALL LEAN
(Gastrocnemius, Soleus)

Weights: heel raise

1. Lean against a wall with the leg to be stretched straight behind you, and the other forward holding most of your weight.
2. Keep the heel of the rear foot on the floor with the toe pointed forward.
3. The farther forward the hips move, the greater the stretch in the calf.
4. To stretch the gastrocnemius, straighten the rear knee. Stretch the soleus by bending the rear knee.

FIGURE 13.18
Wall Lean

REFERENCES

Alter, M. J. *Sport Stretch*. Champaign, IL: Human Kinetics, 1998.

Anderson, B. *Stretching*. Bolinas, CA: Shelter Publications, 1980.

Avela, J., et al. "Altered Reflex Sensitivity after Repeated and Prolonged Passive Muscle Stretching." *Journal of Applied Physiology* 84, no. 4 (1999): 1283–1291.

Bompa, T. *Periodization of Strength*. Toronto: Veritas Publishing, 1993.

Bompa, T. *Theory and Methodology of Training*. Dubuque, IA: Kendall/Hunt, 1994.

Brzycki, M.. "Strength Testing—Predicting a One-Rep Max From Reps to Fatigue." *Journal of Physical Education, Recreation and Dance* 64 (1993): 88–90.

Fowles, J. R. and D.G. Sale. "Time Course of Strength Deficit After Maximal Passive Stretch in Humans." *Medicine and Science in Sport and Exercise* 29, no. 5 (1997): S155.

Gleim, G. W. and M. P. McHugh. " Flexibility and Its Effects on Sports Injury and Performance." *Sports Medicine* 24, no. 5 (1997): 289–299.

Goldspink, D. F. "The Influence of Immobilization and Stretch on Protein Turnover of Rat Skeletal Muscle." *Journal of Physiology* 264 (1977): 267–282.

Hickson, R. C., et al. "Potential for Strength and Endurance Training to Amplify Endurance Performance." *Journal of Applied Physiology* 65 (1988): 2285–2290.

Hickson, R. C., et al. "Strength Training Effects on Aerobic Power and Short-Term Endurance." *Medicine and Science in Sports and Exercise* 12 (1980): 336–339.

Holly, R. G., et al. "Stretch-Induced Growth in Chicken Wing Muscles: A New Model of Stretch Hypertrophy." *American Journal of Physiology* 7 (1980): C62–C71.

Hortobagyi, T., et al. "Effects of Simultaneous Training for Strength and Endurance on Upper- and Lower-Body Strength and Running Performance." *The Journal of Sports Medicine and Physical Fitness* 31 (1991): 20–30.

Johnston, R. E., et al. "Strength Training for Female Distance Runners: Impact on Economy." *Medicine and Science in Sports and Exercise* 27, no. 5 (1995): S47.

Kokkonen, J. and S. Lauritzen. "Isotonic Strength and Endurance Gains through PNF Stretching." *Medicine and Science in Sports and Exercise* 27, no. 5 (1995): S 127.

Kokkonen, J., et al. "Acute Muscle Stretching Inhibits Maximal Strength Performance." *Research Quarterly for Exercise and Sport* 69 (1998): 411–415.

Kraemer, W. J., et al. "Compatibility of High-Intensity Strength and Endurance Training on Hormonal and Skeletal Muscle Adaptations." *Journal of Applied Physiology* 78, no. 3 (1995): 976–989.

Marcinik, E. J., et al. "Effects of Strength Training on Lactate Threshold and Endurance Performance." *Medicine and Science in Sport and Exercise* 23, no. 6 (1991): 739–743.

McCarthy, J. P., et al. "Compatibility of Adaptive Responses with Combining Strength and Endurance Training." *Medicine and Science in Sports and Exercise* 27, no. 3 (1995): 429–436.

Nelson, A. G., et al. "Consequences of Combining Strength and Endurance Training Regimens." *Physical Therapy* 70 (1990): 287–294.

Sale, D. G. and D. MacDougall. "Specificity in Strength Training: A Review for the Coach and Athlete." *Canadian Journal of Applied Sport Sciences* 6 (1981): 87–92.

Sale, D. G., et al. "Comparison of Two Regimens of Concurrent Strength and Endurance Training." *Medicine arid Science in Sports arid Exercise* 22, no. 3 (1990): 348–356.

Schatz, M. P. "Easy Hamstring Stretches." *Physician and Sports Medicine* 22, no. 2 (1994): 115–116.

Stone, M. H., et al. "Health- and Performance-Related Potential of Resistance Training." *Sports Medicine* 11, no. 4 (1991): 210–231.

Vanderburgh, H. and S. Kaufman. "Stretch and Skeletal Myotube Growth: What Is the Physical to Biochemical Linkage?" *Frontiers of Exercise Biology*, K. Borer, D. Edington, and T. White (Editors). Champaign, IL: Human Kinetics, 1983.

Wallin, D., et al. "Improvement of Muscle Flexibility, A Comparison Between Two Techniques." *The American Journal of Sports Medicine* 13, no. 4 (1985): 263–268.

Zatsiorsky, V. M. *Science and Practice of Strength Training*. Champaign, IL: Human Kinetics, 1995.

UNIQUE NEEDS

Racing is not for everyone, but there are more opportunities out there for women my age to be successful because there are fewer of us. I'd tell any woman who has kids and a job that mountain bike racing is something you can do for yourself.

—KATHY SESSLER

Since they are humans, all mountain bikers share certain physiological traits. This allows me to write a book full of generalizations about how to prepare to race. But as you recall from Chapter 3, when it comes to many of the fine details of training, there are enough differences between riders that it is not possible for everyone to do exactly the same things and get the same results. This is the principle of individualization. These differences often have to do with genetics, upbringing and current lifestyle.

Unique needs of subgroups are based on the principle of individualization.

Throughout the previous chapters, I've tried to make it clear that each individual rider must discover what works best, given his or her unique set of circumstances, when it comes to the fine points frequency, intensity, volume and mode of training. It's certainly not possible to write a book that meets each person's exact needs in these areas, but by looking at smaller groups that have much in common, it is possible to further refine some of the guidelines offered previously. Consequently, training recommendations for five clusters of athletes are examined in this chapter—women, veterans, juniors, novices and neo-pros.

Much of what is presented here is based on my observations as a coach and not on scientific research. I have coached male and female athletes, both young and old and with widely varying experience levels, for nearly 20 years. With each of those athletes I've had to make some adjustments in training—no two followed exactly the same program. Some of the adjustments were small, while others were significant. This chapter summarizes the most important changes to what you have read in the previous chapters.

WOMEN

Throughout most of the 20th century there were few sports that women were officially allowed to compete in on a scale even approaching that of men. They were "protected." The most popular—and "ladylike"—sports throughout most of this period were tennis, golf, gymnastics and figure skating. At about midcentury, women began challenging the restrictions placed on them, especially when it came to endurance sports. As a result, women made considerable progress toward full acceptance in endurance sports in the latter years of the last century.

Women were excluded from Olympic endurance sports throughout most of the last century.

The change was quite evident in the sport of track and field. In the 1928 Olympic Games in Amsterdam, for example, the longest race in which women were allowed to compete was the 800-meter run. In that Olympiad, three female runners broke the world record for the distance, but finished in "such a distressed condition" that horrified officials dropped the event from future competition. "Women just weren't meant to run that far," was the position of many male officials and even scientists. It wasn't until the 1964 Tokyo Games that the women's 800-meter run was resurrected in the Olympics.

Cycling has had its ups and downs when it comes to equality of the sexes, but has generally reflected the same attitudes. In the 1890s, the "Golden Age" of cycling, at a time when society often closeted and sheltered "the weaker sex," women were nonetheless accepted into mass-start races alongside men. It wasn't until many years later that this attitude of near-equality changed and women were discouraged from racing bikes. Then, in the last few decades of the 20th century, attitudes began to shift. While prize money is now usually equal for male and female pros in nearly all mountain bike races, most continue to offer shorter events for women than for men.

UNIQUE CONSIDERATIONS

The changing attitudes toward women in society have led, over the years, to the currently accepted view that there is really little difference between the sport-related capacities of male and female athletes. There are, of course, a few obvious, physical distinctions more characteristic of women, such as greater hip width, a shorter torso relative to leg length, a lower center of gravity and a more knock-kneed stance. All these differences affect the cycling equipment selected by women.

In terms of significant, performance-specific differences between the sexes, women, on average, have a smaller aerobic capacity resulting from a smaller heart, and lower oxygen-carrying capacity of the blood relative to males. Also, in comparison with male athletes, women riders carry a higher percentage of body weight as fat, and can generate less absolute force due to their smaller muscle mass. These differences result in about a 10-percent variance in the results of world-class competitions involving males and females, in events ranging from weight lifting to sprinting to endurance sports like mountain bike racing.

Given these basic differences, men and women athletes are really more alike than they are dissimilar. While their velocity may not be as great, women can and do train at the same volumes and intensities as their male counterparts at every level of competition. They're fully capable of doing the same workouts as men. And they respond to training loads in the same way. There are very few reasons why women athletes shouldn't train just as men do.

Women can train in much the same manner as men.

In mountain biking, women usually don't train to compete with men, but with other women. So making training comparisons to men is of little value to the female athlete. The question she ponders is how to improve relative to her female competition. Generally, I've found, there are three areas women should consider concentrating on in order to train better and race more competitively—strength, psychology and diet.

Strength

Most women athletes are relatively stronger in their legs than in their upper bodies. This weakness affects hill climbing. While standing on the pedal, the force generated by the leg in powering the bike uphill must be counterbalanced by the arm pulling against the handlebars on the same side, with stability provided by the abdominal and back muscles. If the arms and midsection are weak, the unbalanced force will tip the bike over or force the rider to restrict leg drive. Upper-body strength, therefore, is required for powerful climbing, and also for handling the bike through technical sections of the course.

Upper-body strength benefits climbing and bike handling.

Upper-body strength work to improve this relative weakness involves pushing and pulling exercises that use all the arm joints plus the back and the abdominals. Abdominal strength also needs emphasizing due to the size and shape of the female pelvis. Whenever possible, work the arms in conjunction with the abdominal and back muscles, rather than in isolation. The seated-row exercise described in the previous chapter is a good example of a multijoint exercise that benefits cycling. This station builds the arms and back in a way similar to climbing on a bike. The chest press will also provide muscular balance.

I generally recommend that women riders continue to lift weights year-round, even in the summer racing months. Otherwise, strength may soon be lost after a winter of focused weight-room work.

Women should lift weights year round.

Psychology

I've found that women are usually better at dealing with defeat than are men. But when it comes to poor performance, a woman is likely to blame it on a lack of ability. In contrast, men are more inclined to chalk up a poor race to lack of effort or "a bad day." This self-doubt is not unusual for women where sports performance is concerned—after all, society has taught them in subtle ways that they are not good at athletics. If you don't agree, just compare the size of crowds at boys' and girls' high school athletic events.

Confidence is as important for success in sport as physical ability. No matter how talented you are, if you don't believe you can, you won't. A good example of this is a woman rider I once coached. She frequently had reasons why she couldn't achieve her high goals, and generally thought of herself as inferior to the other women she raced with. She often commented on her limitations and failures. A lack of confidence was her greatest limiter. I suggested that every night after turning the lights off and before falling asleep, she should use those few minutes in bed to review and relive the major success of her day, no matter how small it seemed. It could simply be that she finished a tough workout feeling strong, or that she climbed one hill particularly well, or that one interval felt especially good. She would recapture that experience in her mind, and go to sleep feeling good about her ability. That year she had her best season ever, winning a national championships and finishing fifth at the world championship. It's hard to know exactly what the impetus for her obviously improved confidence was, but I believe part of it came from simply looking for success in her daily rides.

Other ways to improve confidence include keeping a "success log" in which the day's achievements are recorded. Also, learning to "act as if" you are confident, no matter how insignificant and unsure you may feel in a given situation, like at the start of a race, may improve confidence. Observe how the top women pros conduct themselves before and during a race. They exude confidence just by the ways they stand, move and talk. You've got to believe in yourself if you're to succeed.

Diet

Many women athletes overly restrict their food intake, often resulting in low iron levels. It is not unusual for female athletes to eat fewer than 2000 calories a day, while needing 3000. With an average of 5mg of iron per 1000 calories in the standard American diet, that means an intake of about 10mg of iron a day, with a need of perhaps 15mg.

To make matters worse, vegetarian diets favored by many women athletes are even lower in absorbable iron than the standard diet. Exercise and menstruation further decrease iron levels. Iron deficiency or anemia is a definite possibility under such circumstances. Owen Anderson, Ph.D., the publisher of *Running Research News,* estimates

Women tend to lack confidence for sport.

Reviewing and reliving successes helps build confidence.

Iron deficiency may result from restricting calories.

that 30 percent of women athletes have an iron deficiency. Such a condition results in early fatigue and low endurance. One study even linked low iron with an increase in running injuries in high school girls.

Such problems are easily corrected by including red meat in the diet three or four times a week. If you prefer to restrict your diet to plants, include many vitamin C–rich foods in your meals to improve iron absorption, and eat lots of beans and spinach. Avoid drinking coffee and tea with meals. Should you become anemic, such a diet may prove inadequate for correcting the situation, requiring iron supplementation. Do not take iron supplements without the counsel of your health-care provider, as there are many possible complications.

Also frequently restricted in the female diet are foods high in fat. Dietary fat is necessary for peak performance. A body deprived of essential fats is in danger of being run down and susceptible to illness, due to a weakened immune system. If sick, injured or tired, you can't perform at your best. Include fat in your diet every day from good sources such as nuts, nut spreads, avocados and olive oil. Continue to avoid saturated fat and trans fatty acids, which are found in foods with hydrogenated fat, such as snack foods and prepackaged meals. Chapter 16 provides more details on the athlete's diet.

Dietary fat is necessary for peak performance.

VETERANS

Since the 1970s, some athletes well beyond the age of 35—a time when most are slowing down—have continued to train and compete just as they did when younger. This is unprecedented in the history of Western society. The baby-boom generation has refused to grow old gracefully and has instead insisted on staying physically active. Prior to this generation, age 40 was generally considered old. The medical community once advised anyone beyond that ancient age to slow down so as not to damage their hearts. Now athletes in their 40s and even into their 50s, 60s and 70s accomplish physical feats once considered practically impossible for middle-aged and senior citizens. Many of these aging athletes can still do some of the workouts they did in youth, and they often train with riders 20 years their junior—sometimes on an equal basis.

Master athletes are now doing the "impossible."

These athletes are just the tip of the iceberg. Now that the baby boomers are well into their 40s and 50s, we can expect to see the number of older athletes swell to record proportions, and their performances keep improving. Along with this increasing number of active and competitive older athletes, attitudes are changing about what is physically possible in the second half of our lives.

Attitudes about aging are changing.

FORTY PHYSIOLOGY

While it appears that intense physical activity, such as racing a mountain bike, slows the aging process, it doesn't stop us from getting older physically. There's no denying that with increasing age there is an inevitable decline in some aspects of performance. In fact, world records for endurance events seem to confirm this, as the marks drop by about 1 percent per year after age 30.

Since the 1930s, scientists have studied the link between aging and physiological function. One inescapable conclusion has come from this research: Getting older inevitably means some degree of reduced function. Aerobic capacity (VO2 max) decline is a good example of what the studies show.

You may recall from Chapter 4 that aerobic capacity is a measure of how much oxygen the body uses to produce energy at a maximal workload. The higher one's aerobic capacity, the greater the potential for performance in an event like mountain bike racing.

Research shows steady physical decline with aging.

Studies show that starting at about age 20, aerobic capacity begins dropping on average in the general population, partly because maximum heart rate decreases. A lowered maximum heart rate means less oxygen delivery to the muscles, and therefore a lowered aerobic capacity. The usual rate of decline measured in such research is in the range of six to 10 beats per decade.

Similar results have come from aging studies on the pulmonary, nervous, muscular, thermal regulatory, immune and anaerobic systems: Sometime in the third and fourth decades of life, functional decreases begin, with losses of up to 10 percent per decade. Compounding the problem is what appears to be a normal increase in body fat after the early 20s, obviously made worse by a sedentary lifestyle. Again, this is for the general population—not those who race mountain bikes.

THE AGING MYTH

A little skepticism is a healthy thing when it comes to research. Most studies of aging are based on "cross-sectional" analysis. This means, for example, that a group of 30-year-olds and a similar group of 40-year-olds are tested for some parameter of fitness, and the difference is assumed as the normal loss.

How aging research is generally done.

The alternative is "longitudinal" research, which involves following a group of subjects for several years, testing regularly to see how they change. This method has many benefits. Time is an obvious downside, however, so there are few longitudinal studies of athletes.

Research on aging also raises the question of who the subjects are. Many studies characterize the subjects as "trained endurance athletes." This vague description is usually based on measures of training volume, such as years of activity, or hours trained in a week. Definitions vary. One study's trained endurance athlete may be another study's novice. Seldom is the intensity of training used to categorize the groups studied, as it is hard to quantify. But since it appears that intensity is the key to maintaining race fitness, this is a crucial issue.

The few longitudinal studies that have been done show that when the intensity of training is maintained, aerobic capacity and other selected measures of fitness decline as little as 2 percent per decade. This is roughly a third to a fifth of what is usually discovered in sedentary subjects, or even in those who maintain their health and continue exercising at low intensities.

Intensity is the key to improvement as a veteran.

The "normal" decline in performance of six to 10 percent per decade is probably more a result of self-imposed training and lifestyle limitations than it is of human physiology. Aging may actually only account for a fourth of the losses, while disuse takes the bigger bite.

TRAINING IMPLICATIONS

The bottom line is that intense training keeps the heart, nerves, muscles, lungs and other systems all working to their genetic potential. If you never exercise at high intensity, you will lose fitness, and possibly health, more rapidly than is necessary. For those beyond the age of 40, the following training guidelines will help to keep fitness high and, for some, even improving.

Training guidelines.

Train Intensely

Build and maintain endurance, but give a higher priority to intense workouts. This doesn't mean training anaerobically all the time, but rather planning the most intense sessions meticulously. Know exactly what it is you intend to achieve, and then ride with that purpose in mind. "Intense" doesn't mean "killer" efforts—intervals until you throw up, or even redlining, necessarily. Intense workouts are those incorporating the heart rate 4 and 5 zones and the CP60 through CP0.2 power zones (see Chapter 4 for descriptions of these zones). Training near and above lactate threshold is an effective way to train occasionally. Intense workouts should stress you without leaving you wasted. Always stop before reaching failure. Save the maximum efforts for races.

Use Intensity Sparingly

While intensity in training is important, don't get carried away with it. Do no more than three high-intensity workouts in a week. Some veterans should only do two. How quickly you recover is the key to knowing what frequency is best. You should go into each intense workout feeling ready and eager. The other days are devoted to recovery, aerobic fitness maintenance and the development of skills.

Plan Frequent Rest

Train hard for two or three weeks and then take several days to a week for recovery and rest. Some veterans can use Table 7.2 to schedule their hard training and rest weeks. For those who need more frequent recovery—which is most masters, I believe—Table 14.1 is a better guide. Frequent R and R is the best way for the serious master to improve steadily. Frequent rest time means not only breaks from training every two or three weeks, but also taking two or even three days of easy training between high-intensity sessions. Masters may also find greater improvement by allowing more recovery time between intervals within a workout.

Strength Train Year-Round

This is usually weights, but could be focused hill work on a bike. Older riders who live in the flatlands will improve their hill strength by lifting weights year-round. Aerobic training on flat terrain is insufficient to prevent the loss of muscle mass, especially after the age of 50. One advantage of weight training is that you can also work the upper body, which slows the loss of muscle mass above the waist.

Maintain Leg Speed

Don't be content with grinding up the hills in big gears to develop strength and ride competitively. Also work at developing or maintaining the ability to pedal at high cadence, as this ability tends to decline with disuse and aging. You may find this makes you more efficient and reduces your risk of injury while also aiding nervous system maintenance. Every week do one or more rides at a high-cadence and also include workouts such as fixed-gear riding, spin-ups, and isolated leg training throughout the year (see Appendix B for details).

Continuing to race successfully as you grow older means refusing to accept loss of physical function as normal, always setting challenging goals and never slowing down. It also means redefining "over the hill" to describe a workout, rather than an age.

		Annual Hours										
Period	Week	200	250	300	350	400	450	500	550	600	650	700
Prep	All	4.0	4.0	5.0	6.0	7.0	7.5	8.5	9.0	10.0	11.0	12.0
Base 1	1	4.0	5.0	6.0	7.0	8.0	9.0	10.0	11.0	12.0	12.5	14.0
	2	5.0	6.0	7.0	8.5	9.5	10.5	12.0	13.0	14.5	15.5	16.5
	3	4.0	4.0	4.5	5.0	5.5	6.5	7.0	8.0	8.5	9.0	10.0
Base 2	1	4.0	5.5	6.5	7.5	8.5	9.5	0.5	12.5	12.5	13.0	14.5
	2	5.0	6.5	7.5	9.0	10.0	11.5	12.5	14.0	15.0	16.5	17.5
	3	4.0	4.0	4.5	5.0	5.5	6.5	7.0	8.0	8.5	9.0	10.0
Base 3	1	4.5	5.5	7.0	8.0	9.0	10.0	11.0	12.5	13.5	14.5	15.5
	2	5.0	6.5	8.0	9.5	10.5	12.0	13.5	14.5	16.0	17.0	18.5
	3	4.0	4.0	4.5	5.0	5.5	6.5	7.0	8.0	8.5	9.0	10.0
Base 4	1	5.0	6.5	8.0	9.5	10.5	12.0	13.5	14.5	16.0	17.0	18.5
	2	6.0	7.5	9.0	10.5	11.5	13.0	15.0	16.5	18.0	19.0	20.5
	3	4.0	4.0	4.5	5.0	5.5	6.5	7.0	8.0	8.5	9.0	10.0
Build 1	1	5.0	6.5	8.0	9.0	10.0	11.5	12.5	14.0	15.5	16.	17.5
	2	5.0	6.5	8.0	9.0	10.0	11.5	12.5	14.0	15.5	16.0	17.5
	3	4.0	4.0	4.5	5.0	5.5	6.5	7.0	8.0	8.5	9.0	10.0
Build 2	1	5.0	6.0	7.0	8.5	9.5	10.5	12.0	13.0	14.5	15.5	16.5
	2	5.0	6.0	7.0	8.5	9.5	10.5	12.0	13.0	14.5	15.5	16.5
	3	4.0	4.0	4.5	5.0	5.5	6.5	7.0	8.0	8.5	9.0	10.0
Build 3	1	5.0	6.0	7.0	8.5	9.5	10.5	12.0	13.0	14.5	15.5	16.5
	2	5.0	6.0	7.0	8.5	9.5	10.5	12.0	13.0	14.5	15.5	16.5
	3	4.0	4.0	4.5	5.0	5.5	6.5	7.0	8.0	8.5	9.0	10.0
Peak	1	5.0	5.5	6.5	7.5	8.5	9.5	10.5	11.5	13.0	13.5	14.5
	2	4.0	5.0	5.0	6.0	6.5	7.5	8.5	9.5	10.0	11.0	11.5
Race	All	4.0	4.0	4.5	5.0	5.5	6.5	7.0	8.0	8.5	9.0	10.0
Tran	All	4.0	4.0	4.5	5.0	5.5	6.5	7.0	8.0	8.5	9.0	10.0

TABLE 14.1

Weekly training hours by period for veterans.

JUNIORS

Teenagers who take up the sport of mountain bike racing often ask me if they should participate in other school-sponsored sports throughout the year or focus only on riding. I encourage them to continue in at least one other sport, as that is a great way to develop the general fitness and mobility skills necessary for competitive mountain biking. I've seen too many junior racers who decide to cut out everything except riding and soon burn out. Nearly all the best riders in the world cut their competitive teeth on one or more sports such as running, swimming and soccer.

Mountain biking is not something that should be taken lightly. If you decide to race off-road you must be willing to train conscientiously when school sports are done for the year. Fat-tire racing often requires hours of difficult training. The races aren't over in a few seconds, and there are no time-outs. When the race starts, it is a long, difficult effort. It takes serious commitment to be good in this sport.

You're undoubtedly serious about mountain bike racing since you've gone so far as to buy and read this book. That, in itself, is an expression of commitment. Now you may be wondering if everything this book has described so far applies to you. With some exceptions, it does. Let's examine the details of training for juniors.

HOW TO IMPROVE QUICKLY

Working with a coach is a smart decision.

The best way to advance in multisport, just as with your school sports, is by working with a coach, especially one who lives close by. A good coach will help you progress by offering tips on technique, nutrition, race strategy and sports psychology. These are all things you would undoubtedly figure out, but a coach will speed up the learning process. He or she will also design a training program that fits your personal needs. This is important, since mountain biking is an individual sport—there are no others to rely on, or to slow you down. With a coach you'll also develop more quickly, because there will be fewer setbacks due to injury, burnout or overtraining.

Camps are great for growth as an athlete.

Another way to speed up your progress is by attending a camp for juniors. These are usually staffed with one or more coaches and, perhaps, with elite riders. In a few days you can learn a lot about training and racing. Check in the advertising sections at the backs of cycling magazines for camps that may be available in your area. The camp doesn't have to be just for mountain biking; a road cycling camp is also a good option. If the only camps available in your area are for senior riders, call the camp director and ask if it would be appropriate for you to attend.

A local club can provide support and experience.

Cycling clubs are also good for providing support, expertise, racing experience and the camaraderie of other juniors. Join a club if there is one in your region, and try to train with the members as often as you can. You'll learn a lot just from being around more experienced athletes. Also ask the club to provide events for juniors at their sponsored races, if they don't already do so.

On a slightly different note, you and your parents have probably come to realize that mountain biking is an expensive sport. Don't be concerned with having the latest and greatest frame, suspension system, wheels and pedals. Instead, concentrate on becoming the best motor and the most skilled in your category. When it's time to replace a bike you've outgrown, talk with other juniors about purchasing a bike for which they've also gotten too big. In the same way, see if younger athletes can use your old bike. Regardless of what you may read in the magazines and what others say, the key to improvement is not equipment, but fitness and skills.

Focus on fitness and skills, not expensive equipment.

TRAINING GUIDELINES

When your school sports end for the year and mountain bike training starts, it's necessary to keep things in perspective. Remember that you're not an accomplished athlete yet; there is a lot of room for improvement, and steady growth is necessary to eventually achieve your potential. Professional mountain bikers didn't start off training with huge volumes and lots of intense workouts. They progressed steadily from year to year, a little at a time. The following are my suggested guidelines for maintaining a healthy perspective and steady growth.

Skills Before Fitness

Develop good pedaling technique and handling skills before increasing mileage. Efficient and effective form ultimately means faster race times, and less training time lost to injuries. You also won't waste time by developing bad habits that must be broken later. A coach's feedback is the best way to accomplish this. Exercise caution with volume increases, as high mileage is more likely to cause breakdowns from injury and burnout than occasional high-intensity workouts.

Be wary of high volume.

Be Patient

The most important aspect of racing at this point is participation and learning race strategy, especially pacing. Think of races as hard workouts at which you get to watch and learn from other, more experienced athletes. The best adult athletes were seldom the best as juniors, and, in fact, were often not even close. For example, did you know that Michael Jordan was cut from his junior high school basketball team?

Think Long Term

Rather than simply trying to beat other athletes in every workout and race, develop long-term, personal-improvement goals that focus on advancing to the next level of racing. Such a goal might be to improve your handling skills and climb better by the time you turn 17 in two years. Realistic goals established for your weakest race abilities, and consistent work to accomplish them, will make you a better rider. This takes the pressure off you to always be the best at the next race, and allows you to focus on what is really important—steady progress.

Speed Before Endurance

Develop speed skill with pedaling drills and practice on maneuvering through technical sections of a course. These will train your nervous system and muscles to develop more efficient and effective patterns of movement. Short, fast workouts, especially those intended to improve skills, should be done frequently and are better for you now than are very long, slow endurance workouts.

Form Before Weight

Improve total-body strength, especially for hip-extension (leg press, squat, step-up), by doing body-weight and light-weight workouts in the gym. Stay with the Anatomical Adaptation (AA) weight phase (see Chapter 13 for details) until you are 17. Concentrate more on perfecting form than on the amount of weight lifted. Even if you don't start weights until age 17, spend the first year only doing AA workouts. Always stretch following each set.

Get a Physical

Before the start of each season, do what the pros do—get a complete physical examination done by your doctor. This will allow you and your coach, if you have one, to feel good about starting the year without anything holding you back. If your school requires a physical to participate in your other sports, check this off as already completed.

Have Fun

Always remember why you race. It certainly isn't for money or glory—these are far more abundant in sports like football and basketball. You're probably racing mountain bikes for the personal challenge, for the enjoyment of having exceptional fitness, and, most of all, for fun. Keep that perspective. Win with humility, lose with dignity, congratulate those who beat you without offering excuses, and learn from mistakes.

NOVICES

Although success in cross-country racing is often easy at first, at some point every sport-class rider decides it's time to get serious about training. But other than simply adding more saddle time, few know what it takes to improve racing performance. The following is a brief primer on the essentials of preparing for sport-class mountain bike racing.

RIDING POSITION

Before getting into the nitty-gritty of training, let's first make sure that your position on the bike is conducive to effective riding. If the bike is set up correctly, you pedal efficiently, have good balance, are capable of delivering power to the rear wheel in a wide variety of situations, and feel comfortable for the duration of the race.

The key to all of this is saddle position. Many sport riders set theirs too high, which diminishes performance. Compared with a road bike set-up, the mountain bike saddle is lower—perhaps as much as 1 or 2 centimeters (a half-inch or so). When sitting on the bike on an indoor trainer with shoes off, you should be able to pedal backward with the heels and have a bend in the knee at the bottom of the stroke. Or, sitting on the saddle at a full stop, you should easily reach the ground with your foot for balance. Such a position lowers the center of gravity and allows the use of the feet as skids on tricky descents and off-camber turns.

How to set saddle height.

If you feel the saddle is too high now, make changes of no more than a quarter of an inch (0.5cm) every three to four rides. This will allow you to adapt gradually to the new position.

In the first year of racing, it's advisable to sit a little more upright than the pros do by using a slightly raised handlebar and a short stem. This will improve vision, take the stress off the neck, and help you feel more confident on technical courses.

HANDLING SKILLS

One of the things that sets mountain bike racing apart from road racing is the need to develop excellent handling skills. No matter how good your fitness is, if you can't maneuver the bike effectively through loose soil, over wet roots, down rock-strewn descents and on narrow single-track with trees standing guard just inches from the bar ends, you'll never make it in cross-country. Many a road racer has tried mountain bike racing and felt pretty cocky leading the race over the first climb only to wind up in last place at the bottom of the first gnarly descent.

Handling skills are something every rider should work on weekly throughout the season. Such training starts with refining pedaling skills in the early winter months. Climbing a steep grade on loose terrain demands constant tension on the chain. Great surges of power on the downstroke with huge "dead" spots at the top and bottom and on the upstroke cause you to lose traction and spin out. To work on this most basic skill, pedal on an indoor trainer with one leg while the other rests on a stool or chair. Notice where the dead spots are and work to minimize them by pedaling smoothly. It will take several such sessions to develop this skill. Be patient.

Minimize "dead" spots in the pedal stroke for smooth climbing.

Also in the winter months, work on basic bike control in a grassy park once or twice each week. Skills you can include are bunny hopping, jumping obstacles, track stands, wheelies, slalom runs around closely spaced obstacles, taking tight corners by leaning the bike, mounting and dismounting, and double shifting at the start of a hill. Little or no structure is needed for this workout. In fact, the more like play it is the more you'll get out of it. Doing this with a friend will make it even more fun.

Work on basic handling skills in the winter.

In mid- to late winter, ride trails two or three times a week to integrate the early winter skill development into race-specific abilities. Start with easy trails, but challenge yourself to try more demanding ones every week. Discover how to relax and move with the bike rather than fighting it. Learn to look where you want to go rather than focusing on obstacles to avoid. Find out how far forward to sit on the saddle in order to keep the front wheel down when climbing on loose or bumpy terrain. Riding a technical section over and over within a workout will help you hone these skills. It's also helpful to occasionally follow the line of a more experienced mountain biker as he or she maneuvers through a course.

In late winter, hone technical handling skills.

FITNESS

So far, I haven't talked about race fitness. In the early winter it will develop to a small extent just from riding regularly while working on skills. But fitness can be helped along by riding on the roads two or three times each week, since intensity is steadier and easier to control on pavement than on hilly trails. For these rides a road bike is beneficial, but slick tires for your mountain bike are cheaper. If you detest riding on the road and gently rolling fire roads are available, it's okay to ride them instead.

Ride on the road regularly.

Get a heart rate monitor or power meter and learn how to use it (see Chapter 4 for details). For steady-effort rides, monitoring heart rate or power will help to ensure that the intensity is neither too high or too low. It's still important, however, that you develop a sense of effort from listening to your body. One way to do that is to rate your perceived exertion frequently while riding, using a 0 to 10 scale with 0 being a walk in the park and 10 your maximum effort. You'll soon develop the ability to gauge effort so precisely that you will know just how much energy to expend over the duration of a race in order to finish in the best possible time.

The sport-class rider should work on three elements of base fitness in addition to the speed skill already mentioned. The most basic is aerobic endurance. This is where the road rides or fire roads come in. A two- to three-hour ride once a week in the late winter and spring will produce excellent aerobic fitness. Make these rides low-effort, low–heart rate, and low-power. The course should be flat to gently rolling, meaning grades that are short and shallow enough so that you stay in the easy-to-moderate-effort range all the way. Be careful of doing these rides with others. Too many allow testosterone rather than brains to control their riding effort.

Develop Aerobic Endurance.

After about 12 of these weekly long rides, you can cut back to one every 10 to 14 days if you're racing or pressed for time on the weekends. Otherwise, keep doing one long ride a week throughout the season.

The second element of fitness that the sport rider must build is strength. It starts in the weight room during the early winter months. Improving strength by pumping iron will help your arms and legs absorb shock and allow you to lift the front wheel effortlessly over obstacles and climb like a mountain goat. I recommend that the first-time weight lifter stay with light loads and high repetitions throughout the season. This is the Anatomical Adaptation (AA) phase described in Chapter 13.

Include weights in the program.

During the winter months, lift twice a week religiously. It is best to space these weight room sessions with 72 to 96 hours between them. For example, lift on Mondays and Thursdays. Once the race season arrives, cut back to one strength day each week for maintenance. I recommend Mondays.

The other part of strength to be developed comes from riding hills once a week in the late winter and spring. Separate these rides from weight-training days by 48 hours. So if you're on a Monday-Thursday lifting pattern, hit the hills on Saturdays. Most of this climbing should be done seated to develop hip-extension power while learning to balance the bike. Once aerobic endurance is well established, hills can be included in your long rides. As with long rides, every 10 to 14 days for such a ride will maintain endurance and hill strength once the racing starts or if you are pressed for time.

The third element of fitness to develop is muscular endurance—racing stamina. As explained in Chapter 6, this is the combination of aerobic endurance and force—the ability to maintain a fairly high effort for a long time. It's the most important aspect of fitness for the cross-country racer. There are three workouts that should be done in late

**Develop muscular
endurance.**

winter and spring to build muscular endurance. These are also described in Appendix B under "muscular endurance."

The first workout is tempo riding. Once a week for four to six weeks, ride 20 to 30 minutes at a heart rate in the 3 zone or power output of CP90. This should feel moderately hard, hard enough that you'll look forward to the conclusion of the effort, but know you could have gone longer. These are best done on the road on a flat course. Wednesday is a good day for this workout if you're on a Monday-Thursday weight room routine with hills on Saturday and a long ride on Sunday.

When tempo efforts start coming easy, it's time to take muscular endurance to the next level by replacing tempo with cruise intervals. On a flat road, do intervals that are six to 12 minutes long with two- to three-minute recoveries. The effort is slightly higher than was used for tempo—heart rate 4 to 5a zones or CP30 power zone. This is just below or right at your lactate threshold, or the point at which you first begin to breathe heavily.

After four to six weeks of cruise intervals, it's time to take them off-road. Do the same workout on a hill with a moderate grade. It's okay to shorten the intervals to match the length of your hill so long as they're at least three minutes. The recoveries may be somewhat longer than specified, as you'll need to descend quickly after each one. This will hone your climbing ability, which is so key to success in cross-country.

HAVE FUN

While I've laid out a fairly structured plan for you here, don't let the details get in the way of having fun. It's all right to change things around from week to week, if for no other reason than variety. Back off every fourth week or so and just ride strictly for fun with no thought of fitness or training. Take days off when you don't feel like riding or it would be a hassle to fit into your day. If riding ever becomes drudgery, you'll be known as a former mountain bike racer.

NEW PROFESSIONALS

Elite endurance athletes are gifted individuals who were born with the physiology to excel in long-distance events. They were also fortunate enough to have been steeled for competition throughout much of their youth. While the mix varies from athlete to athlete, they are the product of both nature and nurture.

Elites have an amazing capacity for physical work, and are blessed with an ability to improve fitness quickly. Most have a well-developed work ethic that borders on obsession. They are highly motivated and dedicated to training and to their goals, which causes them to persevere through the most demanding workouts and extraordinary environmental conditions. It is because of such qualities, combined with genetic luck and a spirit of adventure, that they have risen to the top one-tenth in sport.

Some of these same qualities, however, are also their worst enemies. It is not uncommon for elite athletes, especially those relatively new to the elite ranks, to drive themselves into an overtrained state with regularity. Many leave the sport disheartened, never realizing their full potential, due to their overzealous and unbridled training methods. This section explores ways in which the new elite mountain biker may avoid such calamity, and steadily progress toward his or her innate fitness summit.

A propensity for training hard is a double-edged sword.

COACHING

For many, perhaps most, elite riders, training under the guidance of a wise coach is the best way to avoid the twin calamities of overtraining and burnout and ensure steady growth accompanied by a long and successful racing career. A coach with both experience and a good understanding of the science of training interprets and applies the latest concepts and methods to meet the unique needs of the elite competitor. And by planning and managing training from a more objective point of view than the athlete is capable of the coach guides the athlete's racing career toward the achievement of personal goals and long-held dreams.

A good coach can steer the elite rider toward long-term success.

A good coach offers many skills and services above and beyond writing workouts. He or she also helps the athlete clearly define goals and objectives, maintain the vision of the future, and cope with unusual psychological stresses. The concerned coach provides a sympathetic ear for problems ranging from financial woes to interpersonal relationship problems. A coach with an extensive network of contacts may recruit others whose unique skills and services assist with the athlete's development, such as doctors, exercise physiologists, physical therapists, nutritionists, bike mechanics, sports psychologists, and others who may be a part of the athlete's "team."

A "team" approach improves the athlete's chance of success.

Two (or more) heads are better than one. When new challenges arise, as they are certain to do during a season, an experienced coach offers fresh views for dealing with them. He or she often has a gut-level solution, based on years of experience, that might never have occurred to you. In addition, a good coach may even anticipate problems before they appear, and correct your course to avoid them altogether.

Having a coach in your corner lightens the burden of training, and transforms your athletic career from an often frustrating and solitary pursuit into a team effort. All of this means that you are able to put your entire energy and time into what you are already

A coach takes the guess-work out of training.

good at—training and racing. A coach also allows you more free time for recovery since less time is spent trying to determine what you will do next in training.

TRAINING

To the up-and-coming elite athlete, it's obvious that he or she must work very hard to have success in mountain bike cross-country racing, as the competition is tough. That's not a problem for most. The typical self-coached elite athlete's approach is to do

Don't overtrain!

more—more volume, more intensity, or both, with the last being the usual choice. Coupling this decision with inadequate rest and frequently poor diet leads down an inevitable path to overtraining. Elite athletes must avoid such breakdowns at all costs.

The leading cause of overtraining is inadequate recovery time. The elite athlete who has been around for some time knows how to balance the stresses of training with growth-producing rest. Neo-pros often don't have a feel for this yet. The second most common factor in overtraining among elite competitors is excessive volume. Constantly

Inadequate recovery and excessive volume are common causes of overtraining.

placing demands on the body for greater frequency and duration of training is a more probable cause of overtraining than excessive intensity in the absence of high volume. Periodization, as discussed in several previous chapters, is the best way to avoid over-training, since rest, volume increases, and gradual step-ups of intensity are all planned in relation to the highest-priority races.

Other lifestyle factors also contribute to overtraining in the elite athlete. These include diet, social, occupational, academic, travel and financial stresses. Especially notable on this list, and easily controlled, is diet, especially one low in nutrients and high in sugar (see Chapter 16). A less well-understood, psychological cause may be monoto-

Lifestyle also contributes to overtraining

nous training from doing the same basic workout routine day after day, week after week. The mix of these stresses that produces overtraining is a highly individual matter. Just because a training partner easily handles a certain mix of physical and psychological stress doesn't mean that you can. Find what works for you.

When overtraining is suspected, disease and inadequate diet must be eliminated as causes before deciding how to modify training. This is why a close working relationship with a health-care provider or full-service testing facility is recommended, as is a baseline blood test during the early winter months when health is sound and training stress is low.

On the positive side, there are several other training considerations that lead to competitive racing form. The following are training considerations for the elite rider.

Train "Professionally"

When first joining the professional ranks, it's common for riders to fall into the trap of planning their day as if they are on vacation. They all too often go to bed late, sleep in, have a long and casual breakfast, take care of a few chores and errands, and finally, sometime late in the day, go for a ride. Such a lifestyle makes it practically impossible to do two-a-day workouts when they could boost fitness, or to get in a very long ride in the winter months when days are short. This is unprofessional.

Instead, treat training as you would any other job you might have. Plan your days around riding by treating it as the highest priority. The training day starts with going to bed at a decent hour so you can make the best use of daylight rather than squandering it by sleeping in. After digesting breakfast, the first order of the day is training; everything else is secondary to this. Training is now your job—treat it as such.

Train like a professional.

Use Training Time Wisely

The athlete who wins the race is not always the one who trains with the most volume, yet many elite multisport competitors seem to approach training with such a belief. Peak race performance, however, *always* results from finding the optimal balance between workout stress and rest. At this level, training volume is not determined merely by how much time you have available, but by what you do with that time. More is not always better. The athlete who is hungry to win and physically fresh as a result of being slightly undertrained will almost always beat another who is mentally and physically fatigued from chronically overreaching.

Doing less can mean attaining more.

That said, it is also obvious that the best endurance athletes in the world typically employ a relatively high volume of training. Part of the reason for this high volume is that they have the time to do so. There are fewer demands on the pro rider's time than on that of an amateur who also works 40 to 50 hours per week. This means that the pro must find a way to fit in all the training necessary to produce steady growth while avoiding overtraining. One way of doing this that doesn't work well for part-time athletes is to vary the length of microcycles.

In Chapter 7 I described how to train using the system of periodization. Recall that in this system the season is divided into periods, the shortest of which are called microcycles. That chapter suggested the length of a microcycle as seven days. The reason for this is that most riders' lives revolve around seven-day weeks due to commitments such as school, work and other responsibilities. For the elite rider this is usually not the case, which means there is more freedom to manipulate the lengths of microcycles to optimize training time.

Microcycle lengths may be changed to make the best use of time.

Seven days often doesn't fit well into a training plan meant to use time efficiently. After all, the more hard workouts you can fit into a given block of time and still adequately recover, the greater your fitness will be. Microcycles can be of any length that works well for you. For example, you might train on a six-day cycle by alternating hard and easy days in this manner: hard-easy-hard-easy-hard-easy. That's a 1:1 work-recovery ratio. This fits well when it seems that frequent recovery is necessary due to the magnitude of the stress on the hard days, such as in Build periods. This is a very simple and effective pattern.

Another six-day pattern, for when recovery is not great issue, is hard-hard-easy-hard-hard-easy. This 2:1 work-recovery ratio may work well in the early Base periods when the stresses are not great. The hard-hard-easy pattern may be repeated one more time to produce a nine-day microcycle. Another long pattern is hard-hard-hard-easy-easy-hard-hard-hard-easy-easy. A 10-day cycle such as this allows for six hard sessions and four days of recovery—a 3:2 ratio. There may even be combined patterns, such as hard-hard-hard-easy-easy-hard-hard-easy-easy (3:2 and 1:1) to provide more frequent rest. There are many other possibilities.

Experiment to find the best patterns for you at various times in the season.

The point of all of this is that you don't have to restrict training to seven-day microcycles. Experiment to find what works best for you at different times of the year. Keep in mind, however, that changing the patterns like this does not reduce or eliminate your need for extended rest and recovery every fourth week or so.

"Crash" Training

Chapter 3 explained that after a training stress is applied, and the body is allowed to recover, fitness soon develops to a level somewhat higher than originally enjoyed. This process is known as overcompensation. Recent studies show that when the training stresses are closely spaced for an extended period, followed by a long rejuvenation phase, the degree of overcompensation is enhanced. This is known as "supercompensation." Such a risky flirtation with overtraining is sometimes called "crashing." It can be quite effective for the elite rider who needs to boost fitness quickly, but it must be done cautiously.

Supercompensation results from crash training.

Two studies in the early 1990s explored the benefits of crash training. In 1992 a group of seven Dutch cyclists trained excessively (for them) for two weeks by increasing their training volume from a normal 12.5 hours per week to 17.5. Their volume of high intensity went from 24 to 63 percent of total training time. At the end of the two weeks there was a decrease in all of the measurable aspects of their fitness—they were overreached. But after recovering for two additional weeks they posted a 6-percent improvement in power and a 4-percent improvement in time trials, and they produced less blood lactate at race speed compared with precrash levels.

Another study in Dallas had runners overtrain for two weeks and then recover for two weeks. The fitness results were similar to those in the Dutch study, plus there was an increase in aerobic capacities. Further research suggests an increase in blood volume, greater levels of hormones that produce muscle growth, and an improved ability to metabolize fat result from a high-stress crash-recovery period and the ensuing supercompensation.

These and other studies have revealed three guidelines that help in designing a crash cycle. The first is that it takes about three weeks to produce overtraining in young, well-trained athletes. (In a study of elite rowers preparing for the world championship, three hours of daily training for three weeks were necessary to produce overtraining.) Therefore, crash cycles must not go that long, and should probably be far shorter, falling in the range of 7 to 14 days.

The second guideline is that large volume increases are not nearly as effective at producing supercompensation as dramatic increases in intensity. For example, researchers doubled the weekly mileage of a group of well-trained runners for three weeks as the number of highly intense miles remained the same. At another time, they doubled the number of miles that they ran at high intensity for three weeks as volume stayed constant. Following the high-volume phase, endurance and running performance plateaued, but they improved following the increased-intensity period.

Finally, studies reveal that it takes one-half to one full day of active recovery for every day spent crashing. Short crash cycles of, for example, five to seven days are best followed by an equal number of recovery days. Longer crash cycles, in the neighborhood of 14 days, may be matched with

Guidelines for designing a crash cycle.

FIGURE 14.1
Example of 15-day crash cycle culminating with a race. Workouts are listed by category as shown in Appendix B. This is an example only. Actual workouts should be determined based on individual limiters. Note that Day 1 follows a period of recovery.

Overreaching Phase	
Day 1 (Hard)	Power + Muscular Endurance
Day 2 (Hard)	Anaerobic Endurance + Muscular Endurance
Day 3 (Hard)	Force + Muscular Endurance
Day 4 (Easy)	Endurance
Day 5 (Hard)	Power + Muscular Endurance
Day 6 (Hard)	Anaerobic Endurance + Muscular Endurance
Day 7 (Hard)	Force + Muscular Endurance
Day 8 (Easy)	Endurance
Day 9 (Hard)	Anaerobic Endurance + Muscular Endurance
Day 10 (Hard)	Force + Muscular Endurance
Recovery Phase	
Day 11 (Easy)	Off
Day 12 (Easy)	Recovery
Day 13 (Easy)	Recovery
Day 14 (Easy)	Power
Day 15 (Easy)	Recovery
Day 16	Race

fewer recovery days, about one-half day for every day of crashing.

With these guidelines in mind, Figure 14.1 provides an example of a crash cycle for an elite mountain biker. Remember that this is only one way of many in which a crash cycle may be organized.

Crash training must be approached with caution.

Be extremely careful with crash training. The risk of overtraining rises dramatically during such a buildup. It's important that your fitness base (endurance, force, speed skill and muscular endurance) is well established before attempting a crash cycle. If the typical signs of overtraining appear, cut back on the workload immediately (see Chapter 11 for overtraining markers). It is probably best not to attempt a crash cycle more frequently than once for each racing peak in the season. In addition, the last crash workout should probably be no closer to the goal race than two weeks.

EXTENDING YOUR CAREER

Motivation is necessary for success at the highest level of sport, and may determine who will place in the money on a given day. If you aren't mentally driven and absolutely in love with training and racing, there is little chance of a long and successful career in mountain bike racing. But high motivation is also a double-edged sword. Because of it the elite athlete will push through any formidable training session deemed important for producing faster races. This can lead to burnout, recurring injuries, illness and frequent overtraining. Such interruptions break patterns of training consistency, and force a return to previous levels. Consistency is the single most important component for producing peak race fitness. Inconsistent training results in poor race performances. Promising careers sometimes end early when motivation gets in the way of clear thinking.

Motivation needs to be bridled.

Treat your body with respect—it's a fine instrument, not a blunt object. Be cautious with anything that has high risk and the potential to interfere with training stability. Paying close attention to recovery in order to balance stress is the starting point for optimal training and a long, successful career. When rest is adequate, the problems of inconsistency diminish, and you feel positive, confident and eager to race.

Gradual increases in workload reduce the risk of breakdown.

Other than the timely inclusion of rest, the best way to prevent breakdowns is by increasing the training workload incrementally over a period of several weeks. Use a program of periodization, as discussed in Chapters 7, 8 and 9. Sudden and unusually large increases in volume or intensity, such as the crash training described above, must have predetermined time limits and the body's response mut be carefully monitored. At the first sign that something is not right, such as a scratchy throat or inability to recover, decrease the workload despite the training goal's not being achieved. To continue is to risk setback.

Also important to extending your career in multisport is thinking and planning for the long term. It's easy to get caught up in preparing only for the next race, regardless of how insignificant that event may be to your stated long-term goals. The athlete with training myopia sees every race as having equal importance, and tries to attain peak fitness levels for each. This is physiologically, and perhaps even psychologically, impossible. Know what is important for your career not only for this season, but for the next three or four years—such as a berth on the Olympic team or making the national team for world's. Keep such long-term goals uppermost in your thinking when determining your annual training plan design and weekly workout patterns. As discussed earlier, this is where a wise and experienced coach is of great value.

Never lose sight of where you're going

It's also interesting to note that when successful pro athletes are asked the secret of their longevity in the sport, they almost always mention having fun. If you're not having a good time riding a mountain bike and going to races, something needs to change or your career is destined to be a short one. The change needed may be training with others instead of always alone, or moving somewhere you've always wanted to live, or including a significant other in your life.

Most important of all, have fun!

REFERENCES

Atwater, A. E. "Gender Differences in Distance Running." In P.R. Cavanagh (ed.), *Biomechanics of Distance Running*. Champaign, IL: Human Kinetics, 1990.

Balaban, E. P., et al. "The Frequency of Anemia and Iron Deficiency in the Runner." *Medicine and Science in Sport and Exercise* 21 (1989): 643–648.

Bemben, D. A., et al. "Effects of Oral Contraceptives on Hormonal and Metabolic Responses During Exercise." *Medicine and Science in Sport and Exercise* 24, no. 4 (1992): 434–441.

Bompa, T. *From Childhood to Champion Athlete*. Toronto, ONT: Veritas Publishing, 1995.

Brown, C. and J. Wilmore. "The Effects of Maximal Resistance Training on The Strength and Body Composition of Women Athletes." *Medicine and Science in Sports and Exercise* 6 (1975): 174–177.

Budgett, R. "Overtraining Syndrome. *British Journal of Sports Medicine* 24 (1990): 231–236.

Child, J. S.,et al. "Cardiac Hypertrophy and Function in Masters Endurance Runners and Sprinters." *Journal of Applied Physiology* 57 (1984): 170–181.

Clark. "Red Meat: To Eat or Not To Eat." *National Strength and Conditioning Association Journal* 15 (1993): 71–72.

Cohen, J. and C. V. Gisolfi. "Effects of Interval Training in Work-Heat Tolerance in Young Women." *Medicine and Science in Sport and Exercise* 14 (1982): 46–52.

Costill, D. L., et al. "Effects of Repeated Days of Intensified Training on Muscle Glycogen and Swimming Performance." *Medicine and Science in Sport and Exercise* 20 (1988): 249–254.

Cunningham, D. A., et al. "Cardiovascular Response to Intervals and Continuous Training in Women." *European Journal of Applied Physiology* 41 (1979): 187–197.

Deuster, P. A., et al. "Nutritional Survey of Highly Trained Women Runners." *American Journal of Clinical Nutrition* 45 (1986): 954–962.

Dill, D., et al. "A Longitudinal Study of 16 Champion Runners." *Journal of Sports Medicine* 7 (1967): 4–32.

Drinkwater, B. L., et al. "Bone Mineral Content of Amenorrheic and Eumenorrheic Athletes." *New England Journal of Medicine* 311 (1984): 277–281.

Drinkwater, B. L. "Women and exercise: Physiological aspects." *Exercise and Sports Sciences Reviews* 12 (1984): 21–51.

Drinkwater, B. L. (ed.). *Female Endurance Athletes.* Champaign, IL: Human Kinetics, 1986.

Dufaux, B., et al. "Serum Ferritin, Transferrin, Haptoglobin, and Iron in Middle- and Long-Distance Runners, Elite Rowers, and Professional Racing Cyclists." *International Journal of Sports Medicine* 2 (1981): 43–46.

Dutto,D. J. and J.M. Cappaert. "Biomechanical and Physiological Differences Between Males and Females During Freestyle Swimming." *Medicine and Science in Sports and Exercise* 26, no. 5 (1994): S1098.

Ekblom, B. "Effect of Physical Training in Adolescent Boys." *Journal of Applied Physiology* 27 (1969): 350–353.

Fry, R. W., et al. "Overtraining In Athletes: An Update." *Sports Medicine* 12 (1991): 32–65.

Fry, R. W., et al. "Biological Responses to Overload Training in Endurance Sports." *European Journal of Applied Physiology* 64, no. 4 (1992): 335–344.

Fry, R. W., et al. "Periodization and The Prevention of Overtraining." *Canadian Journal of Sports Science* 17 (1992): 241–248.

Gibbons, T. P., et al. 1996. "Physiological Responses in Elite Junior Triathletes During Field Testing." *Medicine and Science in Sports and Exercise* 28, no. 5 (1996): SA756.

Hamilton, N. et al. "Changes In Sprint Stride Kinematics With Age In Masters Athletes." *Journal of Applied Biomechanics* 9 (1993): 15–26.

Heath, G. A. "Physiological Comparison of Young and Older Endurance Athletes." *Journal of Applied Physiology* 51, no. 3 (1981): 634–640.

Hooper, S. L., et al.. "Hormonal Responses of Elite Swimmers to Overtraining." *Medicine and Science in Sports and Exercise* 25 (1993): 741–747.

Jeukendrup, A. E., et al. "Physiological Changes in Male Competitive Cyclists After Two Weeks of Intensified Training." *International Journal of Sports Medicine* 13, no. 7 (1992): 534–541.

Kirwan, J. P., et al. "Physiological Responses to Successive Days of Intense Training in Competitive Swimmers." *Medicine and Science in Sport and Exercise* 20 (1988): 255–259.

Koltyn, K. F., et al. "Perception of Effort in Female and Male Competitive Swimmers." *International Journal of Sports Medicine* 12 (1991): 427–429.

Koutedakis, Y., et al. "Rest in Underperforming Elite Competitors." *British Journal of Sports Medicine* 24 (1990): 248–252.

Koutedakis, Y. "Seasonal Variation in Fitness Parameters in Competitive Athletes." *Sports Medicine* 19 (1995): 373–392.

Leake, C. N. and J. E. Carter.. "Comparison of Body Composition and Somatotype of Trained Female Triathletes." *Journal of Sports Science* 9, no. 2 (1991): 125–135.

Legwold, G.. "Masters Competitors Age Little in Ten Years." *The Physician and Sports Medicine* 10, no. 10 (1982): 27.

Lehmann, M. P., et al. "Training-Overtraining: Influence of a Defined Increase in Training Volume vs. Training Intensity on Performance, Catecholomines and Some Metabolic Parameters in Experienced Middle- and Long-Distance Runners." *European Journal of Applied Physiology* 64 (1992): 169–177.

Lehmann, M. P., et al. "Training-Overtraining: An Overview and Experimental Results in Endurance Sports." *Journal of Sports Medicine and Physical Fitness* 37, no. 1 (1997): 7–17.

Malarkey, W. B., et al. "The Influence of Age on Endocrine Responses to Ultraendurance Stress." *Journal of Gerontology* 48, no. 4 (1993): M134–139.

Malwa, R. M. "Growth and Maturation: Normal Variation and Effect of Training." In C. V. Gisolfi and D. R. Lamb (eds.), *Perspectives in Exercise Science and Sports Medicine: Youth, Exercise and Sport.* Carmel, IN: Benchmark Press (1989).

Mayhew, J. and P. Gross. "Body Composition Changes in Young Women and High Resistance Weight Training." *Research Quarterly* 45 (1974): 433–440.

Nelson. "Diet and Bone Status in Amenorrheic Runners." *American Journal of Clinical Nutrition* 43 (1986): 910–916.

Newby-Fraser, P. *Peak Fitness for Women.* Champaign, IL: Human Kinetics, 1995.

Pate, R. R., et al. "Cardiorespiratory and Metabolic Responses to Submaximal and Maximal Exercise in Elite Women Distance Runners." *International Journal of Sports Medicine* 8 (S2) (1987): 91–95.

Parizkova, J. "Body Composition and Exercise During Growth and Development." *Physical Activity: Human Growth and Development,* 1974.

Pollock, M., et al. "Effect of Age and Training on Aerobic Capacity and Body Composition of Master Athletes." *Journal of Applied Physiology* 62, no. 2 (1987): 725–731.

Pollock, M., et al. "Frequency of Training as a Determinant For Improvement in Cardiovascular Function and Body Composition Of Middle-Aged Men." *Archives of Physical Medicine and Rehabilitation* 56 (1975): 141–145.

Richardson, A. B. and J.W. Miller. "Swimming and the Older Athlete." *Clinical Sports Medicine* 10, no. 2: 301–318.

Rogers, et al. 1990. "Decline in VO$_2$ Max With Aging in Masters Athletes and Sedentary Men." *Journal of Applied Physiology* 68, no. 5 (1990): 2195–2199.

Rushall, B. S. "Some Psychological Considerations for U.S. National Swimming Teams." *American Swimming,* Feb-Mar: 8–12 (1994).

Seals, D. R., et al. "Endurance Training in Older Men and Women." *Journal of Applied Physiology* 57 (1984): 1024–1029.

Shangold, M. M. and G. Mirkin (eds.). *Women and Exercise: Physiology and Sports Medicine.* Davis Publishing, 1988.

Shasby, G. B. and F. C. Hagerman. "The Effects of Conditioning on Cardiorespiratory Function in Adolescent Boys." *Journal of Sports Medicine* 3 (1975): 97–107.

Speechly, D. P., et al. "Differences in Ultra-Endurance Exercise in Performance-Matched Male and Female Runners." *Medicine and Science in Sports and Exercise* 28 (1996): 359–365.

Thorland, W. G., et al. "Strength and Anaerobic Responses of Elite Young Female Sprint and Distance Runners." *Medicine and Science in Sports and Exercise* 19 (1987): 56–61.

Wells, C. L. *Women, Sport, and Performance: A Physiological Perspective.* Champaign, IL: Human Kinetics, 1991.

Weltman, A., et al. "The Effects of Hydraulic Resistance Strength Training in Pre-Pubertal Males." *Medicine and Science in Sports and Exercise* 18 (1986): 629–638.

Wilmore, J., et al. "Is There Energy Conservation in Amenorrheic Compared With Eumenorrheic Distance Runners?" *Journal of Applied Physiology* 72 (1992): 15-22.

Wilmore, J. and D. Costill. *Physiology of Sport and Exercise.* Champaign, AL: Human Kinetics, 1994.

THE TRAINING DIARY

I know myself through mountain biking.
That's how I center myself if things are out of whack personally.
—MYLES ROCKWELL

If you have not been following a methodical, periodized program, it's likely that you have not come close to realizing your potential for race performance. It's obvious from observing how elite riders manage their training that nearly all of them pay strict attention to the cycles of stress and recovery, with their long-term plan pointed at peaking for certain events. Such a methodical approach demands not only planning, but also requires a constant feedback of information for effective decision-making.

A well-kept training diary meets both needs. Without a record of your workouts and racing experiences, you must rely on memory, which all too often is spotty or recalls exaggerated or watered-down versions of what you did a year ago, last month or even yesterday. A training diary is also invaluable for avoiding overtraining.

A diary is especially helpful to the self-coached, time-constrained mountain biker who must make every hour of training count. It's a source of information about what has or hasn't worked in the past, the progress you're making, the need for recovery, how your body responds to a given workout, and how much recovery is necessary following hard workouts and races. The training diary motivates as it builds confidence whenever you review obstacles mastered, difficult workouts completed and high workload weeks sustained, and see how you are overcome other training constraints that happen to everyone from time to time. Confidence grows when successes are written down and reviewed later on. These successes may also include excellent workouts, personal racing bests and objectives accomplished.

In its simplest form, the diary is a log of workouts, races, goals, objectives and dis-

The benefits of keeping a training diary.

tances covered, but it can also provide an early warning system for overreaching and overtraining, which generally announce themselves, if you are paying attention. Tracing the origins of these setbacks to the circumstances that caused them will educate you so that these same problems are avoided in the future. A diary is also a planning tool. Use it to schedule your training week based on the annual training plan you developed in Chapter 7 and the weekly routines worked out in Chapter 8.

A diary is not an end in itself. If all you do is write down training information, but never use the data, its full potential to help you achieve peak racing fitness is not realized. In fact, it's probably a waste of time. But a well-kept and utilized diary is a valuable tool on your journey of personal discovery. It may show you why things aren't going well, or why they are. By paying attention to it, you learn how long it takes to get into race shape following a certain routine. Used wisely, the diary allows you to remember, analyze and modify, motivate and build confidence, plan and hold yourself accountable, all of which sounds surprisingly similar to what a good coach does.

But be aware that there are also downsides to the training diary. It's possible to record too much data, and then spend more time analyzing the data than you did creating it in workouts. The other common shortcoming of some diary keepers is the compulsion to see it as a "score card." Avoid the urge to use your diary this way.

Where should you record all the data? The mode you choose is likely to determine how diligent you are with record keeping. If you get a charge out of high technology, and enjoy detailed analysis, one of the computer-based, software diaries may be just what you need. But if you don't think you will boot up the computer immediately following a workout, then an electronic diary is not the way to go. Choose a standard, paper format instead.

There are several types of diaries.

Many elite athletes prefer to use a simple notebook in which they record anything they want without being forced into a mold by a standard layout. Others design their own by laying out basic pages, and then making copies, which are kept in a loose-leaf notebook.

Appendix C offers a format which follows that suggested in this chapter. You may copy it for your own use. Or you can purchase the *VeloNews Training Diary,* based on this same format from the Velo catalogue, at 800/234-8356, or from the Web, at www.velogear.com.

WHAT TO RECORD

How should you train? There is unlimited information available from training partners, magazines, books, television programs, videotapes and even Web sites to help answer this question. But since you are an individual with unique needs, how do you know which ideas to keep and which to disregard? The best way is to do what any good scientist does with something suspected of having promise—experiment and observe. In this study, however, you are the only subject. What works or doesn't work for you is all that matters when it comes to deciding what workout to do, when to rest, what to eat, and the many other details that define training. Think of your diary as the place where the data from the ongoing experiment is recorded and observed. The more systematic you are in collecting the data, the greater the chance that you will learn your best answers to the "how to train" question.

Training is an experiment with one subject.

Although data is required if you are to train scientifically, writing down too much is as bad as not recording enough. If you have to wade through every minute detail of every workout, you'll have a difficult time drawing conclusions. Record only that which is important and that you're likely to use. The diary should be simple and succinct, or you won't get any value from it.

The following five categories provide a general framework for collecting information that may help you make daily decisions and analyze what you need to improve. Don't feel you have to record all of this. Only keep track of those items that you can quickly write down after a workout, and that you are likely to use later on.

BASIC LOG ENTRIES

This is the information that is brief and easiest to record and analyze. It includes the workout date, course or venue, distance, duration, weather conditions, time of day, equipment used and training partners. Also make note of the quality indicators of the workout, such as interval times, pace or vertical feet gained. Note anything unusual. This might be a knee that felt "funny" or a slight headache.

MORNING WARNINGS

Following the collapse of the Berlin Wall, one of the administrators of the East German Olympic sports program came to the U.S. and spoke about the training methods of the Eastern Bloc athletes. While banned drugs apparently played a role in their success, he explained how individual attention was given to each athlete who lived in the state-sponsored dormitories, and how this contributed to the medal count. He described how each elite athlete's day began with a visit by a staff of professionals and a quick evaluation of readiness to train. This included medical and psychological evaluation, which guided the coaches in refining the day's training plan. The purpose was to have the athlete do only what was appropriate that day—nothing more or less.

Wouldn't it be nice if you had such personal guidance every day? Since it's unlike-

Learning to listen to your body improves training.

ly to happen, the next best option is to learn to make these decisions for yourself. One way to do that is to start each day with a self-evaluation of your physical and mental readiness. Every morning when you wake up, there are clues that indicate if you're up to the scheduled workouts that day. The problem is, most riders don't pay attention.

According to an Australian study, there are daily log entries that may help you pay close attention to the clues. The researchers found that rating sleep quality, fatigue, psychological stress, and muscle soreness on a scale of 1 to 7, with 1 representing the best condition and 7 the worst, was highly predictive of readiness to train. All the ratings are subjective, but if you're honest, a rating of 5, 6 or 7 for any two of these warning signs means that something is wrong, and the workload should be reconsidered that day. Three or more such warning signs are probably a good indication that a day off is needed.

Other indicators that are sometimes helpful in making training decisions are waking pulse and body weight. Find your average waking pulse for a week in which you are healthy and rested. Any time your heart rate is five or more beats above this number, take that as a warning. Another warning is your body weight dropping two pounds in 24 hours. This is usually the result of dehydration, but could also signal excessive training or a diet that does not match your caloric needs. Be sure to weigh under the same conditions each day, such as just after waking and using the toilet.

Forces other than training may affect your warning signs. These could include, for example, travel, work stress, relationship issues, financial problems, heat, humidity and home responsibilities. It makes no difference what causes the warning signs, the bottom line is the same: You must reduce the training workload that day.

Another simple system for evaluating readiness to train is based on recording two ratings every day. The one that you're familiar with from a previous chapter is the Rating of Perceived Exertion (RPE). The other is a subjective rating of recovery—Total Quality Recovery (TQR) scale. At the end of every training session, record how hard it seemed using this RPE scale:

Comparing RPE and TQR.

Ratings of Perceived Exertion (RPE)

6		14	
7	very, very light	15	hard
8		16	
9	very light	17	very hard
10		18	
11	fairly light	19	very, very hard
12		20	
13	somewhat hard		

Every day also record how well recovered you feel using the TQR scale:

Total Quality Recovery (TQR)

6		14	
7	very, very poor recovery	15	good recovery
8		16	
9	very poor recovery	17	very good recovery
10		18	
11	poor recovery	19	very, very good recovery
12		20	
13	reasonable recovery		

Any day in which the RPE rating exceeds the TQR rating is an indication of excessive training and the need for more rest. For example, if RPE for a workout is 13 (somewhat hard) but the TQR is 9 (very poor recovery), the relatively high RPE indicates the need for more rest.

PHYSICAL NOTES

Also record data from your heart rate monitor and power meter following a workout.

Heart rate information may be how many minutes you spent in each training zone. As the season progresses from the Preparation to the Base and Build periods, the higher 3, 4 and 5 zones should make up increasingly greater percentages of your total weekly time. Exactly what those percentages are varies a great deal between athletes, and also varies according to the type of event for which you're training. This is one piece of personal data that is ripe for analysis.

Record heart rate data.

You may also want to include other intensity-related workout data such as peak heart rate achieved, average heart rate and how much your heart rate dropped in one minute at the end of the workout.

If using power measurement on the bike, record average watts and total energy expended. At the end of the week, total up the energy expenditure, in kilojoules, to get an indicator of the workload magnitude that includes both volume and intensity in one number.

Record power data.

MENTAL NOTES

Most athletes think of training as a strictly physical activity and ignore what's happening with the mind and emotions. But sometimes feelings and thoughts are revealing, especially when things aren't going well. For example, low motivation as evidenced by

Emotions are all too often ignored by athletes.

diary comments such as "I didn't feel like working out today" may signal overreaching—an early stage of overtraining. Again, noting and paying attention to these sometimes hormonally dependent emotions keeps you in tune with the inner workings of the body.

In addition to physical development, workouts should also provide training for mental skills that are necessary for successful racing. For example, how good are you at staying focused during a race? Do you find your pace dropping as your mind wanders? If so, work on concentration in certain key workouts. Those that simulate race effort, such as intervals and threshold workouts, are great times to practice staying in tune with what your body is doing. Other mental skills that may need development are confidence, relaxation, attitude and visualization. Record daily accomplishments in these areas in your diary.

Mental skills also need training.

MISCELLANEOUS NOTES

Other training and racing elements you may include in your diary from time to time are travel, environmental factors such as altitude and humidity, work hours or other work-related stresses, weight-training records and family activities that impact training. You could also comment on gears used in climbing a challenging hill; race information including strategy, results, field size and conditions; or the effects of different types of prerace meals. The possibilities are endless and limited only by what you find possibly important to your "experiment."

Record for later comparison any other information you believe may be important.

PLANNING WITH A DIARY

Another way to use your training diary that is quite effective, but seldom done, is as a planning tool. At the end of each week, decide what you need to accomplish in the next week to work toward your season objectives on your annual training plan. Write them down in your diary as training goals for the week. For example, you may set a goal of improving your cycling hill strength by climbing steadily for 10 more minutes this week than you did last week at heart rate zones 4 or 5a, or power zone CP30. Or perhaps one of your annual objectives is to improve lactate tolerance and buffering for faster starts. So a goal for a given week may be to complete a certain number of lactate tolerance repetitions. The idea is that a weekly goal should bring you one step closer to the training objectives necessary to accomplish your seasonal, race-related goals.

Weekly goals lead to the accomplishment of season goals.

Once you know what needs accomplishing in the coming week, decide on the supporting workouts, and the days on which you will do them. Chapter 8 provides guidance in making these decisions so that recovery is adequate. These planning notes could use a shorthand system of your own making, or the workout codes suggested in Appendix B.

For example, a planned workout might be jotted down with a shorthand such as, "40' of M2." This means doing the "cruise interval" and accumulating 40 minutes of high-intensity effort. Then, each day before starting the training session, flip to the scheduled workout in Appendix B to finalize the details. You might, for example, decide to do five, 8-minute cruise intervals with 3-minute recoveries that day. Always keep in mind that it may be necessary to change the workout once you start if you just don't feel right for whatever reason. Overtraining and injury start with the inability to pay attention to the body, and a willful disregard for the future.

Plan workouts based on weekly goals.

At first, this planning for the entire week may take you 20 to 30 minutes. But as you get into the routine, it will only take 10 minutes or so. As far as your progress goes, this is the most important 10 minutes you will spend each week. Such weekly planning will do more to improve your racing than anything else you do other than working out, eating and sleeping.

USING A DIARY FOR ANALYSIS

Now that you've recorded all this information, what do you do with it? The answer depends on what situation you're experiencing. It could be problem-related, such as seeking the cause of an injury, determining why you are chronically tired, or finding out the cause of a poor race. The situation needing analysis might be planning-oriented; for example, deciding what has and hasn't worked in the past in order to peak at the right time for an important race. There is an endless array of situations that you may need to use a diary to delve into as you pursue performance excellence. Hopefully, you've kept your entries brief so that analysis doesn't require sifting through excess verbiage.

TRAINING ANALYSIS

When obstacles appear, as they invariably do, lessening their impact on training and returning to normal workouts is imperative. Injuries, illnesses and overtraining are the most common obstacles for the endurance athlete. The roots of these problems are often found in some combination of excesses in training and lifestyle. Knowing the mistakes you made that caused the setback helps you prevent the same pattern from developing again. The training diary is the key to this knowledge.

Understanding what causes setbacks makes you a wiser self-coach.

Recording changes made in bike set-up, especially saddle position, may prove valuable if a few weeks later a knee flares up. Perhaps the cause is the changes you made, but how much did you move the saddle up, down, fore or aft? Have you ever had it in that position before and experienced anything like this with your knee? Are you able to put it back in the exact same position it was before? Or did something change with your training that may lead to a cause such as more hills in a high gear?

Sometimes there are simply nagging questions that beg for answers. Have you done enough training of certain abilities, such as force development? Are you allowing adequate recovery between workouts? What workout sequences produce the best results for you? What taper procedure seems to work? Looking back through your diaries for recent years often provides answers and new directions in training.

Careful analysis may lead to better training.

RACE ANALYSIS

Want to improve your race performances? After cooling down, ask yourself: Why did it turn out as it did? Was there any particular aspect of it that was especially strong or weak? What role did the prerace meal, warm-up, start, pacing, power, technical skills, endurance, refueling and mental skills play in the outcome? Did you have a sound strategy and follow through on it? The answers to such questions come from nothing more than your memory and conversations with other riders following the race. The longer you wait to answer such questions, the more your memory erodes. To enhance recall, and especially to create a record for the future when you return to this same race, it will help to write down what happened as soon as possible after finishing. The Race Evaluation form suggested in Figure 15.1 helps with this.

Assessing race performances provides insight for training and racing.

Race days on which you felt really good or bad deserve special attention. Examine the preceding days to determine what may have led to this high or low. Perhaps it was a certain pattern of workouts, a period of good rest or excessive stress, or a particular diet that contributed to your results. If such trends are identified, you are one step closer to knowing the secret of what does and doesn't work for you. Reproducing the positive factors while minimizing the negative is valuable for race peaking and performance.

Look for trends, both good and bad.

A diary helps you see the bigger picture by keeping all the details in focus. When used effectively, it serves as an excellent tool for planning, motivating and diagnosing. It also provides a personal history of training and racing accomplishments. A well-kept diary ranks right up there with training, rest and nutrition when it comes to developing a competitive edge.

Race name:_____   _____

Date and start time:_____

Location: _____

Type/distance: _____

Competitors to watch:_____

Weather:_____

Course conditions: _____

Race goal: _____

_____

Race strategy: _____   _____

_____

Pre-race meal (foods and quantities): _____

Warm-up description: _____

_____

Start-line arousal level (circle one):   Very low   Low   Moderate   High   Very high

Results (place, time, splits, etc.): _____

What I did well:_____

What I need to improve:_____

Aches/pains/problems afterwards: _____

Comments on or description of how race developed: _____

_____

_____

FIGURE 15.1
Race Evaluation Form

REFERENCES

Borg, G. "A Simple Rating Scale for Use in Physical Work Tests." *Kungliga Fysiografiska Sallskapets i Lund Forhandlingar* 2, no. 32 (1962): 7–15.

Hooper, S. L., et al. "Markers for Monitoring Overtraining and Recovery." *Medicine and Science in Sports and Exercise* 27 (1995): 106–112.

Kentta, G. and P. Hassmen. "Overtraining and Recovery. A Conceptual Model." *Sports Medicine* 26, no. 1 (1998): 1–16.

Rushall, B. S. "A Tool for Measuring Stress Tolerance in Elite Athletes." *Applied Sport Psychology* 2 (1990): 51–66.

FUEL

*I try to take care of myself by eating really well, avoiding sugar and soda and junk.
It gives me an edge. If I didn't have that goddamn latte I wanted for three months,
then I deserve to win the goddamn race.*

—Missy Giove

Other than training, nothing affects performance more than diet. The body's cells require proteins, fats, carbohydrates, vitamins, minerals and water for health, energy and growth. Chronically eating a diet that is deficient in any of these nutrients compromises your capacity for training and racing, and increases susceptibility to illness. Most riders are aware of the significance of good nutrition, but many don't know what to eat for peak fitness.

So what should you eat? Loren Cordain, Ph.D., professor of exercise and sport science at Colorado State University, believes that the answer is found in the distant past, when Mother Nature shaped our ancestors with the hard facts of evolution. He points out that modern-day endurance athletes already have a lifestyle that closely replicates that of Stone Age men and women of 25,000 years ago. His studies reveal that these prehistoric "athletes" probably burned more than 3000 calories daily coping with the rigors of existence in a demanding environment. The men would often spend much of the day tracking and hunting animals at a steady clip, and would then carry the carcass back to camp. Cordain estimates that they may have run and jogged 10 miles in a day, much of it with a 25-pound load. The women were also active, as they carried children while finding and hauling vegetables and other foodstuffs back to camp. Life was physically difficult by today's standards, but humans evolved to meet the challenges of their environment.

Dr. Cordain points out that the genetic changes evolution wrought still shape our dietary needs today, some 2 million years after man first appeared as a separate genus in the anthropological record. He believes that since evolution is a slow and steady process

Modern and prehistoric athletes have much in common.

requiring tens, if not hundreds, of thousands of years to produce even a 1-percent change, our ancient genes are still best adapted to a Stone Age diet although we live in the space age. We long ago developed the mechanics, chemistry, and gut to process the foods our forebears ate for millennia—and these haven't changed significantly. So what our Stone Age ancestors ate is what we should eat now.

Evolution shaped our dietary requirements.

By comparison with today's notions, they ate a simple diet consisting primarily of meats and organs from wild game, fruits and vegetables. Nuts, seeds, berries and eggs were also eaten. There were no grains or dairy products—substances to which many humans still have adverse reactions. Animal products accounted for most of the calories, perhaps 40 to 50 percent, Dr. Cordain estimates. But the saturated fat content was much lower than what we see in most meats now. These animals were not fattened on corn in feed lots, their growth enhanced with drugs, so the meat was far different from what is currently found in the local supermarket. For example, today a cut of USDA prime beef contains 560 percent more saturated fat than the same amount of meat from wild game such as elk, which is similar to what our ancestors ate for millions of years.

Stone Age people ate less carbohydrate than is commonly recommended now, and what carbohydrate they did eat released its energy slowly. With the exception of infrequent honey finds, they ate no foods that were calorically dense, but nutritionally empty like many of our sugar-rich foods of today. Their foods were fresh and high in fiber, vitamins and minerals. Their primary drink was water with occasional herb or berry teas.

Despite not having a food pyramid to tell them what to eat, they did not suffer from the diet- and lifestyle-induced diseases we now experience: heart disease, hypertension, diabetes and some types of cancers. It appears that they most likely died in their 30s or 40s, usually from accidents or acute illnesses for which there were no cures. While we don't know exactly what the long-term effects of their diet might have been, we do know that many people still following a Stone Age existence in remote areas today live into their 60s, 70s and even 80s. Civilization's common lifestyle diseases do not plague these modern-day Stone Age humans. Apparently, by eating nutrient-dense foods to which they are fully adapted and by having an active and generally low-stress lifestyle, their bodies are in harmony with their environments.

Stone Age humans do not experience civilization's common lifestyle diseases.

With the birth of farming and a gradual shift in diet toward more cereals came higher infant mortality, a reduced life span, iron deficiency, loss of physical height, bone disorders such as osteoporosis, and dental cavities. Modern humans are still afflicted with many of these same disorders.

In only 10,000 years—less in most parts of the world—agriculture reshaped human diet and health. While a hundred centuries may seem long, it's really not in the context of nearly two million years of our time as a genus on earth. If man's existence were represented by 24 hours, farming would have been around for only the last eight minutes, far too little time for the genetic code to adapt. Our currently popular high-carbohydrate diet with its emphasis on starch and sugar is even newer, having been around for only a few decades—mere seconds on our 24-hour clock. Modern athletes have bodies meant for a diet different from what most eat now.

So what should you eat? The short answer is to eat primarily from those foods that your ancestors have eaten throughout most of the last two million years. These include lean meats, preferably from wild game or free-ranging animals, fish, poultry, shellfish, fresh vegetables and fruits in season and close to their natural state, and, in small amounts, nuts, seeds and dried fruit. Those foods that are newest should be eaten in the smallest amounts, expecially those that are highly processed. This will provide you with a simple and nutrient-dense diet to which your body is fully adapted and enhance your capacity for demanding training.

Man's optimal foods.

Let's take a closer look at the details of Mother Nature's training table.

FOOD AS FUEL

While the human genetic code has changed very little, dietary recommendations change often. In the mid-20th century, endurance athletes were advised to avoid starchy foods such as bread and potatoes, and to eat more vegetables and meats instead. In the 1970s, a dietary shift away from protein, began with an increase in carbohydrates, especially starchy grains. The 1980s brought concerns for fat in the diet, and low-fat and fat-free foods boomed, with an accompanying increase in sugar consumption. Now the pendulum is swinging back the other way, with the realizations that certain fats are beneficial and that some carbohydrates are deleterious in large quantities.

Sports nutrition is an evolving science.

The crux of your daily dietary decisions is the relative mix of the four macronutrients you consume—protein, fat, carbohydrate and water. How much of each you include in your diet has a great deal to do with how well you train and race.

PROTEIN

The word *protein* is derived from the Greek word *proteios,* meaning "first" or "of primary importance." That's fitting, because determining macronutrient balance begins with protein intake.

Protein has a checkered history in the world of athletics. Greek and Roman competitors believed that the strength, speed, and endurance qualities of animals could be gained by merely eating their meat. Lion meat was in great demand. In the 1800s, protein was considered the major fuel of exercise, so athletes also ate prodigious quantities of meat. In the early part of the 20th century, scientists came to understand that fat and carbohydrate provide most of our energy for movement. By the 1960s, athletic diets began to change, reflecting this shift in knowledge. In fact, little interest was paid to the role of protein in sports fuel throughout most of the 1970s and 1980s. That changed in the latter years of the 20th century as more research was done on this almost forgotten macronutrient.

Protein has many functions in the athlete's body.

Protein plays a key role in health and athletic performance. It is necessary to repair muscle damage, maintain the immune system, manufacture hormones and enzymes, replace red blood cells that carry oxygen to the muscles, and produce up to 10 percent of the energy needed for long or intense workouts and races. It also stimulates the secretion of glucagon, a hormone that allows the body to use fat for fuel more efficiently.

Protein is so important to the athlete that it may even determine the outcome of races. For example, a study of Olympians by the International Center for Sports Nutrition in Omaha, Nebraska, compared the diets of medal winners and nonmedalists. The only significant difference found was that the winners ate more protein than those who did not medal.

Performance is dependent on dietary protein because the body is unable to produce all it needs from scratch. And, unlike carbohydrate and fat, protein is not stored in the body at fuel depot sites for later use. The protein you eat is used to meet immediate needs, with excess intakes converted to the storage forms of carbohydrate or fat.

Dietary protein is made up of 20 amino acids useable by the human body as building blocks for replacing damaged cells. Most of these amino acids are readily produced by the body when a need arises, but there are nine that the body cannot manufacture. These "essential" amino acids must come from the diet in order for all the protein-related functions to continue normally. If the diet is lacking in protein, your body is likely to

If essential amino acids are missing from the diet, the body cannibalizes tissue.

break down muscle tissues to provide what is necessary for areas of greater need, thus resulting in muscle wasting. This was evidenced in 1988 by the 7-Eleven cycling team during the Tour de France. It was discovered that the circumferences of the riders' thighs decreased during three weeks of racing. After studying their diets, the team doctor determined that they were protein deficient.

The body's demand for protein is quite high, as there is considerable turnover in its protein stores. Approximately 20 percent of your body weight is protein. About two-thirds of a pound (1.5 kg) of this protein is replaced every day. At least a fourth of this daily requirement must come from your diet, with the remainder produced by recycling.

Unfortunately, there is not a general agreement within the nutritional field regarding the recommended protein intake for endurance athletes. The United States recommended daily allowance (RDA) for protein is 0.013 ounces per pound of body weight (0.8gm/kg), but that is likely too low for an athlete. Peter Lemon, a noted protein researcher at Kent State University, suggests athletes eat about 0.020 to 0.022 ounces of protein per pound of body weight each day (1.2–1.4 gm/kg). During a period of heavy weight lifting, such as in the MS phase described in Chapter 13, Lemon recommends a high of 0.028 ounces per pound (1.8 gm/kg). The American Dietetic Association suggests a high-end protein intake of 0.032 ounces per pound (2.0 gm/kg) each day. Nonscientific survey of sports scientists from around the world found a rather broad range of 0.020 to 0.040 ounces per pound (1.2–2.5 gm/kg) suggested for endurance athletes daily. Applying these recommendations for a 150-pound (68kgm) athlete, the possible range, excluding the U.S. RDA, would be three to 6 ounces (84-168gm) of protein each day. Table 16.1 shows how much protein is found in common foods.

The recommendations for protein intake vary widely.

TABLE 16.1

Protein content of common foods per 3.5-ounce (100gm) serving

Food	Protein oz. (grams)	Food	Protein oz. (grams)
Animal sources		**Plant sources**	
Sirloin steak (broiled)	1.05 (30)	Almonds (12 dried)	0.71 (20)
Chicken breast	1.05 (30)	Tofu (extra firm)	0.39 (11)
Swiss cheese	1.01 (29)	Bagel	0.38 (11)
Pork loin	0.92 (26)	Kidney beans	0.30 (9)
Hamburger	0.92 (26)	Rye bread	0.29 (8)
Cheddar cheese	0.85 (24.5)	Cereal (corn flakes)	0.28 (8)
Tuna	0.82 (23)	Refried beans	0.22 (6)
Haddock	0.82 (23)	Baked beans	0.17 (5)
Venison	0.73 (21)	Hummus	0.17 (5)
Cottage cheese (low-fat)	0.43 (12)	Soy milk	0.10 (3)
Egg (whole)	0.42 (12)	Brown rice (cooked)	0.09 (2.5)
Egg white	0.36 (10)	Tomato (red)	0.03 (1)
Milk (skim)	0.12 (3)		

Do you need more protein?

So much for numbers and generalizations. Are you getting enough protein? One way to determine this is to evaluate your physical and mental well-being. Indicators that you may need more protein in your diet include:

- Frequent colds or sore throats
- Slow recovery following workouts
- An irritable demeanor
- Poor response to training (slow to get in shape)
- Slow fingernail growth and easily broken nails
- Thin hair or unusual hair loss.
- Chronic fatigue
- Poor mental focus
- Sugar cravings
- Pallid complexion
- Cessation of menstrual periods

Note that none of these indicators is certain proof of the need for more protein, as each may have other causes. A dietary analysis by a registered dietitian, or by the use of a computer software program such as DietBalancer, may help make the determination if you have concerns. Increasing your protein intake to see how it affects you is another, simple option. It's unlikely that you will eat too much protein. Even at 30 percent of daily calories, as recommended in some diets, the excess, if any, will be converted to glycogen or fat and stored. There is no research suggesting that moderately high protein diets pose a health risk for otherwise healthy individuals, so long as plenty of water is consumed each day to help with the removal of nitrogen, a by-product of protein metabolism.

Animal foods are the most efficient and effective way to get the nine essential amino acids, as ounce for ounce they are richer in protein than plant sources, and they provide all the amino acids in the proper ratios. Animal sources also provide B vitamins and minerals such as highly absorbable iron and zinc, which are lacking in plant foods. Vegetable protein is of lower quality because it is not as readily digestible and lacks one or more of the essential amino acids. It takes large quantities of plant food and smart combining of foods to meet protein needs on a vegetarian diet.

If you eat a vegetarian diet and restrict calories, you are probably protein deficient.

Many athletes think of hamburger, bacon, sausage, luncheon meats and hot dogs when they decide to eat protein. These foods and certain other protein sources, such as cheese and whole milk, are high in saturated fat, which, in research, is closely linked to heart disease. Such foods are best eaten infrequently and in small amounts. Better animal sources of protein are lean cuts of meat from wild game or free-ranging cattle,

Are you really overtrained?

Low dietary intake of the mineral iron may be the most common nutritional deficiency for serious multisport athletes, especially women. Unfortunately, it goes undetected in most.

A 1988 university study of female high school cross-country runners found 45 percent had low iron stores. In the same study, 17 percent of the boys were low. Other research conducted on female college athletes showed that 31 percent were iron deficient. Up to 80 percent of women runners were below normal iron stores in a 1983 study.

Commonly accepted, although still debated, causes of iron depletion include high-volume running, especially on hard surfaces; too much anaerobic training; chronic intake of aspirin; travel to high altitude; excessive menstrual flow; and a diet low in animal-food products. Athletes most at risk for iron deficiency, in the order of their risk, are runners, women, endurance athletes, vegetarians, those who sweat heavily, dieters and those who have recently donated blood.

The symptoms of iron deficiency include loss of endurance, chronic fatigue, high exercise heart rate, low power, frequent injury, recurring illness and an attitude problem. Since many of these symptoms are the same as in overtraining, the athlete may correctly cut back on exercise, begin feeling better, and return to training only to find an almost immediate relapse. In the early stages of iron depletion, performance may show only slight decrements, but additional training volume and intensity cause further declines. Many unknowingly flirt with this level of "tired blood" frequently.

If a deficiency is suspected, what should you do? Once a year have a blood test to determine your healthy baseline levels of serum ferritin, hemoglobin, reticulocytes and haptoglobin. This should be done during the Transition, Prep or Base training period when training volume and intensity are low. This blood test should be done in a fasted state with no exercise for 15 hours prior. Your health-care provider will help you understand the results. Then, if the symptoms of low iron appear, a follow-up test may support or rule this out as the culprit. Your blood indicators of iron status may be "normal" based on the reference range, but low in relation to your baseline. Many exercise scientists believe that even this obvious dip may adversely effect performance.

Should the blood test indicate an abnormally low iron status, an increased dietary intake of iron is necessary. You may want to have a registered dietitian analyze your eating habits for adequate iron consumption. The RDA for women and teenagers is 15mg per day. Men should consume 10mg. Endurance athletes may need more. The normal North American diet contains about 6mg of iron for every 1000 calories eaten, so a female athlete restricting food intake to 2000 calories a day while exercising strenuously can easily create a low-iron condition in a few weeks.

Dietary iron comes in two forms — heme and non-heme. Heme iron is found in animal meat. Plant foods are the source of non-heme iron. Very little of the iron you eat is absorbed by the body regardless of source, but heme iron has the best absorption rate at about 15 percent. Up to 5 percent of non-heme iron is taken up by the body. So the most effective way to increase iron status is by eating meat, especially red meat. Humans probably developed this capacity to absorb iron from red meat as a result of our omnivorous, hunter-gatherer origins. Plant sources of iron, although not very available to the human body due to their accompanying phytates, are raisins, leafy green vegetables, dates, dried fruits, lima beans, baked beans, broccoli, baked potatoes, soybeans and brussel sprouts. Other sources are listed in Table 16.1.

Iron absorption from any of these foods, whether plant or animal, is decreased if they are accompanied at meals by egg yolk, coffee, tea, wheat or cereal grains. Calcium and zinc also reduce the ability of the body to take up iron. Including fruits, especially citrus fruit, in meals enhances iron absorption.

Don't use iron supplements unless under the supervision of your health-care provider. Some people are susceptible to iron overload, a condition called hemochromatosis marked by toxic deposits in the skin, joints and liver. Other symptoms, including fatigue and malaise, may mimic iron deficiency and overtraining. Also note that ingesting iron supplements is the second leading cause of poisoning in children. Aspirin is first.

seafood, poultry and egg whites. Such foods and others high in protein should be eaten throughout the day and not consumed all in one meal. If meat from wild game or free-ranging cattle is not available, be conservative with your intake of red meat and depend more on the other sources.

Eat protein at every meal.

FAT

In the 1980s, Western society painted dietary fat as such a terrifying specter that many athletes still see all types of fat as the enemy and try to eliminate it entirely from their diet. Indeed, there are some types of fat that should be kept at low levels. These are saturated fat, found in prodigious quantities in feed lot cattle, and trans fatty acids, the man-made fats found in many highly processed foods and called "hydrogenated" on the label. Hydrogenated fats lead to artery clogging the same as the saturated variety.

Don't confuse these "bad" fats with all types of fat. There are, in fact, many health benefits associated with eating fat, such as preventing dry, scaly skin and dull, brittle hair. More importantly, fat helps maintain a regular menstrual cycle in women and prevent colds and other infections common to serious athletes. It also assists with the manufacture of hormones, such as testosterone and estrogen, and nerve and brain cells, and is important for carrying and absorbing the vitamins A, D, E and K. Fat is also the body's most efficient source of energy. Every gram of fat provides nine calories, compared with four each for protein and carbohydrate. You may find that eating more fat improves your long-term recovery and capacity to train at a high level, if you previously have been low in fat intake.

The health benefits of fat.

After three decades of believing that very high-carbohydrate eating is best for performance, there is now compelling evidence, albeit in the early stages, that increasing fat intake while decreasing and properly timing carbohydrate consumption may be good for endurance athletes, especially in events lasting four hours or longer. Several studies reveal that eating a diet high in fat causes the body to preferentially use fat for fuel, and that eating a high-carbohydrate diet results in the body relying more heavily on limited stores of muscle glycogen for fuel. Theoretically, even the skinniest athlete has enough fat stored to last for 40 hours or more at a low intensity without refueling, but only enough carbohydrate for about 3 hours at most.

New evidence supports eating more fat for improved endurance performance.

A study at State University of New York illustrates the benefits of fat. Researchers had a group of runners eat a higher-than-usual fat diet consisting of 38 percent fat and 50 percent carbohydrate calories for one week. The second week they ate a more typical high-carbohydrate diet, with 73 percent of calories coming from carbohydrates and 15 percent from fat. At the end of each week the subjects were tested for maximum aerobic capacities and ran to exhaustion on a treadmill. On the higher-fat diet their VO^2max was 11 percent greater than when they were on the high-carbohydrate diet. On the higher-fat diet they also lasted 9 percent longer on the run to exhaustion.

A 1994 study conducted by Tim Noakes, M.D, Ph.D., author of *The Lore of Running* (Leisure Press, 1991), and colleagues at the University of Cape Town in South Africa found that after cyclists ate a diet of 70 percent fat for two weeks, their endurance at a low intensity improved significantly compared with cycling after consuming a diet high in carbohydrates for two weeks. At high intensities, there was no difference in the performances—fat did just as well as carbohydrate.

Other research has shown that our greatest fears associated with dietary fat—risk for heart disease and weight gain—do not occur when eating a diet high in what might be called "good" fats. The good fats are monounsaturated and omega-3 fatty acids, which were plentiful in our Stone Age ancestors' diets. The oils and spreads of almonds, avocado, hazelnuts, macadamia nuts, pecans, cashews and olives are high in these fats. Other good sources are the oils of cold-water fish such as tuna, salmon and mackerel. The red meat of wild game also provides significant amounts of monounsaturated and omega-3 fats.

The bottom line on fat is to select the leanest cuts of meat (from wild game or free-ranging cattle, if possible); trim away all visible fat from meat; include seafood and poultry; eat low- or nonfat dairy foods in small quantities; avoid hydrogenated, trans fatty acids in packaged foods; and regularly include monounsaturated and omega-3 fats in your diet. Eating 20 to 30 percent of your calories from fat, with an emphasis on the good fats, is not harmful, and may actually be helpful for training and racing if your fat intake has been low.

Dietary fat recommendations.

CARBOHYDRATE

Carbohydrate is critical for performance in endurance events, as it provides much of the fuel, in the forms of glycogen and glucose that is converted to useable energy by the body. Low carbohydrate stores are likely to result in poor endurance and lackluster racing.

The zealous athlete who learns this often overeats carbohydrate at the expense of protein and fat. A day in the life of such a person may find that breakfast is cereal, toast and orange juice; a bagel is eaten as a midmorning snack; lunch is a baked potato with vegetables; sports bars or pretzels are eaten in the afternoon; and supper is pasta with bread. Not only is such a diet excessively high in starch with an overemphasis on wheat, but it is also likely to provide dangerously low protein and fat levels. Such a dietary plan could be improved by replacing the cereal with an egg-white omelet and including fresh

Look for ways to add protein and good fat to your otherwise carbohydrate-rich diet.

fruit, topping the potato with tuna, snacking on mixed nuts and dried fruit, adding shrimp to the pasta and dipping the bread in olive oil as the Italians do.

When you eat a high-carbohydrate meal or snack, the pancreas releases insulin to regulate the level of blood sugar. That insulin stays in the blood for up to two hours, during which time it has other effects, such as preventing the body from utilizing stored fat, converting carbohydrate and protein to body fat, and moving fat in the blood to storage sites. This may explain why, despite serious training and eating a "healthy" diet, some athletes are unable to lose body fat.

Carbohydrate causes the pancreas to release insulin.

Some carbohydrates enter the bloodstream quicker than others, producing an elevated blood-sugar response and quickly bringing about all the negative aspects of high insulin described above. These rapidly digested carbohydrates are high on the glycemic

				TABLE 16.3

Glycemic index of common foods

High Glycemic Index (80% or higher)

Bread, French	Molasses	Potatoes, baked	Rice Chex	Rice, white
Corn flakes	Parsnips	Potatoes, instant	Rice, instant	Tapioca
Grapenuts flakes	Pasta, rice	Rice cakes	Rice Krispies	Tofu frozen dessert

Moderate Glycemic Index (50-80%)

All-Bran cereal	Bread, rye	Doughnuts	Pea soup	Pumpkin
Apricots	Bread, wheat	Ice cream	Pineapple	Raisins
Bagels	Bread, white	Mango	Popcorn	Rice, brown
Bananas	Corn chips	Muesli	Potato chips	Rye crisps
Barley	Cornmeal	Muffins	Potatoes, boiled	Soft drinks
Beets	Corn, sweet	Oat bran	Potatoes, mashed	Taco shells
Black bean soup	Couscous	Oatmeal	Potatoes, sweet	Watermelon
Bread, pita	Crackers	Orange juice	PowerBar	Yams

Low Glycemic Index (30-50%)

Apple	Beans, black	Grapefruit juice	Pasta	Rye
Apple juice	Beans, lima	Grapes	Pears	Tomato soup
Apple sauce	Beans, pinto	Kiwifruit	Peas, black-eyed	Yogurt, fruit
Beans, baked	Chocolate	Oranges	Peas, split	

Very Low Glycemic Index (less than 30%)

Barley	Beans, soy	Grapefruit	Milk	Peanuts
Beans, kidney	Cherries	Lentils	Peaches	Plums

index—a food rating system developed for diabetics. Foods low on the glycemic index produce a less dramatic rise in blood sugar, and help avoid the craving for more sugary food that comes with eating high-glycemic carbohydrates. Table 16.3 lists some common high-, moderate-, low- and very low-glycemic foods.

How a carbohydrate food is prepared and what other foods it is eaten with affects its glycemic index. Adding fat to a high-glycemic-index food lowers its glycemic index by slowing down digestion. An example of this is ice cream, which has a moderate glycemic index despite the presence of high amounts of sugar. In the same way, adding fiber to a meal that includes a high- or moderate-glycemic-index carbohydrate reduces the meal's effect on your blood sugar and insulin levels and turns it into timed-release energy.

Notice in Table 16.3 that many of the foods that have a moderate to high glycemic index are the ones we have typically thought of as "healthy" and therefore eaten liberally. These include the starchy foods—cereal, bread, rice, pasta, potatoes, crackers, bagels, pancakes and bananas. No wonder so many endurance athletes are always hungry and have a hard time losing excess body fat. Their blood sugar levels are routinely kept at high levels, causing regular cascades of insulin. Not only does high insulin produce regular and frequent food cravings and excess body fat, it is also associated with such widespread health problems as high blood pressure, heart disease and adult-onset diabetes.

But moderate- and high-glycemic-index foods have an important role in the athlete's diet. During long and intense training sessions and races it is necessary to replenish carbohydrate stores in the muscles and liver. That's why sports drinks and gels are used during exercise. The 30 minutes immediately following a hard training session is when moderate- to high-glycemic-index carbohydrates and insulin are beneficial. This is the time to use a commercial recovery drink or starchy food. Combining protein with a high-glycemic-index food has been shown to effectively boost recovery. Except for during and immediately after exercise, sports drinks, gels and soft drinks should be avoided, however. Other high- and moderate-glycemic-index foods should be consumed in moderation throughout the day, also.

There are appropriate times to eat moderate- and high-glycemic-index foods.

Eating a diet extremely high in carbohydrate is not unanimously supported by the sports science literature. A high-carbohydrate diet may cause your body to rely heavily on glycogen for fuel during exercise, with an associated increase in blood lactate levels, while reducing your use of fat as a fuel for exercise.

WATER

Many athletes don't drink enough fluids, leaving them perpetually on the edge of dehydration. In this state, recovery is compromised and the risk of illness rises. Drinking fluids throughout the day is one of the simplest, yet most effective means of boosting performance for such athletes. Since sports drinks and most fruit juices are high to moderate on the glycemic index, the best fluid replacement between workouts is water.

Dehydration results in a reduction of plasma, making the blood thick and forcing the heart and body to work harder moving it. Even with slight dehydration, exercise intensity and duration are negatively affected. A 2-percent loss of body weight as fluids will slow a racer by about 4 percent—that's nearly five minutes in a two-hour race. When time is critical, as it is in competitive cross-country racing, you must stay well hydrated to keep the pace high.

A 150-pound (68kg) adult loses a little more than a half-gallon (2 liters) of body fluids a day just in living, not including training. Up to half of this loss is through urine at the rate of about 2 ounces (30ml) per hour. Heavy training or a hot and humid environment can increase the loss to 2 gallons (8 liters) daily through heavy sweating.

Unfortunately, the human thirst mechanism is not very effective. By the time we sense thirst, dehydration is already well under way. Following prolonged and intense training or racing, it may take 24 to 48 hours to rehydrate if thirst is the controlling factor. In contrast, a dog will drink up to 10 percent of its body weight immediately following exercise, replacing all lost water. It's important to drink water steadily throughout the day when you are training whether you are thirsty or not.

Get in eight to 12 cups (1 to 1.5 liters) a day, based on your body size and training load. For every pound (450gm) lost during exercise, an additional 2 cups (500 milliliters) of water is needed. You can also use your rate of urination and urine color as a guide. You should need to visit the toilet at least once every two hours during the day and your urine should be clear to straw-colored. If you aren't achieving these standards, drink more.

DIET AND PERFORMANCE

How the macronutrients protein, fat, carbohydrate and water are mixed in your diet has a lot to do with how well you train and race, and, certainly no less important, with how healthy you are.

In recent human and animal studies examining the effects of diet on performance, several have found that increased dietary fat enhances endurance and aerobic capacity. The benefit seems to increase as the duration of the exercise lengthens. During short, high-intensity efforts there appears to be no significant difference, although most studies find a slight advantage for high-carbohydrate ingestion in such events.

Even slight dehydration hurts performance.

Thirst is not a good indicator of the need for water.

Moderate levels of dietary fat may enhance endurance in long events.

One of the downsides resulting from eating a high-carbohydrate, low-fat diet is a greater production of lactic acid by the muscles during exercise, and even at rest. This is probably the result of the body using carbohydrate preferentially for fuel when it is abundantly available. Carbohydrate seems to "turn off" the body's fat-utilization processes.

Additionally, several studies have found the rather surprising result that coronary heart disease risk factors are made worse on a high-carbohydrate, low-fat diet when compared with a more moderate intake of both nutrients that emphasizes monounsaturated and polyunsaturated fats. These negative risk-factor shifts include lowered HDL ("good") cholesterol, increased LDL ("bad") cholesterol, and elevated triglyceride levels. There is much still to be learned about the interaction of diet and health. But for now it appears prudent to include moderate levels of all three nutrients in your diet for both performance and health reasons.

A diet exceptionally low in fat has also recently been shown to depress testosterone levels. Testosterone is an important hormone that assists with rebuilding tissues broken down by exercise. When fat was increased in research subjects' diets testosterone production increased.

A low-fat diet may prolong recovery.

Eating fat in its natural state—for example, in lean meats, plants, nuts, seeds and natural oils—appears to have no deleterious effect on health. Many cultures live quite well on high-fat diets based on such foods. The problem with the standard American diet is that much, if not most, of the dietary fat is saturated, hydrogenated, altered, processed, or artificial. Eating fat is not a problem unless its chemical structure is changed by food producers.

Just as with general health, the foods you choose to eat immediately before a race have a direct effect on how well you do on any given day. It seems a waste to train for weeks for a certain race and then to blow it by eating inappropriate foods as the race approaches. When making final preparations for a race, performance may improve if you're eating a moderate-fat diet in the neighborhood of 30 percent of total calories and by carbohydrate loading for two or three days prior. On the morning of the race, a suggested prerace meal includes up to 200 calories for every hour until race time. So if you eat three hours before starting your warm-up, 600 calories is about the top end. Most of these calories, for events that take two hours or less to complete, should come mostly from low- to moderate-glycemic-index carbohydrates. Small amounts of protein may be included. Performance in longer events may benefit from including more fat in this meal.

Carbohydrate loading and a carbohydrate-based prerace meal may improve race performance.

PERIODIZATION OF DIET

The optimal diet for peak performance must vary with the athlete just as the optimal training protocol must vary from person to person. We can't all eat the same things in the same relative amounts and reap the same benefits. Where your ancestors originated on the planet, and what was available for them to eat for the last 100,000 years or so, is important for what you should eat now.

So the bottom line is that you must discover what mix of foods works best for you. If you have never experimented with this, don't automatically assume you have found it already. You may be surprised at what happens when changes are made at the training table. A word of caution: Make changes gradually and allow at least three weeks for your body to adapt to a new diet before passing judgment based on how you feel and your performance in training. It usually takes at least two weeks to adapt to significant changes before seeing any results. During the adaptation period you may feel lethargic and train poorly. For this reason, changes in diet are best done in the Transition and Preparation periods cycles early in the season. Also, be aware that as you age, changes may occur in your body chemistry requiring further shifts in diet.

That said, an optimal diet to enhance training, racing and recovery involves not only eating moderate amounts of the macronutrients, but also varying the mix of these

Find the diet that's right for you.

FIGURE 16.1
The dietary periodization "seesaw." The percentages are illustration only and will vary between athletes.

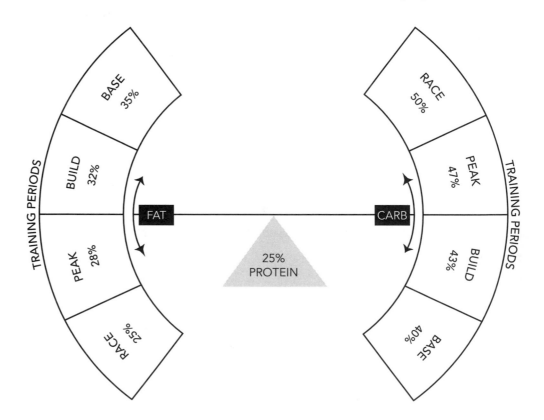

foods throughout the year. In other words, diet should cycle just as training cycles within a periodization plan. Protein serves as the anchor for the diet and stays relatively constant throughout the year as fat and carbohydrate rise and fall and alternately. Figure 16.1 illustrates this "seesaw" effect of the periodized diet. Note that the numbers used in this figure are merely an example, and the right dietary right for you may differ considerably.

ANTIOXIDANT SUPPLEMENTS

Generally it's a good idea to meet your nutritional needs with real foods and use food supplements sparingly. Scientists and supplement designers just aren't as smart as Mother Nature when it comes to deciding what to include and what to leave out of foods. Real food provides everything needed for health and fitness. Adding lots of pills and potions to your diet is usually not wise. The exception is antioxidant supplements. Here's why.

During the process of metabolizing food and using oxygen for exercise, highly chemically reactive molecules called free radicals, which cause damage to healthy cells, are released. This can be compared with the rusting of metal—a breakdown caused by oxidation. Hard training produces large numbers of free radicals, which threaten your health and ability to recover following workouts.

Free radicals hinder recovery.

For example, one study measured by-products of free radical damage in highly trained athletes, moderately trained athletes and a sedentary group. The researchers found that the highly trained athletes had the highest levels of damage, while the moderately trained subjects had the least. The sedentary group was in the middle. A little exercise appears to be a healthy thing when it comes to free radicals, but extensive exercise or none at all causes problems.

In recent years, studies have shown that vitamins C and E reduce this damage and prevent upper respiratory infections associated with extreme physical exertion by combining with the free radicals to stop the oxidative process. The research typically uses large doses of each of these micronutrients, usually hundreds of times the U.S. RDA. The exact amounts needed have not been determined yet, as variables such as age, sex, diet, body composition, body size and training load are involved. Recommended daily intakes based on these studies generally fall into the ranges of 400 to 800 international units (IU) of vitamin E and 300 to 1000mg of vitamin C.

Recommended dosages.

The problem is that in order to get even the lowest of these dosages you would have to eat *all* of these foods *daily*:

• Asparagus 15 spears

• Avocados 31

- Broccoli 4 cups
- Peaches 33
- Prunes 30
- Tomato juice 12 ounces
- Spinach 17 cups
- Wheat germ 1/4 cup

While it's true that serious athletes tend to eat more than the average citizen, they seldom eat enough of the right foods. For example, a 1989 study of serious, same-age-group triathletes found that as a group they had inadequate nutrition due to unusual eating habits. They also demonstrated poor food selection resulting from rigorous training schedules and limited time for eating. All of this means that getting in adequate levels of vitamin C and E is unlikely with busy athletes.

One-a-day multiple vitamins are commonly used, but seldom provide vitamins C and E in large enough quantities, so you may need to supplement your diet with individual dosages, especially of vitamin E. It appears that these supplements should be taken with meals twice a day for best results.

Concerns for using vitamin E.

Vitamin C has a low level of risk at levels of 300 to 1000mg, but high dosages of vitamin E can cause problems for those who are deficient in vitamin K. Those on blood-thinning medications or high doses of pain relievers should also be cautious with vitamin E. Check with your health-care provider before starting supplementation with either vitamin C or E.

ERGOGENIC AIDS

Athletes I train frequently ask if taking a potion or pill they've read about or that someone they know is using would boost race performance. They're looking for that difficult last 1 or 2 percent of improvement that can often mean the difference in a hard-fought race. To help decide, I suggest they answer these five questions that need answering:

1. **Is it legal?** Products are often promoted to athletes despite the fact that they contain a banned substance. There have been many instances of blind trust resulting in a disqualification or worse for an elite athlete. To check on a specific product, call the U.S. Olympic Committee's Drug Hotline at 800/233-0393, or visit their Web site at www.olympicusa.org/inside/in_1_3_7_1.html.

2. **Is it ethical?** Only you can answer this question. Some believe that sport must be conducted in its purest form with absolutely no artificial assistance. But once we begin to ponder such ergogenic aids as carbohydrate loading and vitamin and

mineral supplements, it becomes clear that drawing a line in the sand is difficult.

3. **Is it safe?** Studies on the effects of various sports aids are often limited to a few weeks, as most subjects don't want to donate their entire lives to science. Such short periods of observation may not produce observable effects that might otherwise occur with long-term use. There is also the outside possibility that using multiple substances simultaneously or in combination with common medications may produce undesirable side effects. Another complication is that the U.S. Food and Drug Administration (FDA) safety regulations for supplements are more lenient than for food products. It's always a good idea to check with your family physician before supplementing.

4. **Is its use supported by the research?** There may be an isolated study on any product that demonstrates a benefit, but does the bulk of the literature agree? To search the scientific journals for studies, point your browser at the government's PubMed Web site www.ncbi.nlm.nih.gov/PubMed/, enter the substance of interest, and select "search." You'll be presented with a list of the archived studies and their abstracts. Have fun reading the list—it could be a thousand or more items long. Better yet, ask a knowledgeable and trusted coach, trainer, registered dietitian or medical professional for their insights on the product in question.

5. **Will it help in my race?** Even if generally supported by the research, not all ergogenic aids benefit all people in all events. There are many individual differences that may affect the use of a given product. It may not work well for you because of some combination of your age, sex, health status, medications used, and years of experience in the sport. Some aids have been shown to provide a benefit for short events, such as a 100-meter dash, but not for events lasting several hours.

The following is a discussion of several currently popular and legal ergogenic aids that are *probably* safe for most athletes and beneficial at some level in cross-country mountain bike racing. Before using any of these, consult with your health-care provider. Never use a product in an important race without having first tried it in training or in a C-priority event.

CAFFEINE

This is one of the oldest and most popular ergogenic aids. Caffeine has been shown to increase fatty acids in the blood, thus reducing the reliance on limited glycogen stores in the muscles. It also stimulates the central nervous system, decreasing the perception of fatigue, and may enhance muscle contractions. Most studies show benefits for intense

Legal and beneficial levels of caffeine.

events lasting an hour or longer when 300 to 600mg of caffeine (2 to 4 cups of coffee) are consumed 45 minutes to an hour prior to the start. The benefits last three to five hours. The banned limit requires about 30 to 40 ounces of caffeine an hour depending on the athlete's size. Table 16.4 lists the caffeine content of common products.

Caffeine may also be used to get more out of training. For example, drinking two cups of coffee before interval sessions may increase power output. This increases muscle stress and, given enough time to recover, produces a greater level of fitness.

	TABLE 16.5
Caffeine content in 6 ounces (180 ml) of common products.	
Drip coffee	180 mg
Instant coffee	165 mg
Percolated coffee	149 mg
Brewed tea	60 mg
Mountain Dew	28 mg
Chocolate syrup	24 mg
Coca-Cola	23 mg
Pepsi Cola	19 mg

Possible side effects are numerous.

Side effects may include insomnia, dehydration, heart arrhythmia, anxiety and upset stomach for some individuals. These are not good things to have happen in a race, so definitely try caffeine before a workout first.

BRANCHED CHAIN AMINO ACIDS

During longer and intense workouts as much as 10 percent of the energy expended may come from the amino acids present in the body's protein. Three essential amino acids, ones that must be present in the diet since the body can't synthesize them, make up about a third of muscle protein. These are leucine, isoleucine and valine. Together they are called the branched chain amino acids (BCAA).

Those who eat little protein, especially from animal sources, are likely to get the most benefit from using BCAA. Since vegetarians are often deficient in protein intake levels, BCAA supplementation may prove especially helpful for them.

Possible benefits of BCAA.

Research on the use of BCAA is inconclusive. Some studies have shown that supplementing the diet with BCAA enhances endurance performance in long events, especially those lasting three hours or longer. A few have found that it even helps in events of one-hour duration. When benefits are seen in research they typically fall into these categories:

- You may recall reading in Chapter 11 that high workloads and exhaustive workouts and races are likely to weaken the immune system and lead to illness. BCAA helps to maintain the immune system following such workouts and races, reducing the likelihood of training breakdowns.
- Some studies have shown BCAA to maintain muscle mass, power, and endurance

during exhaustive, multiday endurance events such as stage races or crash training (see Chapter 14).

- BCAA may help to reduce central nervous system fatigue, thus maintaining performance late in a race. This is a recent theory that is still under investigation in the sports science community.
- BCAA promotes the use of fat for fuel while conserving glycogen.

There are four times in the training season when using BCAA may be beneficial: during the maximum strength (MS) phase, in the Build and Peak training periods, for long and intense races, and while training intensely at high altitudes. Here are guidelines for supplementing with BCAA:

How to use BCAA.

- Take about 35mg of BCAA daily for each pound of body weight, but only at the times indicated above. A 150-pound (68kg) athlete would take 5250mg, or about five grams daily. A 120-pounder (54kg) could consume 4200mg, or about four grams a day.
- One to two hours before an MS strength workout, a high-intensity workout in the Build or Peak periods or an A-priority race, take one-half of your daily dose as described in the previous paragraph. Then, one to two hours before bedtime the same day, take the other half.

One potential negative side effect of taking BCAA has to do with imbalances in dietary intakes of amino acids. When eating meat, all of the amino acids are present in the proper ratios, but excessive supplementation with BCAA may upset the balance between them. Some scientists and nutritionists are concerned that this may have long-term health implications.

A possible downside of BCAA use.

MEDIUM CHAIN TRIGLYCERIDES

Medium chain triglycerides (MCT) are processed fats that are metabolically different from other fats in that they aren't readily stored as body fat and they are quickly absorbed by the digestive system, like carbohydrates, thus offering quick energy. They also provide about twice the calories per gram when compared with carbohydrates. Some studies have shown that mixing MCT and carbohydrates in sports drinks can improve endurance and maintain the pace in the latter stages of races lasting two hours or longer.

MCT is best for long races.

In a 1990s study at the University of Capetown in South Africa, six experienced cyclists rode two hours at about 73 percent of maximum heart rate. Immediately after this steady, low-intensity ride, they rode a 40km time trial at maximum effort. They did this three times over a 10-day period, using a different drink for each attempt. One drink was a standard carbohydrate sports drink. Another was an MCT-only beverage. A third ride used a sports drink spiked with MCT.

With the MCT-only drink, their average 40k time was 1:12:08. The carbohydrate sports drink was associated with a 1:06:45. With the mixed MCT-carbohydrate beverage their time was 1:05:00—a significant improvement. The study's authors believe that the MCT spared glycogen during the two-hour steady ride allowing the riders to better utilize carbohydrate during the more intense time trial late in the session.

MCT spares muscle glycogen.

An MCT–sports drink mix may benefit your performance late in races that last two hours or longer. You can create a long-race drink by mixing 16 ounces (500ml) of your favorite sports drink with 4 tablespoons of MCT. Liquid MCT can be purchased at a local health foods store. There are no known side effects for MCT used in this manner.

CREATINE

Creatine is one of the most recent additions to the ergogenics field having its first known usage in athletics in 1993. Since then the number of creatine studies have steadily increased, but a lot of questions still remain unanswered.

Creatine is a substance found in dietary meat and fish, but can also be created in your liver, kidneys, and pancreas. It is stored in muscle tissue in the form of creatine phosphate, a fuel used mostly during maximum efforts of up to about 12 seconds and, to a lesser extent, in intense efforts lasting a few minutes.

Creatine benefits brief, powerful movement.

The amount of creatine formed by the human body is not enough to boost performance, but scientists have found that by supplementing the diet for a few days, certain types of performance are enhanced. In order to get an adequate amount of creatine from the diet, an athlete would have to eat up to 5 pounds (2.3kg) of rare meat or fish daily. Supplementing appears to be effective in increasing stored creatine for most people.

A few years ago scientists from Sweden, Britain and Estonia tried creatine supplements on a group of runners. Following a creatine-loading period, the runners ran a 4 x 1000-meter interval workout at maximum effort. Compared with the pretest results, the creatine-supplemented subjects significantly improved their combined 4000-meter times by an average of 17 seconds, while the placebo-control group slowed by one second. The relative advantage the creatine users experienced increased as the workout progressed. In other words, the creatine supplementers experienced less fatigue and were faster at the end.

Be aware, however, that a few other studies using swimmers and cyclists have found no performance enhancement from creatine supplementation in repeated short, anaerobic efforts.

There is still not a lot known about creatine supplementation, but the benefits are probably greatest for maximizing the gains from brief exercise bouts, such as interval and hill repeat workouts. Some users believe that it decreases body fat, but it may only appear that way since body weight increases due to water retention as fat stays the same. Body-weight gains have been in the range of two to five pounds (0.9 to 2.3kg) Also, creatine does not directly build muscle tissue. Instead it provides the fuel so more power training is possible within a given workout, thus stimulating muscle fiber growth.

The use of creatine by endurance athletes is equivocal. The best times to supplement with creatine for an endurance athlete, if it is used at all, are during the Maximum Strength weight training phase and the higher-intensity Build period of training. Athletes who are low in force and power qualities stand to benefit the most at these times. It is best to avoid its use in the Peak period, when water-weight gains may be difficult to reduce prior to important races. About 20 to 30 percent of those who take creatine experience no measurable physiological changes. Vegetarians may stand to realize the greatest gains from creatine since they typically have low levels due to their meatless diet.

Creatine may help in the MS phase and Build period.

Most studies have used amounts such as 20 to 30 grams of creatine a day taken in four to five doses during a four- to seven-day loading phase. One found the same muscle levels, however, on as little as three grams daily for 30 days. After loading, muscle creatine levels can be maintained at high levels for four to five weeks with two grams taken daily. Dissolving creatine in grape or orange juice seems to improve absorption. In these studies, not all the subjects experienced an increase in muscle creatine levels despite high dosages.

According to scientists who have studied creatine, there is little health risk since it is passively filtered from the blood and puts no extra workload on the kidneys, but the longest study is only 10 weeks. Scientists do know that once you stop short-term use, your natural production of creatine is regained. The only well-established side effect is the addition of body weight during the loading phase, which soon disappears. A greater concern is that creatine may give you a false positive in a urine test for kidney problems. There have also been anecdotal accounts of muscle spasm and cramping in power athletes using creatine on a long-term basis, perhaps due to a lowered concentration of electrolytes in the muscles. Talk with your health-care provider before supplementing with creatine.

Side effects are not fully understood.

SODIUM PHOSPHATE

The German army used sodium phosphate in World War I, and even in the 1930s

German athletes knew of it's worth. It has not been widely publicized in recent years, although some athletes have known about it, but kept the secret.

Sodium phosphate has the potential to improve race performance by allowing you to maintain a high pace longer, and make high-intensity efforts feel much easier.

In 1983, researchers working with elite runners found that sodium phosphate increased aerobic capacity by 9 percent and improved ventilatory threshold, such as lactate threshold, by 12 percent. A more recent study of cyclists in Florida showed that using phosphate improved low-level endurance time significantly, lowered 40km time trial times by 8 percent, and raised lactate threshold by 10 percent while lowering perceived effort. Pretty heady stuff.

Sodium phosphate has great potential for improving endurance performance.

It appears to bring these changes by causing the hemoglobin in the red blood cells to more completely unload their stores of oxygen at the muscle. A greater supply of oxygen allows the muscles to operate aerobically at higher speeds and power outputs that would normally cause an anaerobic state.

Supplementation is similar to creatine loading. Take 4 grams of sodium phosphate for three days before an A-priority race. To prepare your gut for the change, take 1 or 2 grams for one or two days before starting the loading procedure. Spread out the daily dosage by taking one-third of it with each meal. Don't take it on an empty stomach. It's best not to continue using it more than three or four times each season as continued supplementation reduces the benefits. In studies, the gains from sodium phosphate were still apparent one week after the loading stopped, meaning that races over two weeks can reap the benefits.

How to supplement.

A side effect many athletes experience when sodium phosphate loading is an upset stomach. This may not appear until several days into the routine. Feeling sick right before a race is not good for your confidence, so it's best to try the loading procedure the first time before an early season C-priority race or workout. If you find it upsets your stomach, try the following loading procedure:

Days before "A" race	Daily dosage
16–19	1–1.5g
14–15	none
9–13	1–1.5g
7–8	none
6–race day	1–1.5g

Twin Labs makes a product called Phos Fuel that is available in some health food and specialty stores.

If you have a low dietary intake of calcium or have an excessive amount of salt in your diet, sodium phosphate can cause a calcium deficiency. In this case, you'd be advised not to use it. Better yet, increase your intake of dietary calcium and decrease your salt intake. Do not use calcium phosphate, as no performance benefits have been linked with it.

Long-term use may affect calcium levels.

GLYCEROL

Do you wither in the heat? In long, hot races do you cramp up in the last few miles? Do you dread riding or running on days when the temperature reaches the 90s? If so, glycerol may be just what you need.

As your body loses fluid there is a corresponding drop in performance. As pointed out earlier, even a 1-percent drop in body weight due to dehydration reduces maximum work output by about 2 percent. This reduction is a result of decreased blood volume, since the plasma in blood supplies sweat. A 5-percent loss of body weight is common in hot, long races.

Losing seven percent of body weight due to fluid depletion is dangerous to health and may even require hospitalization. Some athletes suffer the effects of heat more than others.

Dehydration prevention maintains performance.

Other than just the heat, other factors may cause you to dehydrate. Sometimes all it takes is a missed aid station, or a dropped bottle on the bike. Beyond these problems, there are also physiological limits on how much fluid the human digestive tract can absorb during high-intensity racing. All of this can lead to disaster in what might have otherwise been an exceptional race.

Glycerol, a syrupy, sweet-tasting liquid, turns your body into a water-hoarding sponge. Used prior to a race, it causes the body to hold onto 50 percent more fluid than when using water alone. Because of this, fluid losses through urination are decreased and there is more water available for sweat.

Glycerol causes the body to retain water.

In one study using cyclists, body temperatures increased 40 percent less when using glycerol as compared with water only. Also, heart rate increased 5 percent less with glycerol and there was a 32 percent improvement in endurance. These are tremendous advantages that could take you from the DNF listing to the top 10. Who wouldn't want these benefits?

In recent years, glycerol products for endurance athletes have become widely available in running stores, bike shops, health food and specialty stores, and through catalog sales. Simply mix and drink the product according to the instructions on the label. Using more will not help you, and may even cause problems.

As with anything new, you should experiment with glycerol before a workout—not a race. It has been known to cause headaches and nausea in some athletes. Better to find that out in training rather than in the most important race of the season.

No side effects are known.

There have been no long-term studies on the effect of large doses of glycerol, but it generally considered safe as it is found naturally in dietary fats.

FINAL THOUGHTS

The supplement industry in the USA is not closely regulated by the government, so product purity may be an issue if any of the above products are purchased from unscrupulous manufacturers. For example, a recent analysis of a widely advertised category of dietary supplements found unidentifiable impurities in most of the products. Buy only from reputable companies whose products are well established in the marketplace.

Bottom line: Use ergogenic aids cautiously and conservatively.

Also, no studies have been done on how any of the ergogenic aids described here may interact if all or most of them are used together, with other supplements, or even with many of the medications commonly used by athletes such: ibuprofen or aspirin. It's always a good idea to talk with your health-care provider before taking any supplement, all the more so if you are on any medications.

When using an ergogenic aid, it's important that you assess the benefits, if any, for your performance. Not only does using several concurrently increase your risk of side effects, it also clouds the issue of which one provided the most performance gain. In addition, you should always be skeptical of faster race times as a result of supplementation. Was it really the pill, or was it the placebo effect? While many athletes probably don't care, coming to understand what helps you and what doesn't will ultimately lead to your best races.

In the final analysis, training and diet provide 99.9 percent of the impetus for performance improvements. Supplements offer only a small benefit. If your training and diet are less than desirable, there is no reason to add any ergogenic supplement to the mix.

REFERENCES

American College of Sports Medicine. "Antioxidants and the Elite Athlete. Proceedings of Panel Discussion." May 27, 1992, Dallas, TX.

American Dietetic Association. "Nutrition and Physical Fitness and Athletic Performance." *Journal of the American Dietetics Association* 87 (1987): 933–939.

Anderson, O. "Carbs, Creatine & Phosphate: If the King Had Used These Uppers, He'd Still Be Around Today." *Running Research News* 12, no. 3 (1996): 1–4.

Appell, H. J., et al. 1997. "Supplementation of Vitamin E May Attenuate Skeletal Muscle

Immobilization Atrophy." *International Journal of Sports Medicine* 18 (1997): 157–160.

Armsey, T. D. and G.A. Green. "Nutrition Supplementation: Science vs. Hype." *The Physician and Sports Medicine* 25, no. 6 (1997): 77–92.

Blomstrand, E., et al. "Administration of Branched Chain Amino Acids During Sustained Exercise—Effects on Performance and on Plasma Concentrations of Some Amino Acids." *European Journal of Applied Physiology* 63, no. 2 (1991): 83–88.

Burke, L. M. and R. S. D. Read. "Dietary Supplements in Sport. *Sports Medicine* 15 (1993): 43–65.

Cade, R., et al. "Effects of Phosphate Loading on 2, 3-Diphosphoglycerate and Maximal Oxygen Uptake." *Medicine and Science in Sports and Exercise* 16, no. 3 (1984): 263–268.

Cerra, F. B., et al. "Branched-Chain Amino Acid Supplementation During Trekking at High Altitude." *European Journal of Applied Physiology* 65 (1984): 394–398.

Clement, D. B., et al. "Branched-Chain Metabolic Support: A Prospective, Randomized Double-Blind Trial in Surgical Stress." *Annals of Surgery* 199, no. 3 (1984): 286–291.

Cordain, L., R. W. Gotshall, and S.B. Eaton. "Evolutionary Aspects of Exercise." *World Review of Nutrition and Dietetics* 81 (1997): 49–60.

Cordain, L. Department of Exercise and Sport Science, Colorado State University, Fort Collins, Colorado 80523. 1999. Personal communication with author.

Davis, J. M. "Carbohydrates, Branched-Chain Amino Acids, and Performance—The Central Fatigue Hypothesis." *International Journal of Sport Nutrition* 5 (1995): S29–S38.

Dufaux, B., et al. 1981. "Serum Ferritin, Transferrin, Haptoglobin, and Iron in Middle- and Long-Distance Runners, Elite Rowers, and Professional Racing Cyclists." *International Journal of Sports Medicine* 2, no. 1 (1981): 43–46.

Eaton, S. B. and M. Konner. 1985. "Paleolithic Nutrition: A Consideration of Its Nature and Current Implications." *The New England Journal of Medicine* 312, no. 5 (1985): 283–289.

Eaton, S. B., M. Shostak, and M. Konner. *The Paleolithic Prescription.* New York: Harper & Row, 1989.

Eaton, S. B. and D. A. Nelson. "Calcium in Evolutionary Perspective." *American Journal of Clinical Nutrition* 54 (1991): 281S–287S.

Eaton, S. B. "Humans, Lipids and Evolution." *Lipids* 27, no. 1 (1992): 814–820.

Evans, W., et al. 1983. Protein Metabolism and Endurance Exercise." *The Physician and Sports Medicine* 11, no. 7 (1983): 63–72.

Goedecke, JH, et al. 1999. "Effects of Medium-Chain Triaclyglycerol Ingested with Carbohydrate on Metabolism and Exercise Performance." *International Journal of Sport Nutrition* 9, no. 1 (1999): 35–47

Graham, T. E. and L. L. Spriet. 1996. "Caffeine and Exercise Performance." *Sports Science Exchange* 9, no. 1 (1996): 1–6.

Grandjean, A. C. "Diets of Elite Athletes: Has the Discipline of Sports Nutrition Made an Impact?" *Journal of Nutrition* 127 (5 Supplement) (1997): 874S–877S.

Green, D. R., et al. 1989. "An Evaluation of Dietary Intakes of Triathletes: Are RDAs Being Met?" *Brief Communications* 89, no. 11 (1989): 1653–1654.

Guilland, J. C., et al. "Vitamin Status of Young Athletes Including the Effects of Supplementation." *Medicine and Science in Sport and Exercise* 21 (1989): 441–449.

Harris, R. C., et al. "Elevation of Creatine in Resting and Exercised Muscle of Normal Subjects by Creatine Supplementation." *Clinical Science* 83, no. 3 (1992): 367–374.

Hawley, J. A. and W. G. Hopkins. "Aerobic Glycolytic and Aerobic Lipolytic Power Systems: A New Paradigm with Implications for Endurance and Ultra-Endurance Events." *Sports Medicine* 20 (1995): 321–327.

Hawley, J. A., et al. 1996. "Effects of Ingesting Varying Concentrations of Sodium on Fluid Balance During Exercise." *Medicine and Science in Sport and Exercise* 28, no. 5 (1996): S350.

Hopkins, W. G. 1996. "Advances in Training for Endurance Athletes. *New Zealand Journal of Sports Medicine* 24, no. 3 (1996): 29–31.

Hu, F. B., et al. 1997. "Dietary Fat Intake and the Risk of Coronary Heart Disease in Women." *New England Journal of Medicine* 337, no. 21 (1997): 1491–1499.

International Dance and Exercise Association. "Antioxidants: Clearing the Confusion." *IDEA Today* Sept. (1994): 67–73.

Kanter, M. M. "Free Radicals, Exercise, and Antioxidant Supplementation." *International Journal of Sport Nutrition* 4 (1994): 205–220.

Lambert, E. V., et al. "Enhanced Endurance in Trained Cyclists During Moderate-Intensity Exercise Following Two Weeks Adaptation to a High-Fat Diet." *European Journal of Applied Physiology* 69 (1994): 287–293.

Lambert, E. V., et al. "Nutritional Strategies for Promoting Fat Utilization and Delaying the Onset of Fatigue During Prolonged Exercise." *Journal of Sports Science* 15, no. 3 (1997): 315–324.

Lapachet, R. A., et al. "Body Fat and Exercise Endurance in Trained Rats Adapted to a High-Fat and/or High-Carbohydrate Diet." *Journal of Applied Physiology* 80, no. 4 (1996): 1173–1179.

Lemon, P. W. R. "Protein and Amino Acid Needs of the Strength Athlete." *International Journal of Sports Nutrition* 1 (1991): 127–145.

Lemon, P. W. R. "Is Increased Dietary Protein Necessary or Beneficial for Individuals with a Physically Active Lifestyle?" *Nutrition Reviews* S4, no. 4 (1996): S169–S175.

Lyons, T. P., et al. 1990. "Effects of Glycerol-Induced Hyperhydration Prior to Exercise on Sweating and Core Temperature." *Medicine and Science in Sport arid Exercise* 22, no. 4 (1990): 477–483.

Maughan, R. J. "Creatine Supplementation and Exercise Performance." *International Journal of Sports Nutrition* 5 (1995): 94–101.

McMurtrey, J. J. and R. Sherwin. "History, Pharmacology and Toxicology of Caffeine and Caffeine-Containing Beverages." *Clinical Nutrition* 6 (1987): 249–254.

Muoio, D. M., et al. "Effect of Dietary Fat on Metabolic Adjustments to Maximal VO_2 And Endurance in Runners." *Medicine and Science in Sports and Exercise* 26 (1994): 81–88.

Nagao, N., et al. "Energy Intake in the Triathlon Competition by Means of Cluster Analysis." *Journal of Sports Medicine and Physical Fitness* 31, no. 1 (1991): 62–66.

Nemoto, I., et al. "Branched-Chain Amino Acid (BCAA) Supplementation Improves Endurance Capacities and RPE." *Medicine and Science in Sports and Exercise* 28, no. 5 (1996): S219.

Noakes, T., et al. "Effects of a Low-Carbohydrate, High-Fat Diet Prior to Carbohydrate Loading on Endurance Cycling Performance." *Clinical Science* 87 (1994): S32–S33.

O'Toole, M. L. et al. "Fluid and Electrolyte Status in Athletes Receiving Medical Care at an Ultradistance Triathlon." *Clinical Journal of Sports Medicine* 5, no. 2 (1995): 116–122.

Peters, E. M., et al. "Anti-Oxidant Nutrient Supplementation and Symptoms of Upper Respiratory Tract Infections in Endurance Athletes." *Medicine and Science in Sports and Exercise* 26, no. 5: S218.

Phinney, S. D., et al. "The Human Metabolic Response to Chronic Ketosis with Caloric Restriction and Preservation of Submaximal Exercise Capabilities with Reduced Carbohydrate Oxidation." *Metabolism* 32 (1983): 769–776.

Robergs, R. A. "Glycerol Hyperhydration to Beat the Heat?" Sportscience web page: http://www.sportsci.org/traintech/glycero/rar.htm, 1998.

Schena, F. "Branched-Chain Amino Acid Supplementation During Trekking at High Altitude." *European Journal of Applied Physiology* 65 (1992): 394–398.

Simonson, J. C., et al. "Dietary Carbohydrate, Muscle Glycogen, and Power Output During Rowing Training." *Journal of Applied Physiology* 70 (1991): 1500–1505.

Somer, E. *The Essential Guide to Vitamins and Minerals.* New York: Harper Collins, 1992.

Stahl, A. B. "Hominid Dietary Selection Before Fire." *Current Anthropology* 25, no. 2 (1984): 151–168.

Taimura, A. and M. Sugahara. "Effect of Fluid Intake on Performance, Body Temperature, and Body Weight Loss During Swimming Training." *Medicine and Science in Sport and Exercise* 28, no. 5 (1996): S940.

Thompson, P. D., et al. "The Effects of High-Carbohydrate and High-Fat Diets on the Serum Lipid and Lipoprotein Concentrations of Endurance Athletes." *Metabolism* 33 (1984): 1003–1010.

Van Zyl, C. G., et al. "Effects of Medium-Chain Triglyceride Ingestion on Fuel Metabolism and Cycling Performance." *Journal of Applied Physiology* 80, no. 6 (1996): 2217–2225

Venkatraman, J. T., et al. "Influence of the Level of Dietary Lipid Intake and Maximal Exercise on The Immune Status in Runners." *Medicine and Science in Sport and Exercise* 29, no. 3 (1997): 333–344.

Walsh, R. M., et al. "Impaired High-Intensity Cycling Performance Time at Low Levels of Dehydration." *International Journal of Sports Medicine* 15 (1994): 392–398.

Weltman, A., et al. "Endurance Training Amplifies the Pulsatile Release of Growth Hormone: Effects of Training Intensity." *Journal of Applied Physiology* 72, no. 6 (1992): 2188–2196.

Wilmore, J. H. and D. L. Costill. *Physiology of Sport and Exercise.* Champaign, IL: Human Kinetics, (1994).

Wemple, R. D., et al. "Caffeine vs. Caffeine-Free Sports Drinks: Effects on Urine Production at Rest and During Prolonged Exercise." *International Journal of Sports Medicine* 18 (1997): 40–46.

EPILOGUE

In completing this project, I'd like to touch on a just a few concerns I have discovered from my previous books.

The problem with writing a book is that it appears definitive, as if everything the author knows, and will ever know, is contained here. Let me assure you that this is not the case. Since I wrote *The Cyclist's Training Bible* in 1995, many of my thoughts on training have evolved. If I had it to do over again, I would say some things differently. It is likely that the same will be true of *The Mountain Biker's Training Bible* in but a few years.

Those who never change their minds on anything once they've said it, and there are many like this, concern me. They live on past glories and fear the future. Change, however, is inevitable, and with it often comes progress.

Another concern has to do with follow-up by readers of this book. There will be many who will contact me by email, fax, or in person to ask very pointed questions about some fine detail of what I have written here and how to apply it to their training. I wish I could help everyone with such a problem, but unfortunately it's not possible. In fact, even when I coach athletes in intensive one-on-one programs it takes days, if not weeks, to know them well enough to resolve the finer aspects of training. The chances of my being able to do that adequately for someone I don't know based on limited information is unlikely.

As I explained a couple of pages earlier, there are no training secrets. The answers to your training questions, and there will be many, are neither mysterious nor known only to a select few. Most questions may be answered with only a little basic information, such as may be found in this book and others, and common sense.

This book was written to help you become better at coaching yourself. Should you find that you are not very good at self-coaching, the best solution is to work with a professional coach. In the U.S. and many other countries, coaching is a growing field. And now that electronic communication through the Internet and by fax has made the world so small, it really doesn't matter where your coach lives. The exception is for novice riders. Those new to the sport should work with a local coach who can regularly see them on the bike and provide guidance on handling skills and the subtle nuances of workouts.

Writing *The Mountain Biker's Training Bible* was a labor of love. Helping athletes reach for their dreams is very rewarding. The highest joy of writing a book is making friends who you haven't met yet. My greatest reward comes when a rider tells me of his or her success in the sport due, in part, to what they have read in my book.

I hope that something I've written here will serve as a seed for others who will nurture and grow a training concept that they can then teach to me. That is as it should be. Only when the teacher and student are willing to exchange roles does real progress occur.

See you on the trails!

RECOMMENDED READING

Baker, A. *Bicycling Medicine.* New York: Simon & Schuster, 1998.

Bompa, T. *Periodization of Strength.* Toronto: Veritas Publishing, 1993.

Bompa, T. *From Childhood to Champion.* Toronto: Veritas Publishing, 1995.

Bompa, T. *Theory and Methodology of Training.* Champaign, IL: Human Kinetics, 1999.

Borysewicz, E. *Bicycle Road Racing.* Brattleboro, VT: Velo-News, 1985.

Burke, E. *High-Tech Cycling.* Champaign, IL: Human Kinetics, 1996.

Burke, E. *Off-Season Training for Cyclists.* Boulder, CO: VeloPress, 1997.

Burney, S. *Cyclo-Cross Training and Technique.* Boulder, CO: VeloPress, 1996.

Elliott, R. *The Competitive Edge.* Mountain View, CA: TAFNEWS, 1991.

Freeman, W. *Peak When It Counts.* Mountain View, CA: TAFNEWS, 1991.

Friel, J. *The Cyclist's Training Bible.* Boulder, CO: VeloPress, 1996.

Howard, J. *Dirt!* New York: Lyons Press, 1997.

Janssen, P. G. J. M. *Training, Lactate, Pulse Rate.* Oulu, Finland: Polar Electro Oy, 1987.

Kreider, R. B., A. C. Fry, and M. L. O'Toole. *Overtraining in Sport.* Champaign, IL: Human Kinetics.

Lynch, J. and C. A. Huang. *Working Out, Working Within.* New York: Tarcher/Putnam, 1998.

Overend, N. and E. Pavelka. *Mountain Bike Like a Champion.* Emmaus, PA: Rodale Press, 1999.

Perry, D. B. *Bike Cult.* New York: Four Walls Eight Windows, 1995.

Phinney, D. and C. Carpenter. *Training for Cycling.* New York: Perigee Books, 1992.

Skilbeck, P. *Single-Track Mind.* Boulder, CO: VeloPress, 1996.

Sleamaker, R. and R. Browning. *Serious Training for Endurance Athletes.* Champaign, IL: Leisure Press, 1996.

Van der Plas, R. *The Mountain Bike Book.* San Francisco: Bicycle Books, 1995.

Whitt, F. R. and D. G. Wilson. *Bicycling Science.* Cambridge, MA: MIT Press, 1995.

Williams, M. *Beyond Training.* Champaign, IL: Human Kinetics, 1989.

Williams, M. *Ergogenics Edge.* Champaign, IL: Human Kinetics, 1998.

Wilmore, J. H. and D. L. Costill. *Physiology of Sport and Exercise.* Champaign, IL: Human Kinetics, 1994.

Ungerleider, S. *Mental Training for Peak Performance.* Emmaus, PA: Rodale Sports, 1996.

Zinn, L. *Zinn and the Art of Mountain Bike Maintenance.* Boulder, CO: VeloPress, 1996.

ANNUAL TRAINING PLANS
2000-2005

THE MOUNTAIN BIKER'S TRAINING BIBLE

Athlete _____

Annual Hours _____

Season Goals

1. _____
2. _____
3. _____

Training Objectives

1. _____
2. _____
3. _____
4. _____

WORKOUTS

WK# MON	RACES	PRI	PERIOD	HOURS	DETAILS	WEIGHTS	ENDURANCE	FORCE	SPEED	MUSCULAR ENDURANCE	ANAEROBIC ENDURANCE	POWER	TESTING
1-Jan-03													
2-Jan-10													
3-Jan-17													
4-Jan-24													
5-Jan-31													
6-Feb-07													
7-Feb-14													
8-Feb-21													
9-Feb-28													
10-Mar-06													
11-Mar-13													
12-Mar-20													
13-Mar-27													
14-Apr-03													
15-Apr-10													
16-Apr-17													
17-Apr-24													
18-May-01													
19-May-08													
20-May-15													
21-May-22													
22-May-29													
23-Jun-05													
24-Jun-12													
25-Jun-19													
26-Jun-26													
27-Jul-03													
28-Jul-10													
29-Jul-17													
30-Jul-24													
31-Jul-31													
32-Aug-07													
33-Aug-14													
34-Aug-21													
35-Aug-28													
36-Sep-04													
37-Sep-11													
38-Sep-18													
39-Sep-25													
40-Oct-02													
41-Oct-09													
42-Oct-16													
43-Oct-23													
44-Oct-30													
45-Nov-06													
46-Nov-13													
47-Nov-20													
48-Nov-27													
49-Dec-04													
50-Dec-11													
51-Dec-18													
52-Dec-25													

Athlete _____

Annual Hours _____

November 2000 - October 2001

Season Goals

1. _____
2. _____
3. _____

Training Objectives

1. _____
2. _____
3. _____
4. _____

WORKOUTS

WK# MON	RACES	PRI	PERIOD	HOURS	DETAILS	WEIGHTS	ENDURANCE	FORCE	SPEED	MUSCULAR ENDURANCE	ANAEROBIC ENDURANCE	POWER	TESTING
1-Nov-06													
2-Nov-13													
3-Nov-20													
4-Nov-27													
5-Dec-04													
6-Dec-11													
7-Dec-18													
8-Dec-25													
9-Jan-01													
10-Jan-08													
11-Jan-15													
12-Jan-22													
13-Jan-29													
14-Feb-05													
15-Feb-12													
16-Feb-19													
17-Feb-26													
18-Mar-05													
19-Mar-12													
20-Mar-19													
21-Mar-26													
22-Apr-02													
23-Apr-09													
24-Apr-16													
25-Apr-23													
26-Apr-30													
27-May-07													
28-May-14													
29-May-21													
30-May-28													
31-Jun-04													
32-Jun-11													
33-Jun-18													
34-Jun-25													
35-Jul-02													
36-Jul-09													
37-Jul-16													
38-Jul-23													
39-Jul-30													
40-Aug-06													
41-Aug-13													
42-Aug-20													
43-Aug-27													
44-Sep-03													
45-Sep-10													
46-Sep-17													
47-Sep-24													
48-Oct-01													
49-Oct-08													
50-Oct-15													
51-Oct-22													
52-Oct-29													

Athlete _____

Annual Hours _____

November 2001 - October 2002

Season Goals

1. _____
2. _____
3. _____

Training Objectives

1. _____
2. _____
3. _____
4. _____

WORKOUTS

WK# MON	RACES	PRI	PERIOD	HOURS	DETAILS	WEIGHTS	ENDURANCE	FORCE	SPEED	MUSCULAR ENDURANCE	ANAEROBIC ENDURANCE	POWER	TESTING
1-Nov-05													
2-Nov-12													
3-Nov-19													
4-Nov-26													
5-Dec-03													
6-Dec-10													
7-Dec-17													
8-Dec-24													
9-Dec-31													
10-Jan-07													
11-Jan-14													
12-Jan-21													
13-Jan-28													
14-Feb-04													
15-Feb-11													
16-Feb-18													
17-Feb-25													
18-Mar-04													
19-Mar-11													
20-Mar-18													
21-Mar-25													
22-Apr-01													
23-Apr-08													
24-Apr-15													
25-Apr-22													
26-Apr-29													
27-May-06													
28-May-13													
29-May-20													
30-May-27													
31-Jun-03													
32-Jun-10													
33-Jun-17													
34-Jun-24													
35-Jul-01													
36-Jul-08													
37-Jul-15													
38-Jul-22													
39-Jul-29													
40-Aug-05													
41-Aug-12													
42-Aug-19													
43-Aug-26													
44-Sep-02													
45-Sep-09													
46-Sep-16													
47-Sep-23													
48-Sep-30													
49-Oct-07													
50-Oct-14													
51-Oct-21													
52-Oct-28													

Athlete _____

Annual Hours _____

| | November 2002 - October 2003 |

Season Goals

1. _____
2. _____
3. _____

Training Objectives

1. _____
2. _____
3. _____
4. _____

WORKOUTS

WK# MON	RACES	PRI	PERIOD	HOURS	DETAILS	WEIGHTS	ENDURANCE	FORCE	SPEED	MUSCULAR ENDURANCE	ANAEROBIC ENDURANCE	POWER	TESTING
1-Nov-04													
2-Nov-11													
3-Nov-18													
4-Nov-25													
5-Dec-02													
6-Dec-09													
7-Dec-16													
8-Dec-23													
9-Dec-30													
10-Jan-06													
11-Jan-13													
12-Jan-20													
13-Jan-27													
14-Feb-03													
15-Feb-10													
16-Feb-17													
17-Feb-24													
18-Mar-03													
19-Mar-10													
20-Mar-17													
21-Mar-24													
22-Mar-31													
23-Apr-07													
24-Apr-14													
25-Apr-21													
26-Apr-28													
27-May-05													
28-May-12													
29-May-19													
30-May-26													
31-Jun-02													
32-Jun-09													
33-Jun-16													
34-Jun-23													
35-Jun-30													
36-Jul-07													
37-Jul-14													
38-Jul-21													
39-Jul-28													
40-Aug-04													
41-Aug-11													
42-Aug-18													
43-Aug-25													
44-Sep-01													
45-Sep-08													
46-Sep-15													
47-Sep-22													
48-Sep-29													
49-Oct-06													
50-Oct-13													
51-Oct-20													
52-Oct-27													

THE MOUNTAIN BIKER'S TRAINING BIBLE

Athlete _____

Annual Hours _____

November 2003 - October 2004

Season Goals

1. _____
2. _____
3. _____

Training Objectives

1. _____
2. _____
3. _____
4. _____

WORKOUTS

WK# MON	RACES	PRI	PERIOD	HOURS	DETAILS	WEIGHTS	ENDURANCE	FORCE	SPEED	MUSCULAR ENDURANCE	ANAEROBIC ENDURANCE	POWER	TESTING
1-Nov-03													
2-Nov-10													
3-Nov-17													
4-Nov-24													
5-Dec-01													
6-Dec-08													
7-Dec-15													
8-Dec-22													
9-Dec-29													
10-Jan-05													
11-Jan-12													
12-Jan-19													
13-Jan-26													
14-Feb-02													
15-Feb-09													
16-Feb-16													
17-Feb-23													
18-Mar-01													
19-Mar-08													
20-Mar-15													
21-Mar-22													
22-Mar-29													
23-Apr-05													
24-Apr-12													
25-Apr-19													
26-Apr-26													
27-May-03													
28-May-10													
29-May-17													
30-May-24													
31-May-31													
32-Jun-07													
33-Jun-14													
34-Jun-21													
35-Jun-28													
36-Jul-05													
37-Jul-12													
38-Jul-19													
39-Jul-26													
40-Aug-02													
41-Aug-09													
42-Aug-16													
43-Aug-23													
44-Aug-30													
45-Sep-06													
46-Sep-13													
47-Sep-20													
48-Sep-27													
49-Oct-04													
50-Oct-11													
51-Oct-18													
52-Oct-25													

Athlete _____

Annual Hours _____

Season Goals

1. _____

2. _____

3. _____

Training Objectives

1. _____

2. _____

3. _____

4. _____

November 2004 - October 2005

WORKOUTS

WK# MON	RACES	PRI	PERIOD	HOURS	DETAILS	WEIGHTS	ENDURANCE	FORCE	SPEED	MUSCULAR ENDURANCE	ANAEROBIC ENDURANCE	POWER	TESTING
1-Nov-01													
2-Nov-08													
3-Nov-15													
4-Nov-22													
5-Nov-29													
6-Dec-06													
7-Dec-13													
8-Dec-20													
9-Dec-27													
10-Jan-03													
11-Jan-10													
12-Jan-17													
13-Jan-24													
14-Jan-31													
15-Feb-07													
16-Feb-14													
17-Feb-21													
18-Feb-28													
19-Mar-07													
20-Mar-14													
21-Mar-21													
22-Mar-28													
23-Apr-04													
24-Apr-11													
25-Apr-18													
26-Apr-25													
27-May-02													
28-May-09													
29-May-16													
30-May-23													
31-May-30													
32-Jun-06													
33-Jun-13													
34-Jun-20													
35-Jun-27													
36-Jul-05													
37-Jul-11													
38-Jul-18													
39-Jul-25													
40-Aug-01													
41-Aug-08													
42-Aug-15													
43-Aug-22													
44-Aug-29													
45-Sep-05													
46-Sep-12													
47-Sep-19													
48-Sep-26													
49-Oct-03													
50-Oct-10													
51-Oct-17													
52-Oct-24													
53-Oct-31													

WORKOUT MENU

MOUNTAIN BIKE WORKOUTS

The following are a few suggested workouts for each ability discussed in Chapter 6. Use these when planning a training week as described in Chapter 8. The alphanumeric code for each of these workouts may be used as a shorthand notation when scheduling a week using a training diary as described in Chapter 15.

Intensities for all workouts are shown as heart rate (HR) and/or power (CP) zones. Chapter 4 explains how to use each of these intensity-gauging systems.

Many of these workouts may be done on either a road or a mountain bike. Those that specifically intended for one or the other are so indicated.

ENDURANCE WORKOUTS

E1: Recovery

Ride on a flat course in the heart rate 1 zone or at half of CP12 zone using small chain ring. This is best if done alone or with another disciplined rider. You may also ride on an indoor trainer or rollers, especially if flat courses are not available. Cross-training can be done for recovery in Preparation, Base 1 and Base 2 periods. An excellent time to do a recovery spin is in the evening on a day when you've done intervals, sprints, a hard group ride, hills, or a race. Spinning for 15 to 30 minutes on rollers or a trainer hastens recovery for most experienced riders. Novices are better advised to take the time off from all training and rest. These workouts are not scheduled on the annual training plan, but are an integral part of training throughout the season. (Periods: All)

E2: Endurance

To develop or maintain aerobic endurance, ride on the road primarily in the heart rate 2 or CP180 zones. Use a rolling course with grades that allow you to stay at the specified intensity. Remain seated on the uphill portions to build or maintain force while pedaling at the high end of your normal cadence range. This can be done with a disciplined group or on an indoor trainer by shifting through the gears to simulate rolling hills. Cross-training is effective during Preparation and Base 1. (Periods: All)

FORCE WORKOUTS

F1: Hilly Endurance

On- or off-road, select a course that includes several hills with moderate grades (4 to 6 percent) that take several minutes to climb. When doing this off-road, fire roads are best. Stay seated on all climbs, pedaling from the hips with a cadence of 60 rpm or higher. Select gears that will keep you in the heart rate 4 to 5a or CP30 to 60 zones on all climbs on this ride. This is a workout that combines endurance with force. (Periods: Base 2, Base 3)

F2: Big-Gear Climbs

Find a hill, either on- or off-road, with steep grades (8 percent or more) that takes one to two minutes to climb. Stay seated on this hill. Select gears that are slightly higher than you would normally use so that cadence is in the 50 to 60 rpm range. Intensity is heart rate 5a to 5b or CP6 to 30. Concentrate on position on the bike and smooth pedaling. Recover for three to five minutes after each climb. Get in 6 to 30 minutes of climbing within a workout. Do not do this workout if it causes knee discomfort. (Periods: Base 3, Build 1)

SPEED SKILLS WORKOUTS

S1: Spin-ups

On a downhill or with a tailwind on the road, or on an indoor trainer set to light resistance, gradually increase cadence to maximum every five minutes over a 30-second period. Maximum is the cadence you can maintain without bouncing. As the cadence increases, allow your lower legs and feet to relax—especially the toes. Hold your maximum for as long as possible. Repeat several times. These are best done with a handlebar computer that displays cadence. Heart rate and power have no significance for this workout, but cadence monitoring is helpful. (Periods: Preparation, Base 1, Base 2, Base 3)

S2: Isolated Leg

On an indoor trainer, place a foot on a chair or stool and pedal with only one leg. Maintain a cadence of 80 to 100 rpm and concentrate on smoothing out the "dead" spot at the top of the stroke by "throwing the knee over the handlebars" and by pushing the toes forward in the shoes as the foot approaches the top position. Change legs when fatigue begins to set in. Repeat several times. While low, heart rate and power are not important for this workout. Monitor cadence. (Periods: Preparation, Base 1, Base 2, Base 3)

S3: Fixed Gear

Set up a road bike with a gear that is appropriate for your strength level and allows a cadence of 90 rpm or higher when riding comfortably on a flat course with no wind. Use a small chain ring (39 to 42) and a large cog (19 to 22). If you are in your first two years of training, don't do this workout. Start by riding flat courses and gradually add gently rolling hills. Intensity should be mostly in the heart rate 2 to 3 or CP90 to 180 zones. This workout is multiability, including endurance, force, and speed skills—all elements required of Base training. (Periods: Base 2, Base 3)

S4: Form Sprints

Early in a road or off-road ride, do 6 to 10 sprints on a slight downhill or with a tailwind. Each sprint lasts about 10 seconds with a recover of several minutes. These sprints are done only for form, so select a lower gear than you would normally sprint in and focus on technique. Power is CP1. Heart rate zones are not applicable. Do these alone. (Periods: Base 2, Base 3)

S5: Off-road Handling Skills

Go to a park and practice bunny hopping, jumping, wheelies, balancing and slalom cornering. As the training year progresses head for the trails and practice those skill elements that cause you the most trouble. These off-road speed skills workouts generally should be done at a low heart rate or power output and early in the training session. The best time to work on skills is when you are well rested. (Periods: Base 1, Base 2, Base 3)

MUSCULAR-ENDURANCE WORKOUTS

M1: Tempo

On a mostly flat road course, or on an indoor trainer, ride in the heart rate 3 or CP 90 zone for 20 to 60 minutes without recovery. Avoid roads with heavy traffic and stop streets. Stay in an aerodynamic position throughout. This workout may be done once or twice weekly. (Periods: Base 2, Base 3)

M2: Cruise Intervals

On a relatively flat road course or an indoor trainer, complete three to five intervals that are each six to 12 minutes long. Intensity is heart rate 4 to 5a and CP30 zones. Cadence is what you would use for a time trial. Recover for two to three minutes after each work interval. Recovery power or heart rate are extremely low—coasting is okay. This workout is best included in the second half of the session when it is a combined workout. The first cruise interval workout of the season should total 20 to 30 minutes of work intervals (for example, 4 x 6 minutes). Increase the duration of each work interval weekly. Stay relaxed and aerodynamic, and closely monitor your RPE by listening to your breathing and paying attention to how you feel. This workout may be done once or twice weekly. (Periods: Base 3, Build 1, Build 2, Peak, Race)

M3: Hill Cruise Intervals

This is the same as cruise intervals except the work intervals are done on a long 2 to 4 percent grade either on the road or trail. Use time trial cadence or slightly lower. Complete two or three cruise interval workouts on flat terrain before doing them on a hill. (Periods: Base 3, Build 1, Build 2, Peak, Race)

M4: Criss-cross Threshold

On a mostly flat road course with little traffic and no stops, ride 20 to 40 minutes alternating between heart rate low 4 to high 5a zones, or with power alternate CP60 and CP30 power zones every 3 to 5 minutes. Use your time trial cadence and an aerodynamic position. (Periods: Build 2, Peak)

M5: Threshold

On a mostly flat road course with little traffic and no stop signs, ride 20 to 40 minutes nonstop at heart rate 4 to 5a or CP60 zones. Stay relaxed, aerodynamic, and monitor your RPE by listening to breathing and paying attention to how you feel. Pedal at the cadence you normally use in a time trial. Don't attempt a threshold ride until you've completed at least four cruise interval workouts. (Periods: Build 2, Peak)

M6: Shifting Cruise Intervals

This is the same as cruise intervals done on the road, except you shift between a higher and lower gear every 30 to 60 seconds. Maintain heart rate 4 to 5a or CP30 zones for 60 seconds and then shift to a higher gear and hold heart rate 5b or CP12 zone for 30 seconds. Repeat this pattern throughout each cruise interval. Cadence is what you would use for a time trial. Maintain an aerodynamic position. The maximum, total interval duration for this workout is about 30 minutes. (Periods: Build 2, Peak, Race)

ANAEROBIC ENDURANCE WORKOUTS

A1: Anaerobic Endurance Intervals

On a mostly flat road course with no stop streets and light traffic, do four to six intervals of three to five minutes' duration each. The cadence is high—higher than what is typical for the hardest portions of a mountain bike race. Intensity of each interval is heart rate 5b or CP6 zone. Recovery at the lowest possible effort while spinning easily. Recover intervals are the same duration as the preceding work interval. (Periods: Build 1, Build 2, Peak, Race)

A2: Pyramid Intervals

These are done the same as the above intervals except the intervals are 1-, 2-, 3-, 4-, 5-, 4-, 3-, 2-, 1-minutes long. Intensity is heart rate 5b or CP6 zone. The recovery after each is equal in duration to the preceding interval. Recover by spinning easily. Do these on a flat road course. (Periods: Build 1, Build 2, Peak, Race)

A3: Hill Intervals

Following a thorough warm-up, go to a steep, off-road hill that takes about three minutes to go up and do four to six climbs. Stay seated with higher cadence than you would normally climb in. Intensity is heart rate 5b or CP6 zone. Recover by spinning easily down the hill, and at the bottom for three minutes. Nine to 18 minutes of total climbing time per workout. (Periods: Build 1, Build 2, Peak, Race)

A4: Lactate Tolerance Reps

Do this on an indoor trainer, or on- or off-road to prepare for fast starts. Find a slight uphill grade, or do these into the wind if no hill is available. After a long warm-up, including several brief, high-power accelerations, do three to five sets of 30- to 40-second repetitions. Intensity is CP1 zone. Heart rate is not applicable. Cadence is high. Recovery between repetitions is half as long as the preceding repetition. For example, after a 40-second rep, recover for 20 seconds. After each set, recover for five minutes with light spinning and very low RPE. The total of all the repetitions in a workout should not exceed 12 minutes. Start with about six minutes total interval time for the first of these workouts within a season, as they are quite stressful. An example of such a workout is three sets of 30-second reps done four times with 15 seconds recovery after each rep and five minutes of recovery between sets. Do this workout no more than once or twice a week and recover for at least 48 hours before attempting another strenuous session. Do not do this workout if you are in the first two years of training for cycling. (Periods: Build 2, Peak)

A5: Long Hill Reps

After a thorough warm-up, go to a 6- to 8-percent grade hill off- or on-road and do four to eight repetitions of 90 seconds each. The first 60 seconds are done seated in the heart rate 5b or CP6 zone. In the last 30 seconds, shift to a higher gear, stand, and drive the bike to the top in the heart rate 5c or CP1 zone. Cadence throughout each rep is relatively high, but should be higher for the last 30 seconds. Recover completely for four minutes after each rep. Do not do this workout if you are in the first two years of training for cycling. (Periods: Build 2, Peak)

A6: Race Simulation

Ride on- or off-road with a group that is appropriate for your ability level. Treat this as a race by utilizing all of the heart rate and power zones. Be aware of how you feel. If tired, sit in or break off and ride by yourself. If fresh, ride aggressively practicing race tactics. (Periods: Build 1, Build 2, Peak, Race)

A7: Time Trial

Find an off-road loop that takes 10 to 20 minutes to complete. The terrain and conditions should be similar to what is expected in your next A-priority race. Complete two to four time trials on this course trying to decrease time on each subsequent attempt. Do up to 40 minutes of total time trialing within a workout. Recover for five to 10 minutes after each. (Periods: Build 2, Peak, Race)

POWER WORKOUTS

P1: Jumps

After a thorough warm-up, do three to five sets of 5 jumps each for a total of 15 to

25 jumps. Concentrate on producing explosive power from the very first pedal stroke. Each jump is 10 to 12 revolutions of the cranks (each leg) while standing on the pedals. These are best done on a mountain bike. Cadence is very high. Intensity is CP0.2 zone. Heart rate is not applicable. Recover by spinning easily for at least one minute between jumps and five minutes between sets. Maintain good form on each jump. (Periods: Build 1, Build 2, Peak, Race)

P2: Hill Sprints

Early in the workout, after a good warm-up, go to an on- or off-road hill with a 4- to 6-percent grade. Do 8 to 12 sprints of 8 to 10 seconds each. Use a flying start for each sprint, taking five seconds or so to build power on the flat approach while standing. Climb the hill applying maximal force by standing on the pedals with a high cadence. Intensity is CP0.2 zone. Heart rate is not applicable. Recover for five minutes after each sprint by spinning at a low RPE. Emphasize good form. (Periods: Build 1, Build 2, Peak, Race)

P3: Crit Sprints

Warm up and then go to an off-road, short-loop course with several tight corners. Do six to nine sprints of 25 to 35 seconds duration each, including one or more corners on each sprint. Concentrate on powerful pedaling while taking the most effective line through each corner. Intensity is CP1 zone. Heart rate is not applicable. Recover by spinning at a low RPE for five minutes after each sprint. This may be done with another rider taking turns leading the sprints. (Periods: Build 2, Peak, Race)

TRAINING DIARY

WEEK BEGINNING: / /   Planned Weekly Hours/Miles _____

WEEK'S GOALS (Check off as achieved)

○ 1._____

○ 2._____

○ 3._____

MONDAY / /	**TUESDAY** / /
○ SLEEP ○ FATIGUE ○ STRESS ○ SORENESS	○ SLEEP ○ FATIGUE ○ STRESS ○ SORENESS
○ PULSE WEIGHT	○ PULSE WEIGHT
WORKOUT _____	WORKOUT _____
DURATION _____	DURATION _____
WEATHER _____	WEATHER _____
ROUTE _____	ROUTE _____
DISTANCE TIME	DISTANCE TIME
TIME BY ZONE [ ]1 [ ]2 [ ]3 [ ]4 [ ]5	TIME BY ZONE [ ]1 [ ]2 [ ]3 [ ]4 [ ]5
WORKOUT RATING 1 2 3 4 5 6 7 8 9 10	WORKOUT RATING 1 2 3 4 5 6 7 8 9 10
NOTES	NOTES

WEDNESDAY   /   /

◯ SLEEP ◯ FATIGUE ◯ STRESS ◯ SORENESS

◯ PULSE   WEIGHT

WORKOUT

DURATION

WEATHER

ROUTE

DISTANCE   TIME

TIME BY ZONE [ ] 1 [ ] 2 [ ] 3 [ ] 4 [ ] 5

WORKOUT RATING 1 2 3 4 5 6 7 8 9 10

NOTES

THURSDAY   /   /

◯ SLEEP ◯ FATIGUE ◯ STRESS ◯ SORENESS

◯ PULSE   WEIGHT

WORKOUT

DURATION

WEATHER

ROUTE

DISTANCE   TIME

TIME BY ZONE [ ] 1 [ ] 2 [ ] 3 [ ] 4 [ ] 5

WORKOUT RATING 1 2 3 4 5 6 7 8 9 10

NOTES

WEEK BEGINNING: / /

FRIDAY / /

◯ SLEEP ◯ FATIGUE ◯ STRESS ◯ SORENESS

◯ PULSE   WEIGHT

WORKOUT

DURATION

WEATHER

ROUTE

DISTANCE   TIME

TIME BY ZONE [ ] 1 [ ] 2 [ ] 3 [ ] 4 [ ] 5

WORKOUT RATING   1   2   3   4   5   6   7   8   9   10

NOTES

SATURDAY / /

◯ SLEEP ◯ FATIGUE ◯ STRESS ◯ SORENESS

◯ PULSE   WEIGHT

WORKOUT

DURATION

WEATHER

ROUTE

DISTANCE   TIME

TIME BY ZONE [ ] 1 [ ] 2 [ ] 3 [ ] 4 [ ] 5

WORKOUT RATING   1   2   3   4   5   6   7   8   9   10

NOTES

SUNDAY   /   /

◯ SLEEP   ◯ FATIGUE   ◯ STRESS   ◯ SORENESS

◯ PULSE   WEIGHT

WORKOUT

DURATION

WEATHER

ROUTE

DISTANCE   TIME

TIME BY ZONE [   ] 1 [   ] 2 [   ] 3 [   ] 4 [   ] 5

WORKOUT RATING   1   2   3   4   5   6   7   8   9   10

NOTES

RACING

RACE 1

CATEGORY

DISTANCE   TIME

RESULT   UPGRADE PTS

NOTES

RACE 2   CATEGORY

DISTANCE   TIME

RESULT   UPGRADE PTS

NOTES

WEEKLY SUMMARY

BIKE TIME   YEAR TO DATE

BIKE MILES   YEAR TO DATE

STRENGTH TIME   YEAR TO DATE

_____ TIME   YEAR TO DATE

_____ TIME   YEAR TO DATE

SORENESS

NOTES

GLOSSARY

Adaptation. Refers to the body's ability to adjust at the cellular level to various demands placed on it over a period of time.

Aerobic. In the presence of oxygen; aerobic metabolism utilizes oxygen. Below the anaerobic-intensity level.

Aerobic capacity. The body's maximal capacity for using oxygen to produce energy during maximal exertion. Also known as VO_2 max.

Agonistic muscles. Muscles directly engaged in producing work.

Anaerobic. Literally, "without oxygen." Exercise that demands more oxygen than the heart and lungs can supply. The intensity of exercise performed above the lactate threshold.

Anaerobic endurance. As used in this book, the ability resulting from the combination of speed skills and endurance allowing the athlete to maintain a high velocity for an extended period of time while anaerobic.

Anaerobic threshold (AT). When aerobic metabolism no longer supplies all the need for energy, energy is produced anaerobically; indicated by an increase in blood lactate. Also sometimes called *lactate threshold.*

Antagonistic muscles. Muscles that have an opposite effect on movers, or that work against other, agonistic, muscles, by opposing their contraction. For example, the triceps is an antagonistic muscle to the biceps.

Base period. As used in this book, the mesocycle during which the basic abilities of endurance, speed skill and force are emphasized.

Bonk. A state of extreme exhaustion during a long ride, mainly caused by the depletion of glycogen in the muscles.

Breakthrough (BT). As used in this book, a workout intended to cause a significant, positive, adaptive response.

Build period. As used in this book, the specific preparation mesocycle during which high-intensity training in the form of muscular endurance, speed endurance and power are emphasized, and endurance, force and speed skill are maintained.

Cadence. Revolutions or cycles per minute of the pedal stroke.

Capillary. A small vessel located between arteries and veins where exchanges between tissue and blood occur.

Carbohydrate loading. A short-term dietary procedure that elevates muscle glycogen stores by emphasizing carbohydrate consumption. Also known as *glycogen loading.*

Cardiorespiratory system. The heart, blood, blood vessels, and lungs.

Cardiovascular system. The heart, blood and blood vessels.

Central nervous system. The spinal cord and brain.

Circuit training. Selected exercises or activities performed rapidly in sequence; used in weight training.

Concentric contraction. The shortening of a muscle during contraction, as when the biceps is used to lift a hand-held weight. See also *eccentric contraction.*

Cool-down. Low-intensity exercise at the end of a training session intended to gradually return the body to a resting state.

Criterium. A multilap race held on a short course.

"Crash" training. A brief period of training marked by excessive stress that is great enough to produce overtraining if continued long enough, and followed immediately by extensive rest. The purpose is to produce *supercompensation.*

Cross training. Training in a sport other than mountain biking.

Drafting. Riding closely behind others in order to reduce effort.

Drops. On a road bike, the lower portion of turned-down handlebars.

Duration. The length of time of a given training session.

Eccentric contraction. The lengthening of a muscle during contraction. For example, slowly setting down a heavy, hand-held weight. See also *concentric contraction.*

Endurance. The physiological ability to persist, resisting fatigue.

Ergogenic aid. A substance, device or phenomenon other than training that can improve athletic performance.

Fartlek. Swedish for "speed play," or an unstructured, interval-type workout.

Fast-twitch fiber (FT). A muscle fiber characterized by fast contraction time, high anaerobic capacity, and low aerobic capacity, all making the fiber suited for high-power activities. See also *slow-twitch fiber.*

Force. The strength evident in a muscle or muscle group while exerting against a resistance. As used in this book, a grouping of bike-specific workouts to improve strength.

Free weights. Weights not part of an exercise machine (i.e., barbells and dumbbells).

Frequency. The number of times per week or per microcycle that one trains.

Glucose. A simple sugar.

Glycogen. The form in which glucose (sugar) is stored in the muscles and the liver.

Glycogen loading. See *carbohydrate loading.*

Glycemic index. A system of ranking carbohydrate foods based on how quickly they raise the blood glucose level.

Growth hormone. A hormone secreted by the anterior lobe of the pituitary gland that stimulates growth and development.

Hammer. Sport slang word used to denote a high-intensity, sustained effort.

Hamstring. Muscle on the back of the thigh that flexes the knee and extends the hip.

Hoods. On a road bike with drop handlebars, the covers of the brake handles.

Individuality, principle of. The theory that any training program must consider the specific needs and abilities of the individual for whom it is designed.

Intensity. The qualitative element of training referring to effort, velocity, maximum strength and power.

Interval training. A system of high-intensity work marked by short, but regularly repeated periods of hard exercise interspersed with periods of recovery.

Isolated leg training (ILT). Pedaling with one leg to improve technique.

Lactate. A substance formed when lactic acid from the muscles enters the blood stream.

Lactic acid. A by-product of muscle work resulting from the incomplete breakdown of glucose (sugar) in the production of energy.

Lactate threshold (LT). The point during exercise of increasing intensity at which blood lactate begins to accumulate above resting levels. Also known as *anaerobic threshold*.

Long, slow distance (LSD) training. A form of continuous training in which the athlete performs at a relatively low intensity for an extended duration.

Macrocycle. A period of training including several mesocycles; usually an entire season.

Mash. To push a big gear.

Mesocycle. A period of training, generally two to six weeks long, made up of two or more microcycles.

Microcycle. A training period of approximately one week.

Muscular endurance. The ability of a muscle or muscle group to perform repeated contractions for a long period of time while bearing a load. As used in this book, a group of workouts that focus on this physical ability.

Overcompensation. An increase in fitness resulting from the application of stress alternated with rest.

Overload, principle of. A training load that challenges the body's current level of fitness resulting in adaptation.

Overreaching. Training at the workload which would produce overtraining if continued long enough, marked by short-term fatigue that is reversible with a few days of rest.

Overtraining. Extreme fatigue, both physical and mental, caused by extensively training at a workload higher than that to which the body can readily adapt; not reversible with a few days of rest.

Peak period. As used in this book, the precompetition mesocycle during which volume of training is reduced and intensity is proportionally increased, allowing the athlete to reach high levels of fitness.

Periodization. The process of structuring training into periods.

Power. As used in this book, the ability resulting from force and speed skill, and a group of workouts that focus on this ability.

Preparation period. The mesocycle during which the athlete begins to train for the coming season; usually marked by the use of cross-training and low workloads.

Progression, principle of. The theory that workload must be gradually increased and accompanied by intermittent periods of recovery.

Quadriceps. The large muscle in front of the thigh that extends the lower leg and flexes the hip.

Race period. As used in this book, the competition mesocycle during which workload is greatly decreased, allowing the athlete to compete in high-priority races.

Rating of perceived exertion (RPE). A subjective assessment of how hard one is working.

Recovery. A period of training when rest is emphasized.

Recovery interval. The relief period between work intervals within an interval workout.

Repetitions (reps). The number of times a task, such as a work interval or lifting of a weight, is repeated.

Repetition maximum (RM). The maximum load that an athlete can lift in one attempt for a given exercise. Also called "one-repetition maximum" (1RM).

Session. A single practice period that may include one or more workouts.

Set. A group of repetitions for a given exercise.

Slow-twitch fiber (ST). A muscle fiber characterized by slow contraction time, low anaerobic capacity, and high aerobic capacity, all making the fiber suited for low power, long-duration activities.

Specificity, principle of. The theory that training must stress the systems critical for optimal performance in order to achieve the desired training adaptations.

Speed skill. Within the context of this book, the ability to move the body in ways that produce optimum performance. For example, the ability to turn the cranks quickly and efficiently on the bike or negotiate technical course sections quickly.

Supercompensation. A greater than normal level of overcompensation as a result of crash training.

Suspension. On mountain bikes, the mechanical device that allows the front and/or rear wheels to move up and down, thus absorbing shock.

Tapering. A reduction in training volume prior to a. major competition.

Tops. The portion of the road bike handlebar closest to the stem.

Training. A comprehensive program intended to prepare an athlete for competition.

Training zone. A level of intensity based on some measure, such as heart rate or power, of the individual's capacity for work.

Transition period. As used in this book, the post-competition mesocycle during which the workload and structure of training are greatly reduced, allowing physical and psychological recovery from training and racing.

Ventilatory threshold (VT). The point during increasing exertion at which breathing first becomes labored, as noted by a sudden increase in the number of breaths per minute. Closely corresponds with lactate threshold.

VO$_2$ max. The capacity for oxygen consumption by the body during maximal exertion, also known as *aerobic capacity* and maximal oxygen consumption. Usually expressed as liters of oxygen consumed per kilogram of body weight per minute (ml/kg/min).

Volume. The quantitative element of training, such as miles or hours of training within a given period. The combination of duration and frequency.

Warm-up. The period of gradually increasing intensity of exercise at the start of a training session; intended to prepare the body for higher intensities.

Work interval. High-intensity efforts separated by recovery intervals.

Workload. The total stress applied in training through the combination of frequency, intensity and duration.

Workout. A portion of a session that is focused on a specific aspect of training, such as power. A session may include more than one workout.

INDEX

NOTES

NOTES

ABOUT THE AUTHOR

Joe Friel has trained endurance athletes since 1980. His clients include elite, amateur and professional mountain bikers, road cyclists, triathletes and duathletes in all corners of the globe. They include U.S. and foreign national champions and world championship competitors. Several are Olympics hopefuls. *Bicycling* magazine says, "Joe Friel is arguably the most experienced personal cycling coach in the U.S."

The author of *The Cyclist's Training Bible* (VeloPress, 1996), *Cycling Past 50* (Human Kinetics, 1998), *The Triathlete's Training Bible* (VeloPress, 1998), and coauthor of *Precision Heart Rate Training* (Human Kinetics, 1998), he holds a master's degree in exercise science and is a certified elite-level USA Cycling coach. Joe also develops and trains others to become coaches. He currently supports and advises three coaches.

He is a contributing editor to *VeloNews* and *Inside Triathlon,* and writes feature stories for *Performance Conditioning for Cycling* and other national publications. He has written a weekly fitness column for the *Fort Collins Coloradoan* since 1981.

He conducts workshops around the country on training and racing for cyclists and multisport athletes, and provides consulting services for corporations in the fitness industry.

From his home at the foot of the Rocky Mountains in Fort Collins, Colorado, Joe enjoys mountain biking in the foothills with wife Joyce, trail running with friends, road riding with teammates in the Fort Collins Cycling and Racing Club and with son Dirk—a professional road racer and coaching associate.

For more information on seminars and personal coaching, visit his Web site at www.ultrafit.com.

OTHER BOOKS FROM VELOPRESS

CYCLIST'S TRAINING BIBLE by Joe Friel.
Now in its 4th printing! Hailed as a major breakthrough in training for competitive cycling, this book helps take cyclists from where they are to where they want to be — the podium! Paperback. 288 pp. Photos, charts, diagrams. 1-884737-21-8. P-BIB $19.95

CYCLO-CROSS by Simon Burney.
A must read for anyone wanting to know all about the techniques, training and equipment necessary in the fastest-growing sport in cycling. Paperback. 200 pp. Photos, charts, diagrams. 1-884737-20-x. P-CRS $14.95

OFF-SEASON TRAINING FOR CYCLISTS by Edmund Burke, Ph.D.
Get a jump on the competition! Burke takes you through everything you need to know about winter training, indoor workouts, weight training, cross-training, periodization and more. Paperback. 200 pp. 1-884737-40-4. P-OFF $14.95

ZINN & THE ART OF ROAD BIKE MAINTENANCE by Lennard Zinn.
The long-awaited companion to Zinn's best-selling mountain bike maintenance book, Zinn & the Art of Road Bike Maintenance explains and demonstrates how to completely and properly maintain every component of a road bike from a simple wheel removal to an overhaul of the new Campagnolo Ergopower levers! Paperback. 296 pp. 295 b&w illustrations.
1-884737-70-6. P-ZYR $19.95

EDDY MERCKX: THE GREATEST CYCLIST OF THE 20TH CENTURY by Rik Vanwalleghem.
This lavish large-format masterpiece reveals the hidden strengths, fears and motivations of the world's greatest cyclist. Paperback. 216 pp. 24 color photos, 165 b&w photos.
1-884737-772-2. P-MPB $29.95

LANCE ARMSTRONG & THE 1999 TOUR DE FRANCE by John Wilcockson and Charles Pelkey.
Lance Armstrong's heroic victory in the world's toughest bike race only two years after nearly dying from cancer was an epic journey of larger-than-life proportions Fortunately veteran cycling journalist John Wilcockson and VeloNews technical editor Charles Pelkey were there to record Armstrong's brilliant comeback. Includes a 16-page color photo section by Graham Watson and the Tour diary of Armstrong's teammate Frankie Andreu. Paperback. 224 pp. Complete Tour maps. 1-884737-69-2. P-99TDF $19.95

JOHN WILCOCKSON'S WORLD OF CYCLING by John Wilcockson.
This great book brings the world of bicycle racing alive through the eyes and experiences of veteran VeloNews editor John Wilcockson. Wilcockson has covered practically every major bicycle race around the globe — including the Tour de France — for 30 years and his writing is a joy for any cycling fan. Paperback. 336 pages. 35 color photographs. 1-884737-77-3. P-WPB $18.95

VELONEWS TRAINING DIARY by Joe Friel.
The world's most popular training diary for cyclists. Allows you to record every facet of training with plenty of room for notes. Non-dated, so you can start any time of the year. Spiral-bound. 248 pp. 1-884737-42-0. P-DIN $12.95

ZINN & THE ART OF MOUNTAIN BIKE MAINTENANCE, Second edition, by Lennard Zinn.
The most popular, up-to-date, and detailed book on mountain bike maintenance available! Technical guru Lennard Zinn shows you in plain English and clear illustrations how you can fix anything on today's mountain bikes. Paperback. 288 pp. Photos and illustrations.1-884737-47-1. P-ZYN $17.95

MOUNTAIN BIKE OWNER'S MANUAL by Lennard Zinn and the technical editors of VeloNews.
This illustrated guide is small enough to pack on trips yet filled with enough comprehensive information to help out with any situation one can encounter including information on bike and trail safety, tools, proper clothing, emergencies, and repair tips on all major components. Paperback. 136 pp. Illustrations. 1-884737-52-8. P-MBO $9.95

THE ATHLETE'S GUIDE TO SPONSORSHIP, 2nd Edition, by Jennifer Drury and Cheri Elliot.
The only comprehensive, step-by-step guide for any athlete, team, or sports event planner who is considering pursuing sponsorship opportunities. Includes worksheets and sample contracts that will help the reader through the sponsorship process. Paperback. 160 pp. Photos and tables. 1-884737-78-1. P-GUI $14.95

THE FEMALE CYCLIST: GEARING UP A LEVEL by Gale Bernhardt.
Foreword by Linda Jackson.
Written for the cyclist who enjoys cycling for fitness, and wants to improve her riding skills and achieve higher goals. Also includes detailed chapters on bike fit and nutrition, as well as training plans and strength training. Paperback. 352 pp. 1-884737-58-7. P-FEM $16.95

SPORT PSYCHOLOGY FOR CYCLISTS by Dr. Saul Miller and Peggy Maass Hill.
Renowned sport psychologist Dr. Saul Miller and former national criterium champion Peggy Maass Hill collaborate on how to improve your cycling through mental training. Using a team of eight cyclists, it follows eight weekly sessions covering the elements of mental training for optimal cycling such as breathing techniques, power thoughts, ìscripting,î what to do under pressure, imagery, and the element of a winning attitude. Paperback. 240 pp. Worksheets. 1-884737-68-4. P-PSY $16.95

WEIGHT TRAINING FOR CYCLISTS by Eric Schmitz and Ken Doyle.
Specifically for cyclists, this guide includes the most current scientific information on strength training, exercise, and technique. Use this book to design your own year-round periodized training program to enhance your cycling performance and fitness. Paperback. 200 pp. 1-884737-43-9. P-WTC $14.95

COMPLETE GUIDE TO SPORTS NUTRITION by Monique Ryan.
Diet plays an increasingly important role with today's athlete and improved performance. Ryan clearly explains the roles menu, meal planning, food strategies, and weight management play in optimizing athletic performance. Paperback. 328 pp. 1-884737-57-9. P-NUT$16.95

THE TRIATHLETE'S TRAINING BIBLE by Joe Friel.
The most extensive training guide available for triathletes. Friel integrates the latest research on training, nutrition, and techniques with everything needed for planning your workouts. A ìmustî book for every triathlete wanting to train smarter, not harder, and achieve their best results! Paperback. 400 pp. Photos, charts, diagrams. 1-884737-48-x. P-TRIB $19.95

DERAILLEUR by Greg Moody.
Moody's third cycling murder mystery follows Will Ross and Cheryl Crane into the world of mountain bike racing in Colorado. Mobsters, mountain bikers, developers and environmentalists are all on a collision course in Moody's latest! Paperback. 368 pp. 1-884737-59-5. P-DER $12.95

TRIATHLON: A PERSONAL HISTORY by Scott Tinley.
This handsome, large-format book features hundreds of photographs accompanied by the two-time Hawaii Ironman champion and triathlon pioneer's passionate and oftentimes humorous prose, tracing the evolution of multisport from its humble birth to Olympic status. Paperback. 288 pp. 1-884737-49-8. P-HOT $39.95

FOR MORE INFORMATION OR TO ORDER:

CALL toll-free 800.234.8356 • FAX 303.444.6788 • Visit our web site at www.velogear.com • VeloPress, 1830 North 55th Street, Boulder, CO 80301
VeloPress books are also available at your favorite bike shop or bookstore.